Your Business
RULES OK

David Holland MBA

© Copyright 2012 David Holland

978-1-291-29099-8
All rights reserved

No part of this book may be reproduced or transmitted in any form or by means, electronic or mechanical, including photocopying, recording, or by any information storage and retrieval system, without permission in writing from the copyright owner.

Printing History

Xlibris Corporation edition published 2011

Results Rules OK Ltd edition published 2013

If you are intending on setting up your own business, have a business that is proving to bit of a challenge to run, or would like to take an already successful business to a higher level of results, this book is definitely for you.

Once you start reading it you will find it hard to put down (I read it in one day) and then you will keep picking it up and dipping in and out as you work through the principles in the book.

A few of things that shine through as you read this book:

* David's obvious level of knowledge on the subject of building and running a successful business.

* His wicked sense of humour. There were times when I was rolling around laughing.

* His genuine approach to helping all business owners, big, small, successful and unsuccessful.

* It's a perfect fit for his other book Life Rules OK.

Kevin G

MPC for Profit

Contents

ACKNOWLEDGEMENTS 7

ABOUT YOUR AUTHOR 9

READING *YOUR* BUSINESS RULES OK 11

INTRODUCTION 15

RULE NO. 1 – IT IS ALL ABOUT YOU 37

RULE NO. 2 – GET THE FOUNDATIONS RIGHT 69

RULE NO. 3 – KEEP ALL YOUR CUSTOMERS 143

RULE NO. 4 – ATTRACT NEW CUSTOMERS 191

RULE NO. 5 – YOU WILL NEED HELP 222

RULE NO. 6 – SYSTEMS RULES OK 240

RULE NO. 7 – YOU HAVE TO INNOVATE 251

RULE NO. 8 – IT'S NOT ABOUT YOU ANYMORE 258

INDEX 262

ABOUT RESULTS RULES OK 272

Acknowledgements

When I wrote **Life RULES OK**, I learned that writing a book is a team effort and one that takes dedication and commitment by not just the author, but their families, friends, and associates. It may be my name on the cover, but Lynn, my wife, has put heart and soul into the journey we have taken that has enabled me to write *Your* **Business RULES OK**. So Lynn – thank you . . .

I dedicated the last book to my two boys, Jon and Rich, and as those of us who are parents understand, everything we do is in some part dedicated to our children. Once I got the approval of my parents for what I had achieved in my life and career, the focus morphed, and I discovered that I wanted my boys to be as proud of me as I am of them. So, now, their approval is important too as are their results and experiences. There is something reassuring about growing older disgracefully; however, I wouldn't want to become an embarrassment to them, at least not all the time. So, boys, this one is for you.

Those of you that have read **Life RULES OK** may recall how my family had a business that had been at the centre of our family life for generations. My mom worked and ran the business with my dad, and they both gave me the knowledge and upbringing that enabled me to embark on a fabulous journey; so, Mom and Dad, thank you . . .

When I decided to write this series of books, I looked back over my life and career so far – just to make sure that there was enough substance to my stories and knowledge to make the books longer than five pages. I also wanted to make sure above all else that they would represent great value, be informative, fun, and inspiring to read – if you are kind enough to invest your money and time in acquiring and reading my book, I have an obligation to make it worthwhile.

What I realised as I looked back, made lots of notes, and contacted people I hadn't spoken to for years is that I and, I guess, all of us are simply a sum of our experiences. I also realised that we are all on the same journey looking for success in our business, our careers, and our relationships. And whilst some of the experiences we have and people we come into contact with may not be those that in hindsight we would choose, they all contribute to who we are and who we will become.

So I'd like to acknowledge everyone who has employed me, worked with me, worked for me, bought from me, or sold to me; I am a sum of all your parts.

I also want to recognise my teachers, those that have guided, taught me and enabled me to have the knowledge and faith to make the choices that have taken me this far. So to Buckminster Fuller, Edwards Deming, Marshall Thurber, Jay Abraham, Michael E Gerber, Tony Robbins, Tom Hopkins, Robert Cialdini, Harry Beckwith, Robert Kiyosaki, Zig Ziglar, Jim Collins, Jeffrey Gitomer, Malcolm Gladwell, Charles Handy and many others; special thanks and acknowledgement, your ideas and concepts are woven into my approach and enrich the fabric of my story.

Finally, *Your* **Business RULES OK** is dedicated to all the people who make the leap and go into business for themselves; we are kindred spirits, and if by reading this book you learn just one thing that helps you and moves you forward, then I will have succeeded.

It is also dedicated to those who take on the responsibility of managing people and resources in all sectors of commerce and industry. Stepping up and being accountable for results take a special talent, and I salute you, entrepreneurs working in businesses as well as owning them.

About Your Author

One of the reasons I decided to get into business coaching and training was my desire to be able to help people in business get a better result. I know how hard business owners work, and what the effects of long hours and stress can do to relationships and family life; I have been there.

My passion is, therefore, to help you – if that sounds patronising, then I apologise; it is not intentional. My dad died on the day after his eightieth birthday in 2010. I loved him and he loved me, but I didn't really know him. He spent all his time and effort working in the business. When he wasn't working, he was thinking about it, worrying about it, or doing the accounts. He was and remains my hero.

Our family business ended in 1989 when Dad retired. In my first book, **Life RULES OK**, I went into more detail about this. In the winter of 1978, Dad realised that whilst the business would sustain him and Mom, it would not be there for me, so I would have to go and build my career somewhere else – bit of a shock to a fifteen-year-old . . .

That is why I do what I do, where the books and materials come from, and the reason I am so passionate. I can help you build your business and improve the quality of life for you and those around you. And, after all, that is why we are here.

My career has been varied. I started out as an engineer with Royal Ordnance and have had the privilege of working with and for great people in a variety of sectors. Looking back, I have been directly involved with businesses as diverse as packaging, transport, clothing, aviation services, recruitment, logistics, wiring harnesses, document management, franchising, business coaching and training.

It is with this knowledge, experience, and passion for your results that we created **Results RULES OK Ltd** and wrote the books and materials that are available on our web site, *www.resultsrulesok.com*.

So please enjoy the book, go to our web site for more information, and email me at *business@resultsrulesok.com* to let me know what you think, and what you have achieved as a result of using the materials, or come to one of our events so that I can thank you personally for investing your time and money in your future and also contributing to ours.

Reading *Your* Business RULES OK

A business has to be involving, it has to be fun, and it has to exercise your creative instincts.

Richard Branson

All businesses are unique. They may follow similar patterns and structures, but they have individual personalities that define them. Whether you are starting your own business or looking to grow your existing business, or whether you are a CEO, manager, supervisor, an ambitious machine operator, or clerk, this is the book for you.

Your **Business RULES OK** is a guide book. Each chapter is intended to build on the previous one and help you develop a process of building a successful business, department, division, or territory. If you are starting a new business, then work through the chapters in sequence, building your plans and activities as you go.

If you have an existing business, then whilst the rules still apply, you can compare what you are doing now with these concepts and see how you are doing. You may have some of them covered off and working really well. You may find that some areas need some tweaking. You may also find that some areas need a complete overhaul.

When recruiting people, we know what we are looking for, or at least we think we do. If I know that a candidate needs to have ten key attributes to be successful in the position, then I can assess the candidates as they attend the selection process, or deselection process as it should be called.

In reality, we also know that of the ten key attributes we want in our ideal candidate, we are probably only going to find people who possess seven of them, and of these candidates, they will each possess a different seven. Same with this book. I have covered a lot of ground from finance to sales, marketing to systematising; all of the people who read this book will already know parts of it and may choose to flip through the parts they have experience and knowledge of. The challenge is that everyone is different and will be able to flip through different parts, and I don't know who knows what.

I have also assumed that you may not have read my first book, **Life RULES OK**, before you start reading this. So for the sake of clarity, there may be some duplication between the introductions to each of the books.

My totally unbiased opinion is that you should buy and read **Life RULES OK** before you read this book.

Whether you are working for someone or working for yourself, whatever you achieve and accomplish, and the manner in which you do it will be a direct reflection of you. If you want to change your results, you may need to start by making some changes yourself first.

So you need to work on yourself as much as, if not more than, you work on your business. **Life RULES OK** will help you - so my recommendation is that you buy it.

Your **Business RULES OK** is written as if you are starting from scratch. I have made the assumption that you are a blank slate and that everything about business is new to you. There may be further reading that you need to do, and you may decide that you need help in putting it all into place, but my hope is that this book will get you started.

I have put a notes page at the end of each chapter so you can scribble ideas and thoughts as they come to you. If this becomes a mini workbook for you, then great.

I have included stories from my own career and business ventures, stories from other people's experiences, and introduced models and concepts that will enable you to take these ideas and implement them in your business. There are other resources and supporting documents available at our web site, www.resultsrulesok.com

We run a series of events, workshops, retreats, and programmes to help you and your teams with understanding how to build a successful business. I also offer keynote, conference, and bespoke training events to clients; please contact me through our web site for more information.

Enjoy . . .

Notes

Introduction

The entrepreneur in us sees opportunities everywhere we look, but many people see only problems everywhere they look. The entrepreneur in us is more concerned with discriminating between opportunities than he or she is with failing to see the opportunities.

Michael Gerber

I never knew what it meant to be an entrepreneur. I heard the term on the news, but it was used in the same tone as 'local businessman' was used when describing someone to whom no other label applied, usually when a crime had been committed and the alleged perpetrator or victim was simply a 'local businessman'.

I knew what owning a business meant. It meant long hours, hard work, and no holidays, or at least that was my experience. The family business was greengrocery, fish, and poultry. The Holland family had been in business since the early 1800s, and we had a number of shops in and around the Birmingham area, from Great Barr to Coleshill, Water Orton to Alum Rock – a truly global empire.

We were in business when Napoleon was retreating from Moscow, during the Crimean War, Boer War, World War I, and World War II. The picture below was taken in about 1910 and was typical of one of the shops. This one was located in Alum Rock in Birmingham; the building still exists and is now a chemist. On the original photograph, parts of the address are visible on the paper carrier bags that are hanging up, and if you look at the architecture, the masonry right-hand side of the shop is higher than that on the left, suggesting that it is built on a gentle incline. So we looked for the only hill in Alum Rock. We found the building and took a framed copy of this picture and presented it to the current business owner who took great delight to show us the ceramic tiles and original fixtures that still remained behind the new shelving and display units.

The big guy in the middle of the photo is my great-grandfather David Holland; on his left shoulder (on the right as you look at the picture) is my grandfather, also David Holland. My great-grandmother can also be seen on the original print, standing in the background. The two young lads in the foreground and the other guy on the left of the photo are unknown. This was family life in the Holland household; everything revolved around the business. The family worked there. Our name was above the shop, and it was an all-consuming activity. My grandfather David had a break from the business; unfortunately, it involved a trip over to Belgium with the Coldstream Guards between 1915 and 1917. He survived the war; however, he was wounded during the Battle of Passchendaele; he returned to the business in 1919. David died in 1943 when my dad, Frank, was just thirteen, meaning that he had to leave school and run the business. A pattern was emerging.

I can't remember if the winters of my childhood in the 1960s and 1970s were any colder than they are now. What I do remember is that going to Smithfield Wholesale Market in Birmingham with my dad was always a very early start. We would be there between 4.00 and 5.00 a.m., and even in June, it was always cold. With the new and improved market opening in 1974, things didn't seem to get any better. I learned that as milk froze, it expanded; pushing the aluminium foil lids off the bottles and that nets of Brussels sprouts would freeze into fifty-pound balls of green ice. There is nothing as cold as the job of splitting sprouts with your bare hands, or at least it seemed this way for a six-year-old.

I learned not to put bananas in the fridge to store them, that mushrooms lose weight as they lose moisture and that if someone wanted one pound of apples, we always weighed five, not four. It always came to more than one pound so we could charge a bit extra every time. We would sell oranges at 10p each or four for 50p and get away with it. From the age of four, when I wasn't at school, I worked in the business – stacking apples and oranges, boiling beetroot in an old top loading washing machine in the backyard, making the tea, flattening boxes, sweeping up, and generally chasing around doing all the grubby jobs. My specialty was cleaning the windows and polishing them up with newsprint; the ink gives a sheen to the glass and leaves the windows free of smears because the paper is so absorbent. And I always got the sympathy of the public – a six-year-old on a stepladder on the high street was always a great way of getting attention.

I learned to drive in an ex-military Bedford TK Truck. From the age of ten, I was loading and unloading, manoeuvring the trucks around the markets and at the back of the shops. I can reverse anything just about anywhere.

I started serving customers at 09.00 hrs. precisely on Saturday, 20 February 1971. This was because on the previous Monday of that week, 15 February, decimalisation was introduced, and I was the only one who actually understood the new system. As with most retailers, we made more money with the new money system.

Confusion on the part of consumers always results in higher margins for the retailers. In the days before EPOS (Electronic Point of Sale) systems and self-service, all transactions were in cash and had to be added up as the produce was weighed, bagged, and handed over the counter. My mental arithmetic skills were honed here, and I can still beat a calculator and add VAT onto values in my head, made easier now by the introduction of 20% VAT in the UK, of course.

At school, I would take orders from my classmates, and the following day, take bags of satsumas, apples, bananas, and nuts, selling them for three times what I bought them from my dad for. Later, when I was working in London, in 1983, when the UK laws regarding the wearing of safety belts was introduced, I had a supplier of Inertia Reel safety belts which I would sell to friends and colleagues, in order to replace the static belts that were fitted as standard to their vehicles back then; I also offered fitting and valet services for an additional investment . . .

Trading was then and now in my blood – it is the thrill of buying something and selling it for more than was paid for it that excites business owners and entrepreneurs, managers, and directors.

People have been trading, buying, and selling goods and services for thousands of years. Bartering was probably one of the earliest methods derived for the exchange of dissimilar goods and services – grain could be exchanged for poultry, a sheep could be exchanged for some tools, etc. The challenge with the barter system was that if I don't want or need what you have to exchange for my goods or services, then the exchange will not happen. There has to be a coincidence of wants for bartering to work. Also, there was no way of fixing an exchange rate. What is a sheep worth in the currency of grain, tools, or furnishings? It depends on the people making the exchange and therefore may not be consistent. Another problem with the barter system was that goods for exchange may not be available at the time the exchange is made. For example, if I want to exchange apples for corn, the apples may not be ripe and ready for eating at the time the corn is harvested. Seasonality of supply could not be accounted for through the barter system.

The Sumerians successfully used 'commodity money' to develop their trading empire. Commodity money is money whose value is derived from the commodity from which it is made. The objects have inherent value in themselves as well as a value for use as money.

There were a wide range of commodities used as money, including copper, salt, shells, gold, and silver, each piece of money having a defined value that could be exchanged for products and services of similar perceived or actual value. Having commodity money removed the limitations that coincidence of wants or seasonality of supply placed on the barter system.

Babylonia was where Iraq is today, in what was known as Southern Mesopotamia. The capital, Babylon, was first mentioned on a clay tablet that dates back to the twenty-third century BC. It was here that systems of trade, rules surrounding debt, property, and legal contracts were first established. The Code of Hammurabi was established around 1760 BC. This, along with other codes, defined the role of money – what levels of interest should be paid on debts and the levels of monetary fines to be imposed for breaking a range of defined laws.

The first commodity money coins that we would recognise as money were produced around 700 BC. It was not until the Song dynasty of the tenth century in China that paper money first appears. The notes produced were given a face value that was determined by an exchange rate for commodities such as silver, gold, or silk. These notes were supposed to be in circulation for a period of just three years when they were supposed to be returned and replaced by new ones upon the payment of a service charge. In reality, not all of the notes were returned, and with new notes being issued, inflation took off, and in spite the government attempting to retrieve the situation, these early notes were eventually discarded.

It would be Kublai Khan, the founder of the Yuan dynasty, who would introduce paper money as a primary means of exchange. The Chao was introduced and was used in restricted areas. However, temptation proved too much, and later, in the dynasty, in order to fund their government, paper money was printed without any restrictions, causing hyperinflation. The Ming dynasty, in a bid to end the hyperinflation caused by the excessive printing of paper money, ended its circulation in 1455.

Fiat money, the system we use today, involves the use of money that has no intrinsic value other than that ascribed to it by government or legislation. The pound note or dollar bill for example, while they have a value prescribed by law, the material they are printed on has no inherent value.

So business has been enabled to operate as it does today because of the development of our ability to exchange value through the use of tokens, coins, and notes. The modern banking system effectively means that we can work, live, and trade in a cashless society – the fiat money model taken to its extreme, where our money is only shown as an electronic entry on a screen, or statement of our account.

Trading is not new. It is one of the oldest professions; even 'that' one included the exchange of goods for a presumably high value service. The business sector of every economy is what drives growth and prosperity. As business people, managers, and entrepreneurs, we have an obligation to be successful and profitable.

Business is based upon the rule of reciprocation. Reciprocation is hard-wired into us. If you buy me a drink at the bar, there are two things that happen (three if you include the act of drinking itself). First, there is an expectation from you that I will reciprocate and buy you a drink in return. Second, there is an obligation placed on me to return the favour and buy you a drink. The only way that the equilibrium can be achieved is when I buy you the drink; then we are even and you have had your expectations met, and I have shed my burden of obligation to you.

At Christmas each year, there is an expectation around the giving and receiving of gifts. Lynn will buy six boxes of chocolates, gift wrap them, attach a blank gift card to each of them, and store them in the garage. If someone turns up unexpectedly to wish us the season's greetings and drop off a gift, Lynn will immediately dash to the garage, fill out the card, and present them with the gift that we had got for them, the box of chocolates. It is an obligation to reciprocate and also not be indebted or obligated to someone that drives us to achieve balance or equity in our relationships. So if you get a box of chocolates from us for Christmas, you know why . . .

The obligation placed upon us to reciprocate is immensely powerful, and it carries over time; the requirement for us to meet our obligations under the rule can last for years. In the book *Influence* by Dr Robert Cialdini, he relays the story of the transfer of aid money between Ethiopia and Mexico in 1985.

In 1985, Ethiopia was experiencing famine. Live Aid was developed and produced by Bob, now Sir Bob Geldof, and Midge Ure. Millions of people in the West donated cash and lobbied government to support the relief effort. The Live Aid multi-venue concerts were held on 13 July 1985 with 72,000 people attending Wembley Stadium and 100,000 people attending the J. F. Kennedy Stadium in Philadelphia. With other supporting concerts in Germany and Australia, an estimated 2 billion people in sixty countries watched the broadcast.

So the intriguing question is why, given that Ethiopia was experiencing one of the worst famines in its history, in 1985 were thousands of dollars in aid money sent to Mexico from Ethiopia?

The answer is simple and shouldn't be that surprising, given the power and endurance of the obligations of reciprocity.

At 7.19 a.m. on 19 September 1985, a massive earthquake of 8.1 magnitude struck the area around Mexico City. Ten thousand people were killed. The infrastructure was severely damaged with millions of people without drinking water, 40% of the population were without electricity, and 70% were without telephone services.

So there was a need for aid to be sent to Mexico. However, the reason that thousands of dollars went from Ethiopia to Mexico was not just that there was a legitimate need. The reason that, when they needed the money themselves, the Ethiopians sent money to Mexico was that in 1935 when Mussolini's Italian troops invaded Abyssinia, now Ethiopia, Mexico helped the Ethiopians. So when Mexico needed help, the Ethiopians were under a contract of obligation to step in.

Now, the rule applies in life and in business, and whilst the obligation to reciprocate is part of our make-up, it works both in the affirmative and the negative.

The well-known phrase 'eye for an eye' comes from the Hebrew Bible and appears in Leviticus, Exodus, and Deuteronomy. The phrase means that if I am injured or harmed by someone, I have 'rights of restitution' such that the compensation I receive should be equitable with the damage I have suffered. In extreme case, this manifests itself as retribution, or the need to 'get even', it's the same rule using a different approach.

What this basically means is that whilst reciprocation works with favours and goods, it also works with damages and loss. So remember that both your negative and positive actions will generate responses. For every action there will be an equal and opposite reaction; if you push, you will receive pushback.

Reciprocation is an underlying principle of business. The understanding of its implications and opportunities are fundamental to how we live, work, and achieve success.

So these are two basic, underlying principles that business relies on:
1. **Money** – The transfer and exchange of value through the use of tokens and currency. We can trade anywhere at any time.
2. **Reciprocation** – We expect to pay for what we get and of course get at least what we pay for. The concept of value and worth is perceived as a consequence of the transaction.

Given there have been people trading and running businesses for thousands of years, why is it that so many don't thrive and reach their full potential or don't survive at all? There are plenty of statistics that will suggest that around 80% of businesses don't make it past the five-year mark, and of those that do, only 80% of them will make it past ten years. These figures are probably overstated and have been used to instil fear in the minds of entrepreneurs.

The rates of business failure depend on the type of business being operated; the rates vary between sectors. It is also worth noting that because a business stops trading, it doesn't mean it has 'failed'. It simply means that the owner has decided to close the business, for example, when retiring.

In my experience, whatever the true failure rate is, it is too high; if you are going into the restaurant business, proceed with caution. Even when a business does survive past the five- or ten-year mark, there are only a few who actually reach their full potential. So there is room for improvement.

Recipe for Success

With all that knowledge and experience, we should be able to start a business, follow the instructions, and become successful – every time.

Franchises attempt to achieve this by offering a ready-made business that provides a product or a service to a proven recipe or process. Providing you follow the process, the business will be successful. This model clearly works; The International Franchise Association lists over 1,100 franchise opportunities business models in over 100 different sectors. Everything from pizzas and burgers to accounting and web design is available as a franchise. There is even a franchise available where clients place their feet in tanks of water containing flesh-eating fish, and they proceed to nibble away at the dead skin cells . . .

A good franchise will have a proven method of not only producing a product or delivering a service but also marketing and selling the products and services so that the franchisee, by following the system, will achieve predictable and consistent results. That is why franchises are able to charge you for using their systems and brand. It is because they have a proven model, which means the risk of running the business is lower and the success rate is higher.

I spent some time living and working in the USA and for two years lived in Las Vegas in Nevada. The US Census Bureau release data showing that in 2010 there were 7.9 million people employed in franchised businesses out of a total workforce of 59 million – just over 13% of the total. So Franchising is indeed big business. McDonald's, Burger King, KFC, and Subway are some of the most recognised brands on the planet.

Does Success Mean Franchising?

In Las Vegas, there are, or at least there were, five fast food restaurants belonging to the 'In-N-Out Burger' company. And as we were new in town, and this brand was new to us, we thought we would try it out. The restaurant we chose to visit was just off the strip on Dean Martin and Tropicana. It has a look of a 1950s diner with yellow and red primary-coloured signs, red awnings covering the outdoor seating area, and palm trees set into the landscaping.

As we entered, we had to join a line of about twenty-five people, patiently waiting to order their food. The line moved along quickly, and we were able to see the menu. First surprise was that there were only five things on the menu, three of them were burgers; one, fries; and one, drinks. At In-N-Out Burger, you have a choice of a double-double burger, a cheese burger, or a hamburger. You can have fries and a drink and that is it – no fish, no cakes, no coffee . . .

When we ordered, next surprise, the food was cooked to order so we had to wait for it again. We were given a numbered ticket, and while we waited, we helped ourselves to drinks, and we dispensed our sauces into small paper cups. In a few minutes, the meal was ready for us to collect and find a seat.

The food was very good, freshly made, served with a smile in a great venue.

I assumed that like so many hamburger chains In-N-Out Burger would be a franchise operation. I was so impressed with the service, product experience of eating there that Lynn bought me a copy of the book titled *In-N-Out Burger* by Stacy Perman, as a gift for me at Christmas 2010, and it became one of the triggers for writing this book.

Now, without going into the details too deeply, it turns out that In-N-Out Burger was founded in 1948 by Harry and Esther Snyder in Baldwin Park, Los Angeles. By ordering food through a unique two-way speaker system, Harry and Esther Snyder developed the first drive-through hamburger stand in California.

There are currently 246 locations through California, Arizona, Utah, and Nevada, all within a day's drive of the Baldwin Park distribution centre. They make all their own patties and bake all their own buns. They are never frozen, and microwaves are not allowed; their burgers were even available at the Academy Awards event with a trailer being brought in for the occasion.

The Snyders' philosophy was simple, and remains, 'Give customers the freshest, highest quality foods you can buy, and provide them with friendly service in a sparkling clean environment.' The business is not a franchise and is owned by Lynsi Martinez, the granddaughter of Harry and Esther.

So it is not franchising per se that is the magic ingredient that supports the success of a venture. In fact, on their web site the company is clear that they have no plans to franchise the business or take it public.

So what is it that makes the In-N-Out Burger such a success? Why haven't they been swallowed up or shut down by the McDonald's or Burger King competitors?

How come they survived and thrived not just the first five years but over fifty years and remain owned by the same family during all that time?

How could they possibly do that and not be a franchise?

The reason is that they follow not just a system; it is more than that. It is a philosophy, a way of doing business, and delivering excellence not just to the customers but to the employees and all people associated with the business. It was the passion, standards, and ethics that were established by Harry and Esther Snyder right from the start that made the company what it is today.

There is a formula for success in business. Some people franchise it and attempt to bottle this formula and sell it creating global empires. Some people 'get lucky' and build great and successful businesses of their own, learning the rules of the formula as they go along. They are not lucky at all – they are hardworking, tenacious, and dedicated to their passion. Harry and Esther, I'm quite sure, didn't have a guide book or instruction manual to help them. They did what they thought was right, applied it consistently, and it worked; this is not luck.

Some people never figure it out, and they bounce from one business failure to another, applying inappropriate systems and methods to a variety of ventures, with equally predictable results. Simply put, they don't know what they are doing.

Let's be clear. Businesses do not fail. It is the people within them that create the environment for failure. Conversely, it is the people within them that also create the environment for success.

In my experience, most businesses that fail, or at least fail to reach their potential, do so because either the owners, leaders, or managers do not have a set of instructions, or if they do, they don't follow them. I struggled to put together the Ikea cabinets we bought for our home in France even with a full set of instructions. So how do we expect people to be able to build a successful business without a set of instructions or rules?

So *Your* **Business RULES OK** is intended to be just that – an instruction manual for building your business, a set of rules that, if you apply them, will enable you to start, build, and grow any business. Treat your business as if you are going to franchise it. Not that I am recommending that you do; just treat it as if you were. Global franchises are not big businesses; they are lots of small- or medium-sized businesses following a set of instructions. In-N-Out Burger is not a Franchise business, but it is effectively run like one.

All franchises are different, because they are operating in a variety of sectors with different products and services; so the systems and procedures that they use will be equally diverse. The common thread that runs through any franchise operation is essentially systematised consistency.

So whilst I can give you the rules and instructions to help, you will have to apply your own ingredients, your own style, philosophy, process, and product. But by applying all these in a systematised and structured way, experience shows that you are more likely to achieve better results in any business.

A Model for Any Business

In order to succeed, there is a basic pattern that, in my experience, all businesses need to recognise and follow. The *Your* **Business RULES OK** Cycle of Business is as shown below:

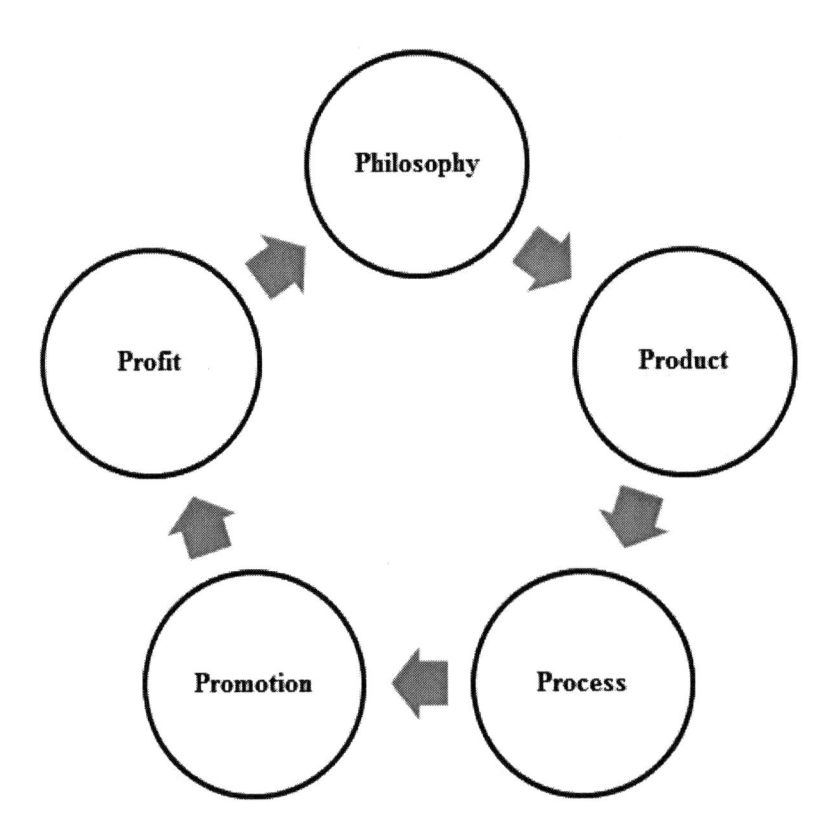

Step One – Philosophy

First, a successful business starts with an idea, dream, or a vision. The business will have a purpose or a mission which when combined with the standards, ethics, and morals of the business owner, define an underlying philosophy. It is this philosophy that will determine how the business is managed, how customers, employees, and suppliers are treated, what standards will be upheld, and how success will be measured.

If, for example, you subscribe to the Milton Friedman philosophy that the primary purpose of a business is to make profit or, as proposed by Peter Drucker, that the purpose of a business is creating satisfied customers, your approach to business will be different.

I would hesitate to say that it doesn't matter what your philosophy is provided that it is applied consistently; however, there are a variety of different approaches that work. Which one or mixture you choose will be up to you.

Personally, I think that a business should have multiple driving forces. My philosophy, if you like, is that whilst profitability and cash generation and shareholder equity are clearly fundamental to the success of any venture, they are only the barometers by which we gauge performance. A business has additional responsibilities – to provide value to its customers, opportunity to its employees, reliability to its suppliers as well as have a social and environmental conscience; more to come.

Step Two – Product

Every business provides a product or service, which it provides in return for cash. Which product or service is provided will of course depend not only on the philosophy of the owner, but their skills, knowledge, interests, and abilities. We will be discussing more around the products and services supplied by businesses later in the book.

We used to live close to Birmingham in the UK and would regularly go there for dinner out, theatre, cinema, etc. There is a development called the Mailbox in the centre of the city which sits adjacent to the redeveloped canal system of central Birmingham. The building itself was converted from a Royal Mail sorting office, and it opened as a retail, restaurant, and residential development in December 2000.

After an evening out, we wandered into the Mailbox and found an interesting Italian restaurant, and decided to give it a try. Now, in my humble opinion, there is only so much you can do with pasta or pizza, so I wasn't expecting anything amazing. However, I was in for a surprise.

The servers were friendly and efficient. The manager, however, was larger than life. He looked like Kojak, the 1970s New York detective character played by Telly Savalas in the TV series of the same name.

He was engaging with all the diners, cracking jokes and being playful with everyone. At one point he came to our table and said, 'Excuse me, sir, but the gentleman at table seven thinks your wife is very attractive and would like to buy her a glass of champagne . . .' having previously told the couple at table seven that I was someone famous, and he would get my autograph for them.

It was a great evening of good food, great service, and good fun.

The moral of this story, and we will be coming back to the mailbox later, is that it is not just the product or service you deliver that is important. It is the context in which you deliver it that is critical.

Your philosophy has to show up in the way you deliver your products and services. It is what defines your business and makes it unique and differentiated from others you may be competing with.

It's not just the pizza; it's the *experience of the pizza* that counts.

Step Three – Process

How will you deliver your product or service with consistency of quality and profitability?

This is where franchises score really well, because they have to sell what is in effect a business in a box that can be operated by anyone suitably qualified; their business models are fully systematised and documented.

Your business process is not just, using the example above, how you cook the pizza. It is everything associated with the running of the business. In a perfect world, any business owner should be able to give me the keys to their business, along with the systems and procedures that show me how it works, and I should be able to run it in their absence while they go away for a twelve-month cruise.

That is the power of process, as we will see in later chapters; the degree of systematising of your business will depend on the stage of development your business is at.

There is a store on the Las Vegas strip within the Fashion Show Mall, called Nordstrom. They are a designer store specialising in apparel, shoes, and cosmetics for men, women, and children.

They sell shoes, so we became regulars there; it appears that Lynn is a collector of them. I even had Fashion Show Mall typed in as a favourite location in my satellite navigation system, so I could always get there when there was an emergency addition to the collection required.

One Saturday afternoon while Lynn was trying on shoes and dresses for an event we were going to, I sat and watched the world go by. I also noticed how the staff were treating the customers. They were attentive, but not pushy; coffee or water was offered, and they seemed to be anticipating the needs of the customers rather than reacting to them. It was impressive, so much so that I approached one of the managers and asked her how it was that they managed to deliver such good service.

She smiled and immediately showed me a small grey card 130 mm × 200 mm on which was the rules of working at Nordstrom that every employee had to adhere to. It was a system.

It read as follows:

Nordstrom Rules:

>#1: Use best judgement in all situations.

>#2: There will be no additional rules.

How can that be possible? How can excellence be delivered without scripts, protocols, procedures, and processes, especially as this was not their only store? They have around 200 stores in twenty-eight different states in the USA. It sounded like a recipe for chaos.

Simply, they trained their people in the philosophy of Nordstrom and then allowed them to interpret and apply it by using their best judgement. They recruited and trained their people such that when given the freedom and trust to deliver excellence, they did because they were empowered to.

The message here is that whilst it is critical to systematise a business in order that it becomes successful, where your business comes into contact with your clients, there has to be freedom. Your customers aren't interested in your systems; they are only interested in your service and products, the value they derive from them, and the experience they have consuming them.

Step Four – Promotion

Even with a great philosophy, world-class product, and a process that delivers both efficiency and relationships, your prospective customers need to know about it. Your job is not to become the best kept secret in the business, so spread the word.

Marketing and sales is all about getting a specific message to your chosen target, not get any message to anyone. In marketing, you need to be a sniper not a machine gunner, especially in the small- and medium-sized business sectors.

Remember, you are not building a brand – you are building a reputation within your niche. Your promotion should be specifically aimed at attracting your ideal clients and should convey the philosophy, product, and process that will define the uniqueness of the experience they can expect when they come to you. It must be congruent. Customers like surprises, but they don't like the shocks associated with unfulfilled expectations.

We once stayed at a hotel in Arcachon, just outside Bordeaux in France. The brochure assured us of sea views. There were sea views but only if you went onto one corner of the roof terrace and were over 6'2" tall. The marketing was accurate in facts but not accurate in spirit. Keep your promotions activity honest.

Treat your marketing as a separate business division. Every pound you invest must result in more profit in pound to the business. If your marketing isn't achieving this, stop doing it.

Marketing is about getting the telephone to ring, getting the first meeting, having them come to your store, or simply getting on the tender list. Selling is about getting to yes, and the first purchase; your philosophy, product, and process should look after the subsequent purchases.

The more promotional activity you do, the more customers you will attract and the business will grow, providing the rule of return on investment is adhered to. We will be exploring more about promoting your business in the following chapters.

Step Five – Profit

The banker's mantra states that 'Sales is vanity, profit is sanity, but cash is reality'. No business ever went bankrupt for lack of sales or profits; it is always lack of cash that kills a business.

Most businesses will know what their sales are and, providing they are using the accrual based accounting system, they should know what their gross and net margins are. Measuring your business performance is critical; sales profit and cash are the barometers or the scorecards that tell you how well the rest of the business is doing.

If profits are down, for example, you can't just 'make more profit'. You will have to adjust the factors that contribute to generating the profit. Profit is an outcome of a series of events that you have control over. Your philosophy, product, process, and promotion are your levers of power and control.

If someone tells me that their profits are down, all they are really saying is that the way they run their business is not producing the results they want. Profits are the symptoms, and the system is the disease. Remember to treat the disease not the symptoms.

When a business is fully systematised, you can check your results, make a change or adapt a process, and see what different results are achieved. If you don't have a system, you don't have control because you don't know what is working and what is not.

You can see on the model that the profits result feeds back into the philosophy part of the model. When your profitability, and of course cash position, is measured, treat it as feedback and consider what in the other stages of the model needs to be adapted or modified to improve the output. It may be that if your profits are not what you want, it is your philosophy that is holding you back.

Your business is a series of systems. The output is profits and cash. If you don't like the profits you are getting, change the system.

Follow the Rules

Treat your business as a person, and give that person a structure to thrive in. The 8 Rules described in this book are really your instruction manual about how to build your business in the most appropriate sequence of steps that will help you maxims each of the 5 P's of the Cycle of Business.

Rule 1 is about you and how you affect your business, and like it or not, if you want to change your business, the change has to start with you. You will have your personal Statement of Purpose, along with the business vision, mission, and rules of the game; your philosophy on business is clear – now it is time to get your business moving.

Rules 2 to 7 are about development and growth, each subsequent chapter will explain the rules and tactics you can introduce to build your business. Following and applying the rules in sequence, each one building on the previous, will enable your business to grow and for you to achieve your own personal goals and dreams.

Rule 8 is the result of everything else that you achieve in your business, by applying the other rules.

The model below shows you the structure of the rules; notice that your philosophy supports everything and that innovation covers every aspect. All the areas are of equal importance, and being particularly strong in one area alone may not be enough to sustain and help your business grow.

```
┌─────────────────────────────────────────────────────┐
│         Rule #8 - Its not about you anymore         │
├─────────────────────────────────────────────────────┤
│         Rule #7 - You have to innovate              │
└─────────────────────────────────────────────────────┘
 ┌────────┐  ┌────────┐  ┌────────┐  ┌────────┐
 │Rule #3 │  │Rule #4 │  │Rule #5 │  │Rule #6 │
 │ Keep   │  │Attract │  │  You   │  │Systems │
 │  all   │  │  new   │  │  will  │  │ Rules  │
 │ your   │  │customers│ │  need  │  │   OK   │
 │customers│ │         │ │  help  │  │        │
 └────────┘  └────────┘  └────────┘  └────────┘
┌─────────────────────────────────────────────────────┐
│       Rule #2 - Get the foundations right           │
├─────────────────────────────────────────────────────┤
│         Rule #1 - It's all about you                │
└─────────────────────────────────────────────────────┘
```

This is your toolkit to build your business and will enable you to bring the Cycle of Business to life in practical stages.

The level of the results your business will be able to achieve will be dependent upon the extent to which the rules are applied. Now, while the rules are in a particular sequence, and when building a business, this is the sequence that ideally should be followed. There may be opportunities for quick wins from introducing an innovation before new customers are attracted for example; there are exceptions to the rules.

In my seminars and workshops we will work through the process of explaining each rule, how to apply it, and what the benefits will be. Regularly, someone will have a scenario in their business that needs the rules to be adapted or bent to suit. That is fine; these are rules not laws.

There is a science and an art to business; the scientist knows the rules, and the artist knows when to bend them.

Notes

Rule No. 1 – It Is All About You

Drive thy business or it will drive thee.

Benjamin Franklin

You own it. It doesn't matter whether you are the owner of the business, a director, CEO, general manager, operations manager, supervisor, or clerk. You own what you do, and you own the results you get. Your business will have a character and personality of its own. It will build relationships with customers, suppliers, and employees as well as other organisations. It is both a living and legal entity over which you have control and responsibility.

Coming from a family business background, ownership was easy for me to understand. When I worked in other people's businesses I always assumed ownership and treated the enterprises as if they were my own. What I came to realise was that, if I take ownership, I also accept responsibility for my performance and that of those around me. I realised that the ownership mentality meant that my heart and soul was put into the job; that it had an effect on those around me and the results I was able to achieve.

First, let's take a look at what you *don't* need in order to run a successful business:

1. **University Degree** – Education and training are important. Knowledge gives confidence and enables us to see opportunities that would otherwise be missed. However, most degrees do not teach you how to run a business, so don't use the excuse of not having a degree to not start your business. I studied for my MBA and achieved a distinction, good knowledge, ideas, and confidence, but not critical for starting or running a business. Steve Jobs – Apple, Bill Gates – Microsoft, Richard Branson – Virgin Group, Henry Ford – Ford Motor Co; didn't have college or university education before they got into business.

2. **£1,000,000 Cash** (or some other significant amount of money) – Actually starting a business is very cheap in the UK via Companies House; to incorporate a new business is just £20 for example. Now all businesses need cash to fund the start-up periods, probably twice as much as you initially anticipate, and there are other set-up costs that need to be considered. However, some of the best businesses have started in garages, spare bedrooms, using weekends and evenings to get things started. Your job can fund your business in the early stages. Some year ago I was talking with someone starting a new venture; he said that he had everything in place including £50,000 in the bank as a safety net, just in case things picked up slower than anticipated. He asked my advice; I was running my own logistics business at the time. I told him to get rid of the safety net – not spend his money but ignore it, put it somewhere he couldn't easily get at it. The reason was that with a safety net the temptation is always to use it. Only when the £50,000 had gone would he actually get on with building the business. He ignored this advice; however, he contacted me to say that in hindsight I had been right. He had got tangled in his safety net. It became a psychological excuse for him not getting on with building his business. Only when the £50,000 had been exhausted did he decide to get clients and build his company.

3. **Ten Years' Experience** – Business is the best college you can attend. You will learn more in twelve months doing it than in five years reading about it. Advice, guidance, and support are critical to your success, but the best way to learn about business is to get into it. Providing you stay open to advice and guidance from those you choose to associate with, they will compensate for any perceived lack of experience you may have.

4. **Know the 'Right' People** – Having friends and associates that can offer support, ideas, and guidance are really helpful. The only 'right' people you really need to get to know well, however, are your customers. When your product or service

is good enough, unique enough, or adds enough value to them, they will be the best supporters you can have. They are your 'right' people every time.

5. **Fancy Car, Watch, and Suit** – These will come in time if you want them. When you are getting into business, the first thing you buy is not the Porsche; it's more likely to be the building you operate from that you will buy first. Invest first, play later. I have met plenty of 'entrepreneurs' who show up at networking events, dinners, or award ceremonies. Before they have customers, or even raised the first invoice, they have bought the Rolex, the Gucci, and Porsche (all of which are fabulous of course . . .). However, they are not at the event year after. Your customers want to know what you can do for them before they care what you do for yourself. What is the difference between a start-up business owner in a new Porsche and a pizza? A pizza can feed a family of four.

6. **Permission** – Interesting one here. In my work and experience, I have seen several instances of budding entrepreneurs that seem to be waiting for someone to tell them to get into business, or give them permission. Now, whilst having the support of family and those close to you is of course important, I would never start a new venture without Lynn being involved for example. Starting your business is your choice, and the best time to start it is whenever you are ready, or probably even when you think you can't afford it.

7. **Shareholders** – Keep the family jewels. You don't need partners in order to get started. It's called 'having your own business' for a reason, because it's *yours*. Wherever possible, avoid multiple shareholders; if you can, keep it all under your name. The reason is that as time progresses, I can almost guarantee that at some point shareholders will fall out. This damages the business, so as a tip, keep all the shares forever. (If you go public of course then the case is different . . .) If you must have shareholders, then make sure

you get a shareholders' agreement drawn up before you get going.

8. **Premises and 'Stuff'** – A business can be started from just about anywhere. You don't always need premises. Now, it's worth checking what you can and can't do from your home. Local authorities, mortgage lenders, and insurance companies are among those that will advise you on what you are allowed to do; so before you start an iron foundry in your garage, check out the rules and regulations first. If you do need premises, then take advice regarding the leases. If you only have a twelve-month business plan, don't sign a twenty-five-year lease. If you want to find new business owners, go to the stationery store. In there you will find them buying 'stuff', staplers, multi-coloured Post-it notes, pens, paper, and all the paraphernalia that they think will demonstrate that they are actually in business. All you may need is a basic computer, web access, and a telephone to get you started. Buy your leather office furniture and designer desk tidy on the way home from collecting your first client cheque that is over £25,000.

What You *Do* Need

It's like searching for the Holy Grail, attempting to define what makes a person successful in business. I don't believe that there is a perfect mould or pattern that can be copied and duplicated such that success can be guaranteed. There are, however, attributes that are critical – the absence of which will almost certainly restrict the likelihood of you being

---

Lynn and I have been together since 1979 and married since 1986. We have one law and one rule that have served us well so far:

1. Law – OK to look, but don't touch.

2. Rule – Never be apart for more than sixteen hours.

Law can't be broken; rule can be broken by agreement.

successful in business. So let's take a look at what you *do* need – in no particular order . . .

1. **Energy** – At least in the early stages, you will be working harder for yourself, for less money than any job you would consider applying for. If you have the attitude that your own business is a 'job' that can be clocked in and out of every day, then maybe it's not for you. Your business will be all encompassing. It will become not only what you do but define who you are; you will need lots of energy. In your own business if you don't make the sale, you don't eat, simple. So you will have to do whatever it takes to make it work. That takes physical energy to do the hours you may need to do, and emotional energy to keep yourself applied and motivated to keep going.

2. **To Win** – Be competitive, having the need to come first – beat the target, beat the competition, beat the deadline. Winning in business is just about the number one priority. It's not just about the money. Sales and profits are the barometers by which you can simply tell how good you are at winning. Win more, make more, and be able to do more.

3. **Commitment** – When you promise yourself and those around you that you will do whatever it takes to achieve your dreams, keep at it until you do. In business you will have days of pure elation, and you will also have days of pure despair. I remember some years ago having to pay our VAT and staff payroll by using my credit cards. I didn't pay the mortgage because I paid my team. If you are prepared to make a commitment then be prepared to keep it. When you shake hands on a deal or agree to something, whether with a customer, supplier, employee, or even an agreement with yourself, stick to it; keep your promises and your promises will keep you.

4. **Focus** – Follow the plan and stay on track. Keep your objectives in mind at all times. When you are clear about your objectives and your purpose, staying on track is easy.

Without clarity, confusion reigns. Combining your attention and intention will get you results. A disciplined approach to your work and activity is important.

5. **Knowledge** – Know your product and service and know your customers and the environment. Ignorance is not bliss. In fact in business it will wipe you out. Knowledge is nothing without understanding; understand what your customers need and want (they are different), what your market environment requires, and how to keep your business ahead of their combined expectations. Keep learning – one of my rules is to read a book every week – I take notes, keep ideas, and keep my knowledge growing. Knowledge itself is not power, but understanding how to use it is.

6. **Intelligence** – It's not just about being smart. Emotional intelligence is a skill that can be learned and refined; having the ability to control your own emotions and influence those of others will help you with your interactions. Remember, we are emotional creatures and having the ability to perceive, use, manage, and understand emotional states of ourselves and others is fundamental to building relationships; and business is all about relationships.

7. **Vision and Goals** – Have these written down and broken down into bite-size chunks. Having these will keep you focussed and give you a benchmark or a target to achieve. Long-term goals should be broken down into short-term objectives and activities. In his book *Be My Guest,* in the first chapter entitled 'You've Got to Dream', Conrad Hilton explains how when he saw a picture of the newly completed Waldorf Astoria Hotel in New York in 1931, although at the time he was nearly bankrupt, he cut out the picture and wrote across it 'The greatest of them all'. When he got his own office and desk, the picture was placed under a sheet of protective glass on the surface of his desk so that he could see it every day – the dream being to own the Waldorf

Astoria. In October 1949, the dream became a reality and the Waldorf Astoria hotel became part of the Hilton Group.

8. **Risk Taking** – If you are not prepared to take a risk, then don't get into business. Risks can be mitigated of course with good planning, research, and implementation, but at some point, you will have to back your ideas with your money or your time, or likely both. There is always a risk that your idea won't work, that you will not achieve the outcome you planned. In fact, I can almost guarantee that in business a lot of your outcomes will not be those you planned, good or bad. What some people see as a risk, others don't, and vice versa. You have to be able to take the wins with the losses and not take it personally. Dust yourself down, get back on the horse, and keep going. Your rewards will be commensurate with the risks you take.

9. **Standards** – I have been fortunate to have had the opportunity to get to know a number of successful entrepreneurs and business people. I have read the biographies and life stories of others that I have not had the privilege of knowing personally yet. The people, who are successful in business, have standards that they adopt and that become fundamental to the way they run their business. How they treat their customers, their employees, and suppliers is a critical aspect of the business operations. It defines the culture of the organisation and is a visible manifestation of their personality and personal philosophy. Now, entrepreneurs and managers are not all saints. However, I have found that the ones who operate consistently and sustainably have high standards of integrity and honesty amongst others. You may not always agree with what they say, or even like what they are saying, but at least you know where you stand.

These areas combine to define your philosophy on, and attitude towards your business. The philosophy of the owners of any business will always show up in how the business looks, feels, and operates, whether you like it or not. By taking control and defining your philosophy, you are setting the standards that everyone can understand and contribute to. Whilst you can choose your philosophy, it must be true; if you are not congruent with the standards and rules that you define, or they are simply written as a piece of marketing to fill a page on the web site, you won't get away with it for long. Your customers, employees, and suppliers will see through it very quickly and the trust will be broken.

So here we have an opportunity to ask ourselves questions about our motives and standards. If these are what define how our business operates, we need to make sure that we are 'fit for purpose'. When you look back on your career, relationships, and business ventures, look for the common factor in all the outcomes – the common factor in all of mine is me, and in all of yours, is you.

Do you need to change anything?

If your philosophy is to simply get every penny from your customers, not care about service, quality, relationships, and reputation, then that is what will show up in your business – regardless of what you write down. Business is a true test of character, and it will reveal your attributes and personality to the world.

However, if your philosophy is to provide excellence in all areas of your business, recognising that profits are simply a result of the amount of value you add to others, this too will be revealed.

It is this philosophy that will define your business, and remember, it will go through stages of growth. Whilst your philosophy may be consistent throughout, the method in which you apply it will adapt over time.

Stages of Growth

Your business will be unique; you and your business will have a relationship – it needs to be a marriage, not a date. Treat your business as if it were a person. Your business will go through stages of development, as a person would; treat your business as such. What stage your business is at will depend on you and the manner in which the business has grown over time.

Remember that your business has to go through these stages. Some will take longer than others and some may be more successful than others, but you have to go through them. Whilst your philosophy may not change fundamentally, the way your business operates almost certainly will.

1. **Conception** – The idea, the spark of creativity, that first sketch on the back of a beer mat or napkin in the pub, the idea that comes to you while you are waiting in the departure lounge of LAX. The excitement and thrill of you having the potential to realise your dreams and visions. Your focus here is time and resources to enable the business to get started.

2. **Birth** – Can take some time. Some births are more difficult than others and may follow lengthy gestation periods of procrastination, deliberation, or second thoughts. Creating your business from nothing, whilst not exactly a miracle, is none the less a significant project. Raising finance, branding, web sites, email systems, and product or service design will take time and will need to be completed if the idea you had at conception is to become a reality. In my experience, single births are less traumatic than multiple births. You open the doors for trade, and your new business is born. As the proud parent, you show of your new addition to all your friends and family, who of course only tell you what a pretty baby you have. All is good with the world; you are now in business and have entered the world of the entrepreneur. Your focus here is sales, where will the first customer come from, who will receive the first invoice from you, and what revenue will you achieve.

3. **Infancy** – Your new business is totally dependent on you; it can do nothing by itself and relies on you to do everything for it. You start to have sleepless nights as your business keeps you awake. You realise that the cute little project you

started actually needs constant feeding with cash and time. It is unpredictable and needs constant care and attention. Your baby isn't as attractive as you thought. Customers aren't flocking to your door, and the phone is not ringing. Instead of being the world's best accountant/lawyer/web designer/manufacturer or restaurateur, you have to become a sales and marketing guru, and at the same time you have to teach your new venture not only how to eat, walk, and talk, but how to be presentable and attractive, more attractive that the other babies that you never knew were around before but who have somehow shown up to upset your plans. Your focus here is gross margins; you start to adapt your pricing to suit the market.

4. **Early Childhood** – The worst is over. Your little darling can now at least walk and talk, eat and dress on her own. Your business has a personality and can actually produce a product or a service that people find attractive. And whilst you still need to give constant care and attention to your creation, you are now considering developing and expanding your repertoire and increasing the pace of development. Your business is turning in a profit; however, you are not taking wages yet because all money is being put back into the development and growth of your baby. Your focus begins to turn to cash flow as the business grows, and you realise that, depending on which sector you are in, your customers pay you later than you pay your suppliers, and the bank is not as friendly as they were before.

5. **Formative Period** – You decide that you cannot cope with all the jobs you have to do as a busy entrepreneur and that you need a nanny for your little angel. You hire a manager to run some aspects of your business so that you can focus on what you do best. The mistake is of course that you hire someone to run the business for you while you do the technical work of being the accountant/lawyer/web designer/engineer or chef, because you forget that you own a business, not a job, and that your role is to manage the

business and build a team to deliver the products and services in a consistent manner, in line with your philosophy, dreams, and objectives. You go through several nannies until you find someone who is better at the technical work than you are, and out of desperation, you hire them to deliver the product, while you concentrate of building relationships with customers, strategic development of the business; you have just become a business owner rather than self-employed. Progress is being made. Now with increased costs, your attention is still on the cash, but also net profitability. You realise that you have to get value from every expense in the business; efficiency and productivity begin to become compelling.

6. **Adolescence** – The difficult time. As your baby matures, and you have more people helping you with her development and growth, you have nannies, teachers, coaches, trainers as well as advice from friends and family, she starts to rebel against your philosophy, and the dreams and aspirations you had for her no longer seem relevant. At some point, your business will go through a process of change. When the period of early development is finished, you will stand back and look at what you have created and wonder what happened. Yes, the business is successful and growing, but it wasn't exactly what you had in mind at conception. You have to make a choice; you have to either acknowledge that your business may have grown in a slightly different way to the one you anticipated, but that it still fits with your philosophy and values and is enabling to achieve your objectives, or not. This is a critical point for you as the business owner; are you going to allow your business to grow and flourish with the ideas and input from your team, customer, and advisors, allowing for innovation of products and services that will keep the business growing? Are you going to allow the science and art to guide your activities, or are you going to decide it is too uncomfortable and put your child up for adoption, or keep it in nappies and not allow it to flourish? Remember that you have to grow and develop as a business

owner/entrepreneur, and at some point, you will have to make the leap from being the directive parent of the business to becoming the consultative uncle. You will have to let go and pass the control to your team, allow them to guide your business, make mistakes, and even do things you don't like occasionally. This is a coming of age for the business, and coming of age for you as the owner. Your focus here will be on the products and services that are contributing to the net profits; the direction of the business may need to change or adapt with the introduction of the new or the discarding of the old.

7. **Adulthood** – Now your child has matured into an attractive, professional, proficient, and charming character. It's time for growth and continued development. As your business matures and you have the people and systems in place so that it runs almost independently, you, as the chairman of the board, can work on strategic development. Now you have choices. You can duplicate the business and open other branches, form alliances with other businesses or buy them and build a group, or you may decide to franchise your models. Or, of course, you can keep it as it is, maximise your returns, and prepare the business for sale or as a legacy for your family. The key here is that you have the luxury of choice, and that once your business achieves adulthood, the possibilities for continued innovation and growth are much greater. Now you will be focussing on shareholder value and become more interested in the balance sheet than the profit and loss statements.

So, your business is all about you, and you will need to learn and develop new skills at a faster pace than your business grows, otherwise it will get out of control, or you find that you become the limiting factor in the success of your own entity; you are on a journey as much as your business is.

Bringing Your Philosophy to Life – Four-Step Process

Assuming that by now you are clear on what your philosophy is, here are the four steps:

Step 1 – Statement of purpose. Universities and professional schools will sometimes require a prospective student to prepare and submit a 'statement of purpose' or SoP, prior to enrolment on a course of study. The reason behind it is that admissions tutors need to be clear regarding the reasons why a student wants to enrol in a particular course of study, what their motivation is, and how success in their chosen field would contribute to their own development and objectives. The same rules apply for us in life and, therefore, in business.

Your SoP should be in the form of a few paragraphs detailing your personal objectives including professional, personal, and financial, and how your business will contribute to these objectives. We all intuitively know what our purposes are. However, writing them down somehow makes them more tangible and real; it is an interesting process to go through and will make you think. Your SoP should establish what is important to you:

- Recognising your key skills, attributes, experience, and knowledge

- Defining what values guide and influence you, why they are important, and how they will manifest themselves in your life

- Bring clarity regarding which beliefs you hold to be true and their importance to you

- Understanding who it is that is important to you and which people you'll need to take on the journey with you

- Committing to how you will contribute and make a difference, to whom and by when. How do you want to be remembered, what legacy will you leave

- Stating what goals and objectives you will accomplish – short term (twelve months) and long term (five to ten years).

It should be a document that inspires you and captures the essence of you as an individual, why it is that you do what you do and what success looks like and feels like to you. Now you can translate this in to your business.

Step 2 – Vision statement for your business. Your business is the vehicle by which you will achieve many of your goals, so your business and personal objectives need to be synchronised. The vision of your business should be synchronised with your personal statement of purpose; they should be complimentary. Remember that you set the scene for your business. It is your choice, and the reason that you are in business is to realise your purpose.

To create a vision for your business, consider what your business will look like in ten years' time. What specific achievements will it have accomplished? The vision is your long-term driver; it defines the results and outcomes that will be achieved by the business and, essentially, determines what success looks like.

Here are a few examples to get you started:

- *Walmart* – Worldwide leader in retail
- *Walt Disney Corporation* – To make people happy
- *Microsoft* – A personal computer in every home running Microsoft software
- *Amazon* – Our vision is to be earth's most customer-centric company; to build a place where people can come to find and discover anything they might want to buy online.

The vision should engage and excite you and the people working with you. For example, when we created our company **Results RULES OK**, we defined our 2020 vision as follows:

> 'To enable everyone to enjoy learning, achieving, doing, and being more . . .'

This is how we constructed and interpret our vision.

- **20:20** - We have a defined time frame in which to achieve the vision, 31 December 2020.

- **Enable Everyone** – Make our materials accessible to the widest possible audience on a global basis.

- **Enjoy** – One of our values is fun, and we believe that learning and professional and personal development should be fun, and people should enjoy working with us.

- **Learning** – We are in the business of educating, entertaining, training, and inspiring people.

- **Achieving** – We recognise that our activities must result in positive and tangible results being achieved. The name Results Rules OK is true; they do . . .

- **Doing** – To get results, we have to do something different than we have been in the past. We will encourage people to do what they didn't think they could in order to achieve what they didn't think was possible.

- **Being More** – Personal growth is a positive objective, and through leadership and inspiration we will encourage people to be the best they can become.

Every word is significant, and it enables us to develop our services and products accordingly. If we have an opportunity, providing it takes us closer to our vision, we go for it, whereas if it takes us away from our vision, we decline.

> Star Trek, Starship Enterprise – 'its five-year mission to explore strange new worlds, to seek out new life and new civilisations; to boldly go where no man has gone before'.

Your vision statement can be a single line, a paragraph, or a whole page – whatever makes sense to you and really defines what you are in business for and the difference you intend to make.

Step 3 – Mission statement. Mission statements have been misused and misunderstood in business. They have tended to become clichéd, particularly in the domain of the marketing and PR departments; do not let your marketing people define the mission for your business; their job is to promote and educate about it, not get involved with the writing of it.

If you want to test out the validity of the mission statement of any business, just ask the employees or better still, ask their customers what it is, most of the time they will not know, so it becomes an irrelevance.

In 2001, one of my clients was a plastic injection moulding company based in Birmingham. In the dreary reception area, displayed on the wall was a framed copy of the company's mission, vision, and values statement, signed by the chairman, no less. I asked the receptionist what the mission, vision, and values of the company were, she had no idea. I asked the production manager, who was my client, what they were, he told me that he didn't know and that it was something that the directors had had to put up as a requirement of achieving Investors in People accreditation (an initiative by the UK Government to help improve business performance) and be allowed to get on the tender lists with large prospective customers. No one cared what they were, and because they weren't defined, everyone made them up to suit themselves. By 2008 they were no longer in business.

In 2007, we stayed in a fabulous resort hotel in Portugal, the Penha Longa Hotel, Spa, and Golf Resort, nestling in the Sintra Mountains near Lisbon, close to the Estoril coastline, and out of interest, Grand Prix circuit too. Part of the Ritz Carlton Group they specialise in luxury spa breaks and providing a five-star experience. About three days into our stay, I noticed a pattern; their team seemed particularly attentive to our needs; they remembered our names and seemed genuinely interested in the experience we were having during our stay with them. They would make decisions regarding our requests without having to speak to 'management' and always checked that our requests had been fulfilled. I asked one of the reception staff how it was that everyone seemed to be able to combine to give such great service; she immediately pulled out of her pocket a small card that was entitled the 'Ritz Carlton Credo', which effectively defined the mission of the company.

Everyone had one of these cards – the bar, restaurant, and cleaning staff. It was a living set of values that everyone not only knew of but understood and worked to the letter and spirit of as well. And it showed. The service was exceptional, and it wasn't because the Ritz Carlton Group wanted to simply get a certificate for Investors in People on the wall; it was because they know that it makes very good business sense. In 2011, they were unsurprisingly still in business.

Your mission statement should define how you will achieve your vision. It doesn't need to be too specific. That will come when you do your business planning as we shall see. It needs to set the ground rules, or the basic standards, compliance with which, will move the organisation nearer to the vision.

This is ours, the **Results RULES OK** mission statement:

> Results RULES OK is a growing, profitable, and successful business. Our growth will be achieved through the design and delivery of the world's best knowledge-based experiences to all of our customers regardless of their size and location, or the type of our programmes or products they buy from us.
>
> We are a team of outstanding, professional, and passionate people who believe and trust in the 2020 vision, mission, and values of Results RULES OK. We are in the business of providing amazing speaking, training, support, and development programmes that will be experienced, enjoyed, and used by everyone on the planet.
>
> All our customers will be attracted to us and stay with us because of our abilities, reputation, the results we enable them to achieve, and the trust-based relationships we develop. We offer value for money, and we adapt our products and services to the needs of our customers, offering a truly unique and bespoke service. We will do whatever it takes to achieve results, both for ourselves, our partners, and customers.
>
> We will impress our customers by exceeding their expectations, and through shock and awe, they will not only remain with us but they will be compelled to refer their customers, suppliers, friends, and associates to us.
>
> We are in the people business and work with like-minded partners and associates to help us achieve our vision. We build long-term relationships and value the feedback we receive from those who work with us. We have fun in our business, and we encourage everyone else to as well. Every one of our team is empowered to make decisions using their best judgement at all times. Customer service is everyone's responsibility. Profit is the result of customers

saying 'wow!' about what we do, not about what we charge.

Our suppliers are our partners, and we will treat them as such. We promise to pay for the services we have requested and work with them to resolve any issues that may arise. We are good people to do business with, and we respect that all businesses have to be profitable; we expect the same in return.

Our strategic and tactical plans are designed to support the 2020 vision of our business and will be reviewed on a regular basis. This mission statement will be reviewed continually but by no later than the end of 2015.

Remember you are introducing your philosophy into your business. If you believe that something is important, include it. Don't include statements of the obvious or those that are negatively positioned.

For example, personally I don't like the inclusion of phrases such as 'prompt, professional, and courteous service'; as opposed to what? The rude and insolent service you used to get before the consultant wrote the mission statement?

You expect to get that as a minimum anyway. It's not your mission to be mediocre; it is your mission, however, to be outstanding.

Here are some examples of what to avoid. These are actual extracts from mission statements, although I have not quoted the names of the companies they came from. I may of course write to them and offer my help.

Hotel – 'Gay Friendly'.

Not sure what this means. However, it suggests that the hotel down the road is actually the 'fascist homophobe friendly' one, so we have a choice of where to stay. Don't have as your mission that which you are compelled to offer anyway. That is not a mission – it is a compliance notice.

Electronics – 'To scout profitable growth opportunities in relationships, both internally and externally, in emerging, mission inclusive markets, and explore new paradigms and then filter and communicate and evangelise the findings.'

What? Your mission needs to be simple and easily understood by everyone; it is a statement of intent not a statement of how many big words you know.

Anyone – 'It's our responsibility to collaboratively engineer economically sound deliverables in order to enthusiastically initiate world-class content to set us apart from the competition.'

OK, so this one was generated by the Dilbert Mission Statement Generator online and doesn't relate to any business, but you get the message.

Step 4 – Rules of the game. Define the general principles that should be understood and complied with by everyone in the business, including the owner. These are not the rules and regulations about what to do if someone is sick, or needs to book a holiday, etc. Those will be in the company handbook. The rules of the game define a code of conduct that people may be expected to be held accountable to. These have been called value statements, culture statements, or as the Ritz Carlton Group call them simply – 'basics'.

Here is where your philosophy actually manifests itself in your business, how you and your team will work together, how they will interact with customers, what expectations are placed upon them, and how your business will be perceived by your customers and suppliers.

For example, South West Airlines have clear rules with regards to customer service, and those rules and the culture of service excellence enabled this moving story to unfold.

On 5 January 2011, Caden Rogers was just two years old when he was admitted to hospital after allegedly being attacked by his mother's boyfriend at his home in Colorado. His injuries were so severe as a result of the attack that he had to be placed on life support, and his parents agreed that within twenty-four hours his life support should be turned off so that his organs could be used for transplant.

After being contacted by the parents with the tragic news, Caden's grandfather, who was in Los Angeles at the time, was told that if he could get to Colorado before Caden's life support was removed, he would be able to say goodbye.

The grandfather arrived two hours early at LAX in order to catch his South West Airlines flight to Denver; however, the queues at the security lines meant that he would very likely miss his plane. He explained to the Transport Security Administration or TSA representatives of his predicament, but they chose to simply ignore him and told him he would have to wait along with everyone else.

So he phoned his wife and told her what had happened. She in turn contacted South West Airlines to see if they could help.

When he finally got through security and arrived at the gate, he was met by the pilot of the plane who said, 'They can't go anywhere without me, and I'm not going anywhere without you. Now relax, we'll get you there.'

The pilot had taken it on himself to commit what is in effect a cardinal sin in the aviation industry; he had delayed a plane for twelve minutes and chosen to wait for this grandfather so he could say goodbye to his grandson before his life support was removed.

That single act of human kindness has had global press coverage, and South West Airlines have received more positive PR due to that pilot taking it upon himself to delay the plane, than any amount of marketing that money could buy.

Living in Las Vegas, I would regularly use South West Airlines as they do have a different and refreshing approach to customer service, and they actually make it fun to fly. They were my airline of choice, and I am not surprised that the pilot chose to delay the plane. Their culture of unique customer service runs throughout the business. It is how they do things, and the difference shows.

On their web site, they state that 'We like to think of ourselves as a customer service company that happens to fly airplanes (on schedule, with personality and perks along the way). How may we help you today?'

If you want your team to deliver the extraordinary, then make sure they know that it is OK to make a decision. If the rule of the game is customer service, then allow them to achieve it. I don't know what fines or financial penalties were levied on South West because of the delay. However, the fact that they got that grandfather to Colorado makes any fines worthwhile. Well done, South West.

Now, the same cannot be said of the TSA. What were they thinking? The amount of good press that South West attracted was only matched by the bad press that the TSA generated because of their attitude. The difference of course is that passengers can choose which airline to use, whereas the TSA is mandatory on everyone and they don't need to attract customers.

So, your rules of the game need to be clear and concise and ensure that your philosophy, purpose, vision, and mission are manifested in your business and that they become true for everyone associated with it.

Our rules of the game:

1. **Respect** – We treat everyone with respect, courtesy, and friendship. We are in the business of building positive lasting relationships with customers, suppliers, partners, and team members.

2. **Fun** – We enjoy what we do, and it shows, and we encourage others to do the same.

3. **Service** – We are here to help our customers with our products and services enabling them to achieve great results. Everyone in the team is empowered to make

decisions using their best judgement that will ensure our customers are amazed by what we do.

4. **Success** – We are a successful business, and we make a profit so that we can maintain our standards and continue to grow and develop.

5. **Excellence** – Only the best is good enough. Our products and services are amazing and so are the results our clients achieve; we will innovate and introduce new concepts and materials only when they add value to our customers.

6. **Ownership** – We take responsibility for our results and accept feedback regarding our conduct. We will always speak about others in the manner we would have them speak about us, and assume the same courtesy in return.

How Does Your Business Reflect You?

The cycle of business from the introduction shows the 'process' of running a business, and in the perfect world, the three operational aspects – product, process, and promotion – would each be the separate responsibility of an individual, team, or department. The reality is that as the owner of the business, your preferences and influence on the business will show up in how the business runs.

Your business, regardless of its size, will be a reflection of you. If you want to know what someone is like, take a look at their kitchen, their bathroom, bedroom, and car – the signs will be there. If you want to know what a business owner is like, simple – just look at their business, their people, and the results they achieve.

Having a business is like the story in *The Picture of Dorian Gray*, the 1891 novel by Oscar Wilde, in which a painted picture of Dorian Gray ages and bears the scars of life, while the actual Dorian Gray remains youthful and vibrant. Your business will reveal and display your knowledge, your fears, your successes, and your failures; it becomes a true likeness. If you want to change your business, the change may need to start with you.

'Work harder on yourself than you do on your job.' – Jim Rohn.

As the owner, you will have direct control of the three key aspects of your business, the orchestration of which will result in the degree of profitability that the business achieves. The model below shows this relationship; the area where the circles overlap represents the level of profit achieved.

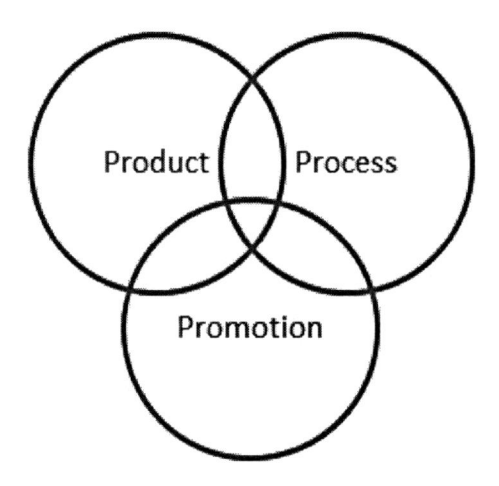

```
        Product    Process

              Promotion
```

That is how it should look; the three circles are the same size, with each area receiving a similar amount of attention and investment, and each one contributing to the result to a similar degree.

Depending upon your background, experience, and training, you may find that you are more comfortable with some of the disciplines of the model more than others, and your preferences will show up in how your business runs, and the focus you and your team maintain.

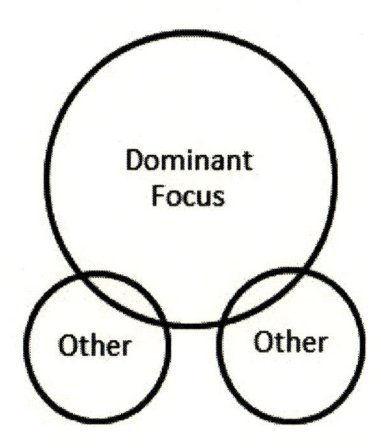

Imagine you have a single dominant focus within your business. It doesn't matter which one of the three you choose – the effect is the same.

Product Focus

Let's say you are naturally gifted at the product aspect of your business. Your expertise and focus lies within the design, process, or engineering aspect of what your business does. Classically, this is where the technicians – the dentists, lawyers, accountants, designers, etc. – find themselves. Your focus on this to the detriment of the other two will mean that you may remain an expert in your field. However, without promotion and process, the business will not grow, and you will be locked into a job, continually having to produce client work or billable hours, rather than have a business that you can manage and develop.

Promotion Focus

Say, the dominant focus was promotion, and your strength was developing marketing and development plans and generating leads and customers on a consistent basis for your business. As you attract the customers through only this focus, you will find that your service levels and client retention levels are poor. You will be attracting new customers only to effectively kick them in the teeth, so your business cycle becomes a self-fulfilling prophecy; you have to keep the promotion activity high all the time because of the inability to keep long-term clients. Your reputation will suffer as word spreads, and it becomes a spiral that becomes ever more difficult to break.

Process Focus

Assume your focus is singularly on the process aspects, then whilst you will have the most systematised business in the world, it will be systematically delivering products that your customers don't want. And without any promotional activity, it will be the best-kept secret in the world as well. You will attract a number of customers that appreciate what you produce and the services you deliver. However, growth will be restricted. Innovation can be the casualty of a singular focus on process.

I once worked with probably the brightest person I have ever come across. He was a brilliant engineer who had developed a unique process of heat treating and moulding waste plastics. The process was truly amazing, unique, and innovative. He would delight in showing me the machines, the control equipment, and the latest jigs and fixtures he had made to improve the productivity. The difficulty was that the process was making a product that no one knew about. There was very little promotional activity happening, because he believed that his process was so amazing that it would automatically attract customers, regardless of the product itself.

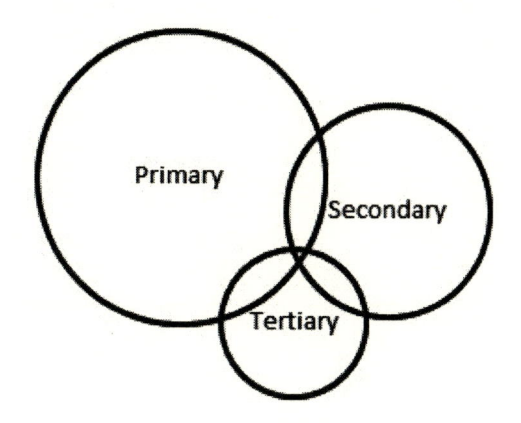

Now what happens in reality is that most businesses don't have a single dominant focus; they generally have one which is dominant, one which is maintained, and one which is neglected – which one will depend on the owner.

There is no such thing as a typical business. However, in my experience, the hierarchy will regularly look like this:

1. Primary Focus – Product
2. Secondary Focus – Process
3. Tertiary Focus – Promotion

The reason for this is that regularly it is the accountants who run accounting practices, lawyers who run legal practices, and chefs who run restaurants. People regularly get into business because they have a technical ability or skill that they want to make into a business, so that is why they keep their primary focus on the product; it is what they know best, what they understand, and where they feel comfortable.

The process of delivering the product or service will receive attention especially as the business begins to grow. However, the challenge that so many businesses face is that the structure of the business doesn't mature into a systematised hierarchy. The business remains in the structure of a monarchy with centralised control and decision making remaining with the owner. The team, whilst being productive, depend on the owner for decision making, technical, and commercial guidance.

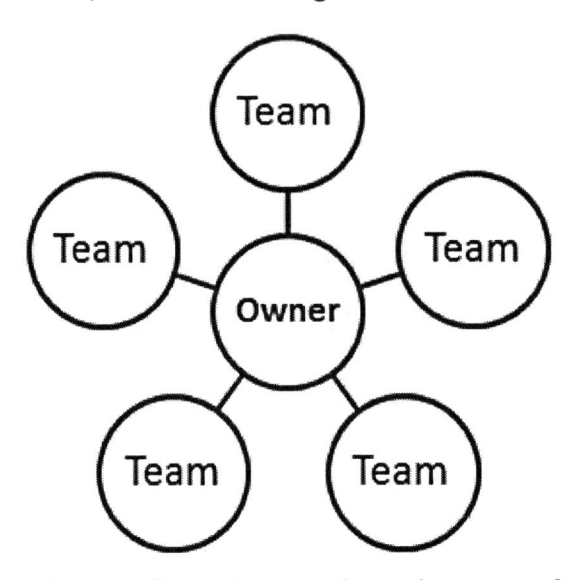

```
        ( Team )
           |
( Team )—( Owner )—( Team )
          / \
    ( Team ) ( Team )
```

This structure is great for projects or the early stages of growth of a business, and it is the natural form of a product or service enterprise. It is, however, restricting on the growth potential of the business, and it will lock the owner into a technical product-focussed job; the business cannot run without the owner. This is why so many owners don't take holidays, or if they do, spend most of the time on the mobile phone talking to the office just to check everything is going as per plan. There is a structural defect in their business.

At some point, the business has to become structured and systematised. There has to be a focus upon the process aspect of the business to enable it to grow. This can be a challenge for the owner as it means that they have to pass authority and control over to someone else. They have to learn to stop being the accountant, lawyer, or chef and become a business owner whose role is the growth and development of the business, not the delivery of the product.

```
        Owner
       /     \
  Manager   Manager
   /  \        |
Team  Team   Team
```

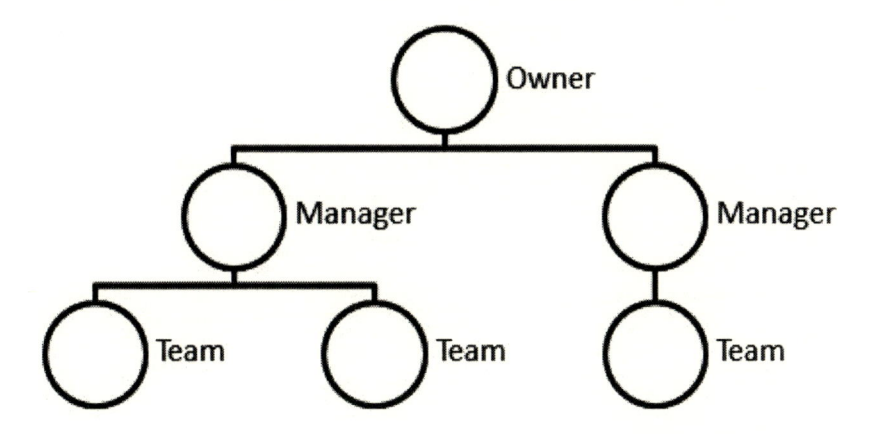

The hierarchy structure requires process. Systems and procedures need to be defined, and people have to be recruited and trained to carry out the roles and delegated responsibilities. To recruit people to effectively replace the activity that the owner has traditionally done requires money, and the level of promotional activity in the business at its current levels may not be generating enough work for the business to be able to afford to hire people.

So the business cycle that many companies get locked into is that constraints of cash would limit the ability of the business to invest in the process and promotional activities that will generate the cash in the first place.

How Do We Put This Right?

At the start of the book, I proposed that your business should be built as if you are going to franchise it and that the combination of your philosophy with product, process, promotion, and the resulting profit is the model to enable this to be achieved.

If I buy a hamburger franchise, my job as the owner is not to serve the customers, flip the burgers, or clean down the ovens. My job is to manage the system such that it produces predictable outcomes of revenue and profits; and this should be the role of a business owner in any sector.

The benefits of a systematised business that has the owner looking after strategy, and the team looking after operations, are

1. More efficient business will return greater shareholder returns on a consistent basis.
2. The model is scalable and the business can grow through duplication.
3. The business is worth more should it come to be sold. Investors will buy themselves a business; they won't want to buy themselves a job.

The first 'mistake' that business owners make, I know because I have done it myself in the past, is that they start the 'wrong' business. What I mean is that the best business for a qualified accountant to own may be a restaurant; a skilled mechanic could own a delicatessen or a salon.

The reason is that, taking the case of the accountant and the restaurant, people who know how to do the technical work will have to be hired from day one. The accountant will not be able to do the cooking or food preparation; qualified staff will have to be hired from the start. The structure of the business that starts like this is different from one that starts with the owner as technician at the centre of the monarchy; this business will have to be in the form of a hierarchy from day one.

Of course this is not very helpful, and I am not suggesting that the way to put this right is to abandon ship and start again. Tempting as that may be . . .

Now again, back in the real world, we start a business because we have a passion, an interest, and a skill, so of course we tend to go for what we know about and enjoy doing. We get in to business for a variety of reasons in the first place – freedom, escape from corporate, to be in control of our futures, or to make a difference, and we are bound to get involved in the product aspects of what we do.

The challenge is that when this approach actually begins to become the limiting factor in the success of our business, we have to change the way we do things and adopt a new approach. The opportunity we have is that we can still do what we love and enjoy with regards to the delivery of a great product, whilst having a business that is more structured, profitable, and able to grow.

We have to start from where we are; we have to effectively reverse engineer your business so that the outcome is the same as if you had started with a fully systematised 'franchise' model. The solution is to build your business in a methodical and structured way, one that enables your existing business to be refined and adapted to maximise its current potential, whilst generating the cash flow that will allow you to invest in the people, processes, and promotional activities that will maintain sustainable growth.

The following chapters will describe the tactics and concepts associated with each of the Eight Rules and, most importantly, define the most effective sequence to apply them. This will enable you to get your business where you want it to be; and so you can take holidays without the mobile phone.

When it comes to building a business, there are a number of key attributes all of which contribute to the steps of the cycle of business described earlier. It is the introduction of these attributes in a planned and structured way that will enable you to grow your business while retaining your core philosophy at its heart.

Notes

Rule No. 2 – Get the Foundations Right

Disneyland is a work of love. We didn't go into Disneyland just with the idea of making money.

Walt Disney

The components of a solid foundation for your business are to

1. Have a plan
2. Get the product right
3. Get the process right
4. Know your numbers

Have a Plan

Most business plans are written not for the benefit of the owners or directors but for the benefit of the bank when a loan is required. The plan is then packed away and consigned to a shelf to gather dust and never gets brought out unless your bank manager pays you a visit. This may be a little extreme but not that far from reality for a lot of businesses. The day-to-day survival activities that are required to keep your business operational mean that medium and long-term planning is one of the first areas to be neglected.

Plans are great as guides and benchmarks against which progress can be compared. However, it is not the issue that we anticipate that cause us the greatest challenges. The global recession of 2008/2009, the BP Deepwater Horizon disaster of April 2010, or the political changes in Egypt in early 2011 all had dramatic and long-lasting effects on people and businesses; and none of them were predicted.

The issues that will present us with either our greatest opportunities or challenges cannot be predicted. As Robert Burns found out in November 1785 whilst ploughing a field and turning up a nest of mice, 'the best laid schemes of mice and men . . .'

Prepare for the unexpected; leave flexibility and contingency in any plans you make so that when you get either a pleasant surprise or an unpleasant shock, there is capacity for them to be dealt with.

So to start with, any plans you make must be simple, clear, and easy to use. Whenever possible, have a single-page business plan, such that they can be put on the wall, circulated to the team, and referred to easily; they become relevant and meaningful to the business and the people in it. That is the key with developing a great plan. Everyone in the business should have and own their plan that contributes to the objectives of the business.

Build your plan starting with your statement of purpose, vision, mission, and 'rules of the game' documents that we have explored in the first chapter. Then looking at where your business is now, compared to where you need it to be in ten years, choose the major objectives that have to be accomplished in order to achieve the vision.

The more comprehensive the plan, the more relevant and practical it will prove to be. Involve your trusted advisors or members of your team in the development of the plans; they may well see things that you don't and come up with some of the best ideas and suggestions, plus people who are involved in putting together the plan are much more likely to take ownership and responsibility for it.

There are a number of ways to put your plans together, the process chart details, and the various stages that need to be completed. The principle of the system is to take your long-term visions and objectives and break them down into specific goals and activities that will help you achieve them.

The planning model shown below gives you an overview of the planning system that will be discussed during this chapter. As you can see, it starts with the vision and results in a daily to-do list with all stages covered in between. There are a range of free documents available on our web site at www.yourbusinessrulesok.com.

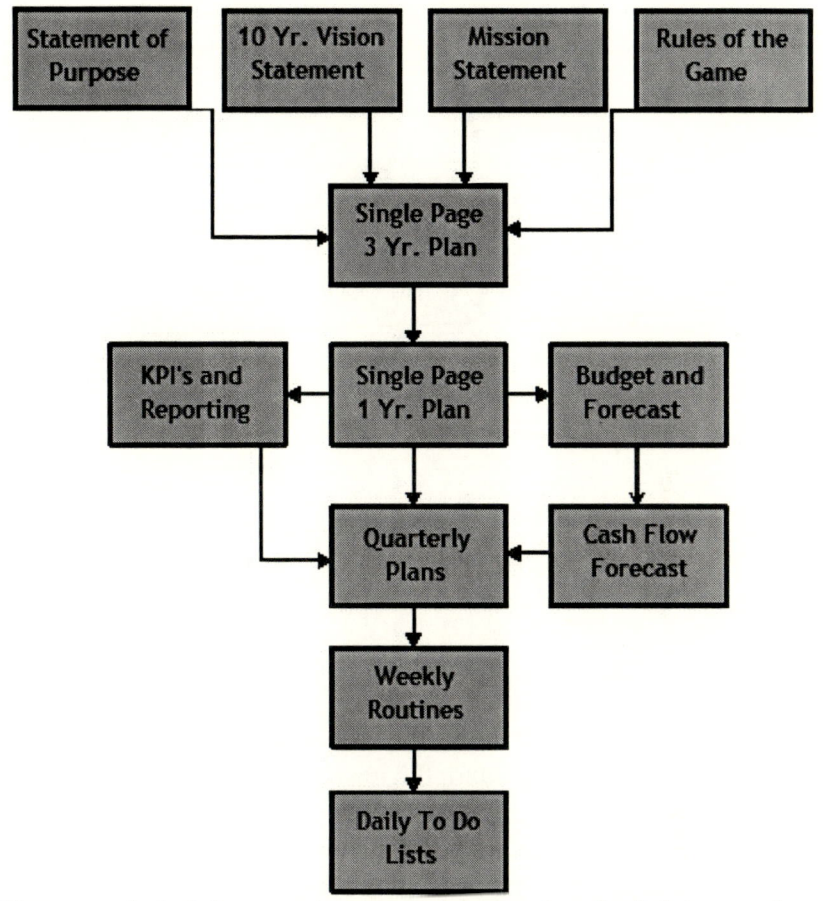

```
┌──────────────┐ ┌──────────────┐ ┌──────────────┐ ┌──────────────┐
│ Statement of │ │ 10 Yr. Vision│ │   Mission    │ │ Rules of the │
│   Purpose    │ │  Statement   │ │  Statement   │ │    Game      │
└──────┬───────┘ └──────┬───────┘ └──────┬───────┘ └──────┬───────┘
       │                │                │                │
       │                ▼                ▼                │
       │        ┌──────────────┐                          │
       └───────▶│  Single Page │◀─────────────────────────┘
                │  3 Yr. Plan  │
                └──────┬───────┘
                       ▼
┌──────────────┐ ┌──────────────┐ ┌──────────────┐
│  KPI's and   │◀│  Single Page │▶│  Budget and  │
│  Reporting   │ │  1 Yr. Plan  │ │   Forecast   │
└──────┬───────┘ └──────┬───────┘ └──────┬───────┘
       │                ▼                │
       │        ┌──────────────┐ ┌──────────────┐
       └───────▶│  Quarterly   │◀│  Cash Flow   │
                │    Plans     │ │   Forecast   │
                └──────┬───────┘ └──────────────┘
                       ▼
                ┌──────────────┐
                │    Weekly    │
                │   Routines   │
                └──────┬───────┘
                       ▼
                ┌──────────────┐
                │ Daily To Do  │
                │    Lists     │
                └──────────────┘
```

Stage one is to take your ten-year vision and make it into a series of three-year plans. This will mean that you have three-by-three-year plans and a final twelve-month plan to complete the process. It is the choices made here when you translate your vision into a practical business plan that the effects of external factors have to be taken into consideration.

Your business has to operate within its environment, and whilst this environment does not necessarily affect your ten-year vision, it will certainly have an effect on how you go about achieving it. The plans need to take account of what you have direct control and influence over and also the relevant factors which you do not.

Politics　　　　　　　　**Economics**

Social　　　　　　　　　**Technology**

Legal　　　　　　　　　**Environmental**

Mission　　　　　　　　**Statement of Purpose**

Rules of the Game　　　**10 Year Vision**

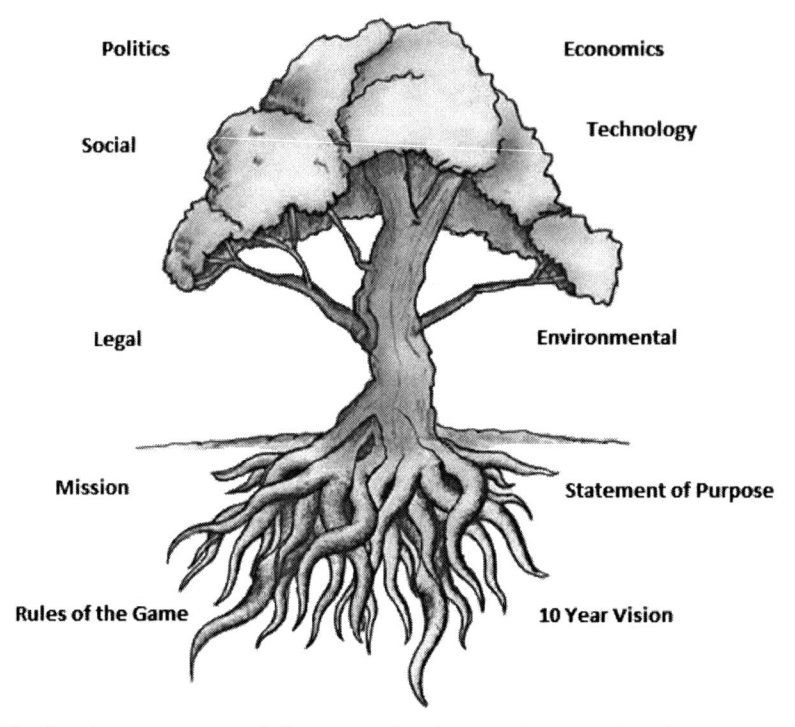

The business tree model shows the issues that need to be considered. Below the ground, the unseen roots of your business are defined by your vision, mission, statement of purpose, and rules of the game. These are your anchors. They are stable, solid, and definite. Whatever happens above ground, these roots will sustain your business and give it a platform for growth.

Above ground, and in order to bear fruit, your business, represented by the visible trunk and branches of the business tree, has to operate and adapt to the environment. The image your business displays above the ground is dependent on what is below it.

Your business cannot operate in isolation; it has to operate within the context of its external environment. Whilst you can influence the environment, the degree of control is really only dependent upon your degree of compliance with the constraints and opportunities it presents to you.

As a tree has to bend with the wind, so your business has to adapt to and engage with its environment. Remember, it is from the external environment that your opportunities and challenges will originate. What they are depends on how you interpret your unseen vision into tangible plans, decisions, and activities.

The three-year plan is where the invisible becomes tangible, where vision is translated into a working and practical document. It is also a reality check where you will need to take into account the external environmental factors that will affect your business.

Scan Your Horizon

In order to put meaningful plans in place, start by taking a look at both the immediate and future environments in which the business is operating and decide upon the appropriate strategy.

PESTLE analysis is a great start when choosing the appropriate strategies that will enable your business to achieve the long-term objectives.

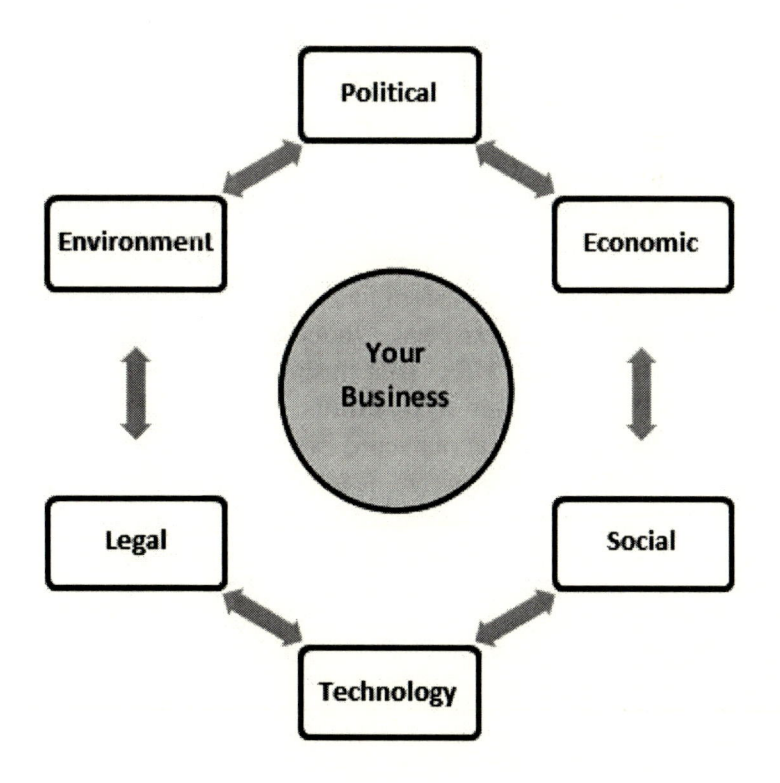

By considering the impact of each of the factors on your business, the model will help you make appropriate plans that will fully capitalise on the opportunities whilst minimising the threats that will become apparent.

1. **Political** – Government policy implications, both domestic and international. Taxation, legislation, and policies regarding the environment and investment.
2. **Economic** – Predicted rates of growth, inflation, interest rates, exchange rates, and commodity pricing.
3. **Social** – Population growth, demographic, and skills availability. Working patterns and expectations of workers for health care and pension schemes, language or translation issues, and cultural and religious considerations.
4. **Technology** – Communication or delivery of services through technology. Sales and marketing through new media, investment in infrastructure, and market awareness of advances.
5. **Legal** – Contract law, employment, and health and safety issues will affect how a business operates.
6. **Environmental** – Climate change and its possible effects, customer perceptions, transport policies, and green policies.

These are just basic guidelines. Of course, you will be able to choose those aspects that will more directly affect your business and the sector in which you operate.

The document below can be used to assess the impact of these external factors on your business. Under each heading put the issues that you feel will affect your business and clarify them in the 'relevant factors' column. Determine whether the effect will be positive or negative and put score over the range −10 for very negative to +10 for very positive. It is the strategic implications that are critical and which should be used to feed into your plans; these are how you will deal with the implications, positive and negative, you identified.

	Relevant Factors	Effect + / -	Importance	Strategic Implications
Political				
Economic				
Social				
Technical				
Legal				
Environment				

Once the PESTLE exercise has been completed, summarise it into a working document that will define your operational plan. The SWOT process puts into context the internal aspects of your business, its strengths and weaknesses, with its external environment and the opportunities and threats it will present. This process just needs you and your team to make a list under each of the headings of those issues that are most important to your business and will help you build your plan.

Strengths Positive Internal	**Weaknesses** Negative Internal
Opportunities Positive External	**Threats** Negative External

Strengths – What inherent strengths does your business have? This could include location, key skills or knowledge, products, and reputation.

Weaknesses – These could include cash availability, marketing, track record, profitability, product, or service.

Opportunities – From the external environment, what are the best opportunities that will take you towards your vision?

Threats – External threats from competitors, legislation, and the economy.

The results of SWOT analysis will enable the plans for your business to be more strategic in that they will take account of external factors as well as the internal ones. Remember that the greatest threats and the biggest opportunities may not be visible to you; we can only plan on the basis of what we know now. Always be prepared for the unexpected and adapt accordingly.

Results RULES OK

Single Page 3 Year Business Plan.

Company	

For the 3 Years commencing	

Year	20xx		Sales	Profit	Cash
Quarter 1	Objective				
Quarter 2	Objective				
Quarter 3	Objective				
Quarter 4	Objective				
		Total			

Year	20xx		Sales	Profit	Cash
Quarter 1	Objective				
Quarter 2	Objective				
Quarter 3	Objective				
Quarter 4	Objective				
		Total			

Year	20xx		Sales	Profit	Cash
Quarter 1	Objective				
Quarter 2	Objective				
Quarter 3	Objective				
Quarter 4	Objective				
		Total			
		Grand Total			

The Three-Year Plan

Understanding your long-term ten-year vision means that you can predict where you need to be at the end of three, six, and nine years, leaving you with a final one-year plan for completion. As we will see later, the pace of growth and the strategies and tactics employed will define the results required at different stages of growth.

Taking your plan in three-year stages, we can set the sales, profit, and cash objectives for each year and break each year down into quarters. Each quarter has a single dominant objective assigned to it, one that is critical to the success of the business, so each year we have just four primary objectives.

Single-page business plans are the best. Here is a template that you can use that gives you a three-year plan with specific objectives and predicted key results all on one page.

Each year is broken down into individual ninety-day quarters, and from your preparation work and research already carried out, you need to select a primary objective that has to be achieved for a ninety-day period. This means that you have to be really specific, as you only have twelve objectives to complete the three-year plan.

At the end of each ninety-day period, in addition to the actual objective, set yourself targets for sales, profit, and cash. These will be your barometers, or your scorecard, that you can use to check that progress is being made and if you have to adjust your plans as you go along.

Results RULES OK
Single Page 1 Year Business Plan

Company	

For the 12 Months commencing	

			Sales	Profit	Cash
Quarter 1	Objective				
	Goal 1				
	Goal 2				
	Goal 3				
		Total			

			Sales	Profit	Cash
Quarter 1	Objective				
	Goal 1				
	Goal 2				
	Goal 3				
		Total			

			Sales	Profit	Cash
Quarter 1	Objective				
	Goal 1				
	Goal 2				
	Goal 3				
		Total			

			Sales	Profit	Cash
Quarter 1	Objective				
	Goal 1				
	Goal 2				
	Goal 3				
		Total			

The One-Year Plan

Now you've got your single-page three-year business plan. It's time to translate it into a twelve-month forecast. For your twelve-month plan, we will need to have a budget, cash flow forecast, and a series of relevant key performance indicators in place. The shorter the horizon of the plan the more specific and detailed the plan needs to become. This exercise is repeated every twelve months.

You should take the four objectives from the first year of your three-year plan for the year and transpose them onto the one-year business plan. Then for each ninety-day period during the year, assign goals that need to be completed in order to achieve the objective. If you have a team, for example, whilst everyone may have the same objective, their individual goals will be different; but they all contribute to the same outcome.

Again, with your budgets and forecasts, put your ninety-day targets for sales, profit, and cash on the plan so everyone knows what the outcome needs to be each ninety days.

Results RULES OK

12 Month Business Budget Tool

Company — **Year Starts**

	Annual Total	Jan	Feb	Mar	Apr	May	Jun	Jul	Aug	Sep	Oct	Nov	Dec	TOTAL
Income		125000	100000	130000	140000	175000	175000	140000	150000	125000	135000	80000	65000	1540000
Direct Costs		62500	50000	65000	70000	87500	87500	70000	75000	62500	67500	40000	32500	770000
Gross Profit		62500	50000	65000	70000	87500	87500	70000	75000	62500	67500	40000	32500	770000
Contribution %		50.00%	50.00%	50.00%	50.00%	50.00%	50.00%	50.00%	50.00%	50.00%	50.00%	50.00%	50.00%	50.00%
Running Costs														
Wages	425000	35417	35417	35417	35417	35417	35417	35417	35417	35417	35417	35417	35417	425000
Energy	8000	667	667	667	667	667	667	667	667	667	667	667	667	8000
Premises	50000	4167	4167	4167	4167	4167	4167	4167	4167	4167	4167	4167	4167	50000
Insurance	7500	625	625	625	625	625	625	625	625	625	625	625	625	7500
Communication	6000	500	500	500	500	500	500	500	500	500	500	500	500	6000
Travel	12000	1000	1000	1000	1000	1000	1000	1000	1000	1000	1000	1000	1000	12000
Printing	8000	667	667	667	667	667	667	667	667	667	667	667	667	8000
Expenses	12000	1000	1000	1000	1000	1000	1000	1000	1000	1000	1000	1000	1000	12000
Hire Charges	18000	1500	1500	1500	1500	1500	1500	1500	1500	1500	1500	1500	1500	18000
Stationery	6000	500	500	500	500	500	500	500	500	500	500	500	500	6000
Depreciation	14000	1167	1167	1167	1167	1167	1167	1167	1167	1167	1167	1167	1167	14000
Marketing	42000	3500	3500	3500	3500	3500	3500	3500	3500	3500	3500	3500	3500	42000
TBA	0	0	0	0	0	0	0	0	0	0	0	0	0	0
TBA	0	0	0	0	0	0	0	0	0	0	0	0	0	0
TBA	0	0	0	0	0	0	0	0	0	0	0	0	0	0
TOTAL		50708	50708	50708	50708	50708	50708	50708	50708	50708	50708	50708	50708	608500
NETT PROFIT		11792	-708	14292	19292	36792	36792	19292	24292	11792	16792	-10708	-18208	161500
%		9.43%	-0.71%	10.99%	13.78%	21.02%	21.02%	13.78%	16.19%	9.43%	12.44%	-13.39%	-28.01%	10.49%
Year to Date		11792	11083	25375	44667	81458	118250	137542	161833	173625	190417	179708	161500	

The Budget

The budget is a prediction of the financial performance of your business over a specific period. The budget can be constructed so that it suits your individual business requirements, and there are plenty of templates and accounting packages that are available to help you.

A basic budget should be for a twelve-month period. The one in the table shows the year from January to December. You can use your own company's financial year or adjust to the tax year if that is more relevant.

Your budget is the translation of your goals and objectives into money targets and is a critical tool for managing your business. The basic measures that your budget should include are listed below:

1. Sales Income – What do you expect the level of sales income to be in each month?
2. Direct Costs – What costs will the business incur as a direct result of achieving the sales. This could be labour and materials, for example, referred to as the 'cost of goods sold'.
3. Gross Profit – Sometimes called gross contribution, it is a measure of the efficiency of the business. Derived from sales income minus direct costs, it is also expressed as a percentage of sales.
4. Overheads – These are also known as operating expenses and are the costs that are incurred regardless of the levels of sales income achieved. Costs such as rent, insurance, staff salaries, etc.
5. Net Profit – This is simply the gross profit minus overheads and is a measure of the overall productivity of the business. It is also expressed as a percentage of sales.

When setting a budget, it is important to involve your team. Each department may need its own budget for expenses as well as sales; they all need to contribute towards the overall objective.

Cahflow Forecast Tool

Results RULES OK

Company

Cash In

Source	Wk 1	Wk 2	Wk 3	Wk 4	Wk 5	Wk 6	Wk 7	Wk 8	Wk 9	Wk 10	Wk 11	Wk 12	Wk 13	Total
														0
														0
														0
														0
														0
														0
														0
														0
														0
														0
Total	0	0	0	0	0	0	0	0	0	0	0	0	0	

Quarter Starts

Cash Out

Destination	Wk 1	Wk 2	Wk 3	Wk 4	Wk 5	Wk 6	Wk 7	Wk 8	Wk 9	Wk 10	Wk 11	Wk 12	Wk 13	Total
														0
														0
														0
														0
														0
														0
														0
														0
														0
														0
Total	0	0	0	0	0	0	0	0	0	0	0	0	0	

Net Movement	0	0	0	0	0	0	0	0	0	0	0	0	0	
Opening Balance	0													
Cash Position	0	0	0	0	0	0	0	0	0	0	0	0	0	

Closing Balance	0
Movement	0

Cash Flow Forecasting

Budgets generally deal with the timing of transactions or received benefits. For example, if you invoice £10,000 in January but don't get paid until February, under the accrual system, the sale is taken in January. The outstanding money creates a debtor which will appear as an asset on your balance sheet; a similar process is applied to expenses.

Cash and sales/overheads are reported in the profit and loss account, but they do not reflect the actual timing of the cash transactions. So in support of the budget, you must have detailed cash flow forecast. This document predicts both the timing and the amounts of cash that will go in and out of your business. Effectively, it is prediction of what your bank statement will look like as your business trades. Again there are plenty of templates and tools around to help with this; the one shown is a simple ninety-day cash flow forecast.

Key Performance Indicators

A key performance indicator or KPI is a measurement that tells you how the business is performing. There are hundreds of things that can be measured within a business, and they would be too complex and time consuming to measure and report on them individually. So select a few important ones that are easy to measure, and they will give you enough information about how the business is doing on a regular basis. It's like the dashboard in a car; all the measurements that can be made are carried out by the sensors and on-board computers.

As a driver, all we need to know are the most important facts such as speed, fuel level, engine temperature, and distance travelled. If we understand these simple facts, then we can assume that everything else is OK and proceed. Same with your business. Choose a number of KPIs that will support your particular business and enable you to track performance in relation to the objectives and budgets that you have set, then monitor them on a regular basis.

There are hundreds of potential KPIs that you can choose from, and the art of this is to select those that are most critical and relevant to you and your business. They do not have to be purely financial. They can relate to anything that has an effect on your business and determine its success. Here are a few real-life examples to help you.

1. **Temp Agency** – The Industrial and Commercial Temporary Employment Agency business is highly competitive. Several agencies may have the same people registered with them for work, so differentiating a business through quality and calibre of worker can be challenging. We guaranteed that all bookings for temporary workers, if accepted, would be filled and that all our workers would show up on time every time; temporary worker attendance became a key KPI for our business. We measured it daily, and the objective was 100% attendance 100% of the time. This focus on service built our reputation with customers and meant that we retained good contracts, and because we could offer long-term consistent work, we also attracted the most reliable workers.

2. **Transport** – Running a fleet of vans delivering parcels and commercial documents means juggling drivers, bookings, and products along with traffic, weather conditions, and mechanical breakdowns. We had several KPIs in this business and two that became part of the 'language' of the business that focussed the team on a consistent basis. First was on-time deliveries, with our target of 100%. In the operations office, each coordinator had two jars on their desk – one with a green label and one with a red label. Every van that was sent on a delivery had a glass marble allocated to it. When the delivery was made, the marble would be put into the green jar for on-time deliveries and into the red jar for late deliveries. At the end of each day, we counted the marbles, and the best performing controller won a prize. Controllers also had KPIs for the safety of the drivers with zero tolerance of speeding, loading, and parking offences; one of these and all the marbles went to the red jar . . .

The second KPI that worked well was 'booked miles'. We charged a rate per loaded mile for each delivery that we did and had fixed rates of charges depending on the size of the vehicle. Knowing the operational costs of the business and marginal costs of running the vehicles meant that we knew how many charged miles had to be driven for the business to break-even. Our break-even point was 1,000 chargeable miles per day, so the KPI became the time during the day that we achieved this. Some days it would be three in the afternoon, while some days it was eleven in the morning; the target was 1,000 miles by twelve. It was something that was tangible and easily measured. It didn't involve money, and when the 1,000 was achieved, a bell rang in the office and celebration tea and biscuits were served; we were in England after all . . .

3. **Web Design** – Some businesses have a delay in their sales process from receipt of order to invoicing and cash collection. In the web design business, whilst deposits are taken, there is generally a delay in the processing of the work as design and coding activity have to be completed before the product is finished. One of the key drivers of not just the web design business but any business where processing or manufacturing is required to complete an order from a customer is 'order intake'. From the budget we knew what the level of sales needed to be each month. So we also knew that the value of orders received had to keep pace. By setting a daily KPI of value of orders received, we knew how strong our order book was and could predict accurately what the sales level would be in future weeks and months. This KPI was an early warning sign. It meant that we knew if sales would increase or decline several weeks before they actually did and we could do something proactive about it and not simply wait for the accountant to tell us three weeks after period ended that we had a bad month.

4. **Just About Any Business** – In his book *The Ultimate Question*, Fred Reichheld suggests that in business we have to ask our customers the ultimate question and measure their

responses to produce a rating or score for the business called the Net Promoter Score or NPS. The question is this: 'How likely is it that you would recommend this company to a friend or colleague?' The responses are measured over a scale of 1 to 10 and the NPS calculated. This is a great KPI for any business, and it's a great book too.

KPIs should focus attention on those activities and results that drive the growth and sustainability of your business. They should support your vision, mission, and rules of the game and help in turning your philosophy into operational reality. If your passion is customer service and excellence, then choose KPIs that support this, not just ones around sales revenue as they may conflict.

Don't have KPIs that encourage corners to be cut or safety to be compromised. Reward and measure excellence, not just efficiency and productivity; remember, profits are the barometer with which you measure your performance, not the single focus of your activities.

W. Edwards Deming was an American statistician, professor, author, and lecturer. He was born on 14 October 1900 and died on 29 December 1993. In 1947, with the Allied powers still occupying Japan, he was invited by the United States Department of the Army to go there to help out with the planning of the forthcoming census due to take place in 1951.

While he was there, he was invited by the Japanese Union of Scientists and Engineers to teach their members about the principles of Statistical Process Control, SPC. From June to December 1950, he trained hundreds of engineers and managers about the concepts of SPC and also his philosophy that improving quality of manufactured goods would actually reduce expenses, increase productivity, and improve market share.

Arguably it was Deming's teachings that had a profound effect on the ability of the Japanese to rebuild their economy. In Japan now the prestigious Deming Prize continues to be awarded for excellence in quality control and management. In 1960, Dr Deming was awarded the Order of the Sacred Treasure, Second

Class, in recognition of his contribution to the transformation of Japanese industry.

In his book, *Out of the Crisis*, he defines fourteen key principles for management, and he is largely credited with the introduction of the concept of Total Quality Management.

One of the key aspects of the transformation of Japanese products was not improved design or marketing, they simply made products that were marginally better. When Ford began using Japanese manufactured gearboxes, in addition to ones made in the USA, in their cars, they noticed that customers started specifying the Japanese built units over the ones manufactured in the USA; they were even prepared to wait until a Japanese built unit was available if that was what it took.

Ford engineers could not understand what was going on. The gearboxes built in Japan were built to the same engineering drawings that were being used in the USA. So why the perceived difference? The difference it turns out was only marginal. However, it was this marginal change that delivered huge improvements to the actual quality of the gearbox. The cars with Japanese gearboxes were quieter and smoother; there was less vibration. They didn't leak oil, and they lasted longer.

What the Japanese did was simple – they built the same gearbox, but only made it better. They did this by 'tightening the tolerances'. In mass production manufacturing, components cannot be made to an exact dimension. There has to be a tolerance, an upper and lower limit, that is acceptable. For example, a steel shaft could have a required diameter of 100 mm with a tolerance of plus or minus 1 mm, which means that, providing the shaft is between 99 and 101 mm diameter when it is completed, it will be accepted. The Japanese simply made the components more accurately, to a smaller tolerance, so they fitted together better, ran smoother, and lasted longer.

Focus on the product and process, and promotion and the profit will look after itself.

Notes About Growth

It is likely that your business will have to grow during the ten-year period, generating profits and cash that will enable your vision to become a reality. There are several ways in which you can grow your business. The franchising model suggests that duplication and geographic expansion is the key to growth, and whilst this may be true and work well for your own business, it's important to consider what other strategies are available to you; here are a few to think about . . .

Igor Ansoff was born in Vladivostok on 12 December 1918; he went to the USA with his family and graduated from the Stuyvesant High School in New York and later studied at both the Stevens Institute of Technology and Brown University where he received a doctorate in applied mathematics. He designed a method of assessing strategic choices in business in a model known as the Product/Market Ansoff matrix.

The matrix will help assess the strategy that suits your business the best and also recognise the relative risks associated with the different choices.

Products

	Existing	New
Markets Existing	Market Penetration	Product Development
New	Market Development	Diversification

Strategy No. 1 – Market Penetration

Existing products and services being sold into a familiar market.

In my experience, especially within the small and medium enterprise or SME sector, there is usually plenty of room for growing the sales and profits by simply doing more of what the business already does. Providing a better product with improved process and proactive promotional activity is the best approach. There is no need to duplicate or diversify until you have maximised what you already have. The risks associated with doing more of what you already know best are the lowest of all the strategies.

Strategy No. 2 – Product Development

New products and services being sold into a familiar market.

If I am selling shoes, then I may as well sell laces and polish. Introducing new products that are complimentary to your methods of sales and distribution is a great way of building sales and profits. You are selling similar products to your existing customers, and it allows you to 'bundle' your products and make offers and promotions. There is some risk here as you will have to educate your existing market that you offer different products and services. However, the market has knowledge about you already, and your reputation will help with the implementation of such strategies.

Acquisition of other companies who offer the products and services that you want to add to your portfolio can be considered here, although partnering, strategic alliances, distributor agreements, and licensing arrangements should also be considered.

Strategy No. 3 – Market Development

Selling existing products into new markets.

Once you have maximised the potential for sales in one market, the time may be right to take your products and services to alternative markets. This could mean geographic expansion (the franchise model), demographics, or the development of new niche markets. The success of this strategy will be dependent upon the marketing and/or distribution strength of your business. The risk here is mainly from the investment and uncertainty surrounding the marketing activity that would be required for demographic changes in the target, or control and management issues arising from geographic separation of operational units. Horizontal integration through the acquisition of competing businesses falls within this strategy.

Strategy No. 4 – Diversification

Selling new products into new markets.

This is the highest risk strategy of them all because there are more degrees of uncertainty with this approach than any of the others, so proceed with caution.

This strategy can include the introduction of new services to new markets through development or acquisition. This is the classic conglomerate model where through centralised control, management, and branding, a diverse array of services and products are provided to an equally diverse array of market sectors. The benefits are that diverse operations and markets reduce dependency upon particular sectors and allow for cross marketing of services between the group. The risk is dilution of control and confusion regarding the identity of the brand.

The Richard Branson's Virgin Group of companies is probably one of the most high profile and most successful diverse companies in the world. The Virgin 'empire' includes businesses as diverse as Virgin Atlantic Airways, Virgin Megastore music and entertainment, Virgin Holidays, Virgin Mobile Phones, and Virgin Radio.

Here's a tip: Before you choose this strategy, make sure you have capitalised on the other areas first.

Pace of Growth

So you have decided on the appropriate strategy for your business. Now consider the implications this will have, and plan not only the type of growth but, of equal importance, the pace and pattern of growth.

What is the most efficient pace of growth for the business, and how will it be predicted?

Will growth be achieved organically or will acquisitions be made?

Using sales revenue as an example, here are some ideas of how to approach the plan.

Vision: In ten years, to have sales revenue of £20,000,000 p.a.

Current Position – Sales Revenue of £5,000,000 p.a.

The pattern of growth will be important. Although you are putting plans together on three-year chunks, it is important to know what the objectives are at the end of each stage so you know you are on track.

Straight-line growth would seem to be the simplest and most straightforward way of growing your business. Simply get a graph and go from current sales to target sales in a straight line. This method is very simple, but it isn't the most practical or realistic method. The chart shows what the sales chart would look like for our £5m business growing to £20m over a ten-year period using the straight-line method.

Straight Line Growth

	Yr 1	Yr 2	Yr 3	Yr 4	Yr 5	Yr 6	Yr 7	Yr 8	Yr 9	Yr 10
Sales	5.00	6.67	8.33	10.00	11.67	13.34	15.00	16.67	18.34	20.00

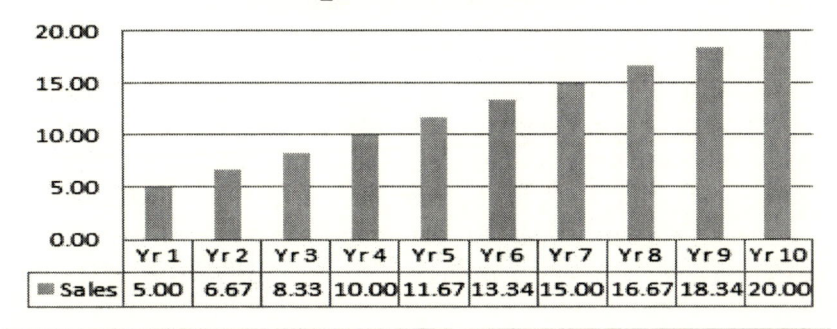

The straight-line growth means that the amount of additional sales made each year is the same. In this case, every year the sales increase by £1.67m, and whilst this looks realistic on a graph, in reality it is unlikely to succeed.

The reason is that the growth in percentage terms is too heavily weighted to the early years of the plan.

As the next chart demonstrates, in year 2 of the plan, the growth rate will need to be 33% whilst in year 10 the growth rate will only need to be 9%. The growth of the business in percentage terms actually slows down over time according to this model, whereas in reality the pace of growth should be consistent or even growing with the maturity of the business.

The principle applies to any rate of growth. The faster the rate the more pronounced the effect.

Straight Line Growth vs % Growth

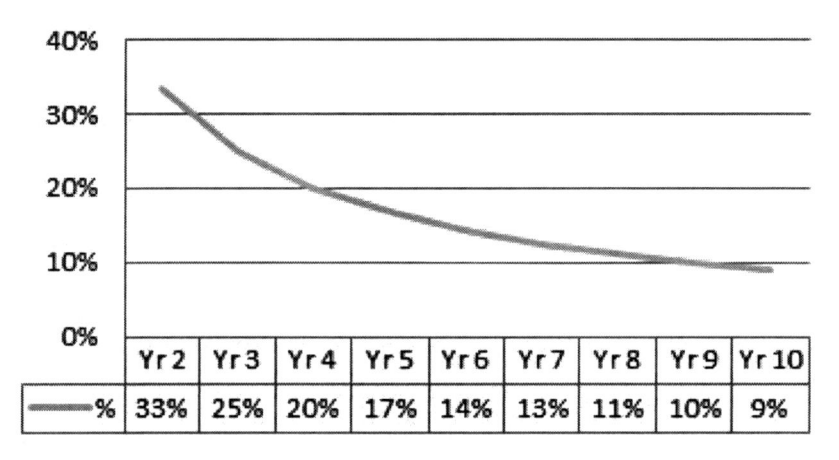

	Yr 2	Yr 3	Yr 4	Yr 5	Yr 6	Yr 7	Yr 8	Yr 9	Yr 10
%	33%	25%	20%	17%	14%	13%	11%	10%	9%

The compound growth model has consistency of percentage increases in sales each year over the period and is more realistic to achieve. The chart shows that in year 2 sales only increased by £830K whilst in year 10 the sales need to increase by £2.85m. The consistent factor is the percentage rate of growth which stays at around 17% every year, not the pound value growth every year; this is operationally more realistic and sustainable.

Compound Growth

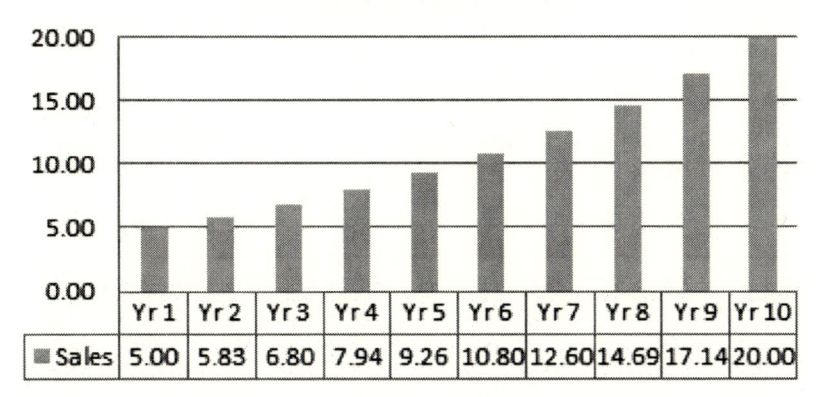

	Yr 1	Yr 2	Yr 3	Yr 4	Yr 5	Yr 6	Yr 7	Yr 8	Yr 9	Yr 10
Sales	5.00	5.83	6.80	7.94	9.26	10.80	12.60	14.69	17.14	20.00

Growing your business through acquisition will result in a series of step changes in the business as new companies come on stream. This will take careful management and control and particular attention to operational and management support.

Growth Through Acquisition

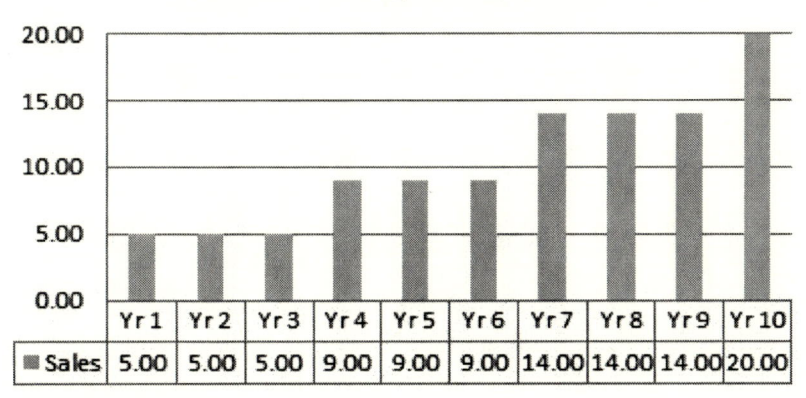

	Yr 1	Yr 2	Yr 3	Yr 4	Yr 5	Yr 6	Yr 7	Yr 8	Yr 9	Yr 10
Sales	5.00	5.00	5.00	9.00	9.00	9.00	14.00	14.00	14.00	20.00

Growing Pains

First thing, with any objective, be clear what you mean, and be careful of statistics. When a business is growing, it will have two aspects to the sales revenue that will affect the results.

1. **Total Revenue** – Total sales achieved in the twelve-month period.
2. **Running Rate** – Pace of sales achieved as a result of the growth of the business during the twelve months.

For example, using a business that has annual sales of £1m to demonstrate the differences between a static and growing business, consider the following two scenarios:

Scenario 1 – The sales of a business are reasonably consistent from month to month; while there are slight seasonal variations they are not significant. The monthly sales figures for this business in thousands (pound) are as shown below:

Jan	Feb	Mar	Apr	May	Jun	Jul	Aug	Sep	Oct	Nov	Dec	Total
80	80	90	85	85	80	80	85	90	85	80	80	1000

The sales graph for this business will look like this. As you can see, the pattern is reasonably flat, and providing the pattern is continued into the following year, the total sales achieved will be similar to these results. This effectively shows a business with a stable £1m in annual sale.

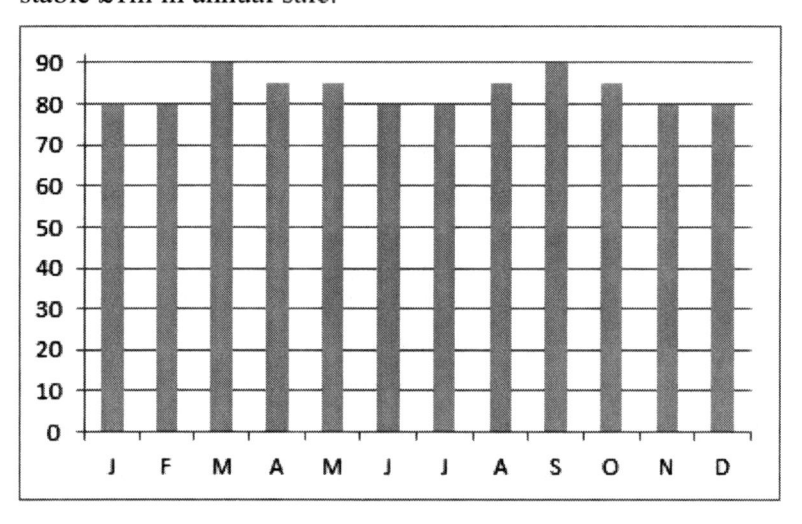

The average sales revenue per month is £83,333.

Scenario 2 – The sales of the business are increasing steadily. Sales and marketing activity and improved customer service has resulted in the sales increasing by approximately 9% every month. The monthly sales figures for this business in thousands (pound) are as shown below:

Jan	Feb	Mar	Apr	May	Jun	Jul	Aug	Sep	Oct	Nov	Dec	Total
50	54	59	65	70	77	83	91	99	108	117	127	1000

The sales graph for this business will look like this. As you can see, the pattern shows a steady month on month increase in revenues. This too shows a business with £1m in annual sales; however, the pattern is not stable.

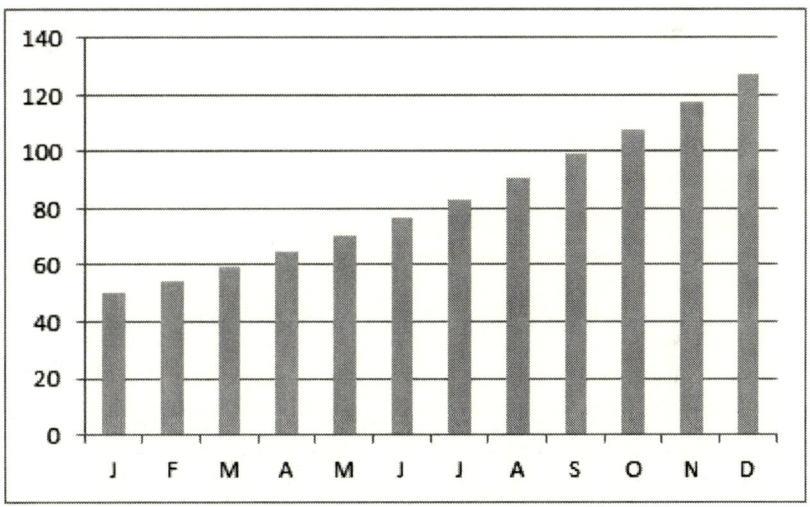

The average sales revenue per month is again £83,333.

What Does This Mean for You?

There are key differences between the two patterns; differences that have to be taken into account at the planning stage because business growth will almost certainly be one of your key objectives.

The growing business has achieved annual sales revenue of £1m, as has the static company. However, the pace or running rate of the static company has remained at £83,333 per month, whereas the growing company has reached a pace or running rate of £127,000 per month at the end of the year.

Whilst it could reasonably be assumed that the static company would achieve similar levels of sales revenue during the following year; all things being equal. The growing company will start off the next year with sales revenue of at least £127,000, the level achieved in December. Even if this business ceases to grow any further during the second year, its annual sales revenue will be in the order of twelve months × £127,000 = £1,524,000. Remember, the infrastructure of the growing business will have been built to cope with a pace of £127,000 per month. If it doesn't at least maintain that level of sales, profitability will decline.

An increase of 52% over the first year; sounds great, doesn't it?

Now, if the growth during the second year continued at the same 9% per month as was achieved in the first year. The total sales during the year will be £2,558,000, with the pace increasing to £328,000 in December; all from just a 9% compound improvement in monthly revenue.

Does This Sound Too Good to Be True?

It may well be too good to be true, because there is a risk that your fast-growing business will run out of cash if you do not plan very well at this stage and understand the implications that growth will have. Beware the fatal attraction of sales increase being the single focus for your business.

There are plenty of businesses that were profitable and growing that went out of business because they ran out of money. Lack of sales and profit does not kill a business; when a business runs out of cash though, it is usually fatal. Remember, sales is vanity, profit is sanity but cash is reality.

Why Does a Growing Business Run Out of Cash?

Growing businesses generally need cash to achieve the growth, not just in marketing and sales activity but operational costs as well.

A growing business can be hit with a triple whammy of reduced gross margins, increased operational costs, and declining cash flow. The actual details may be different for each business type; however, the implications for all businesses are depressingly the same – closure.

Quick Story No. 1 – Vanity Kills

A business sells and distributes stationery products to retailers and turns in the following results:

1. Sales Revenue – £4,000,000 p.a.
2. Gross Profit – 40% or £1,600,000 p.a.
3. Overheads – £1,000,000 p.a.
4. Net Profit – 15% or £600,000 p.a.

In a bid to increase sales, your sales manager, who is paid a bonus on the sales revenue he generates for the business, decides to offer an incentive to existing customers to buy more products, so 20% discount is given on all sales to those customers who will buy above a minimum order value. A similar introductory offer is made to new customers to entice them to switch from their current supplier.

The gross margin originally being achieved on all sales was 40%; for every £100 of product sold, with material costs of £60, the gross profit was £40.

With the 20% discount applied to the same product, whilst the material costs remain the same at £60, with the new discount price of £80 (£100 – 20%), the new gross profit is just £20 or 25% gross margin.

The sales increased by £1,000,000, or 25%, to £5,000,000 after the discount was introduced. This is a significant increase in revenue and one which could be celebrated.

What this meant in operational terms was that because of the discount, in order to achieve a 25% increase in sales, 56% more products had to be shipped to customers. This resulted in an increase of 35% in overheads as shift working was introduced and additional warehouse space was rented. The increase in sales revenue also meant that bonuses were paid to the sales manager, again increasing the costs of the business.

The new results achieved by the business now looked like this:

1. Sales Revenue – £5,000,000 p.a.
2. Gross Profit – 25% or £1,250,000 p.a.
3. Overheads – £1,350,000 p.a.
4. Net Profit – 2% or £100,000 p.a.

Now, this business will start to eat cash. Remember – as the owner derives income from dividends taken out of profits, it is not a £100,000 problem the company has, but a £700,000 one as all the original profits have been wiped out. The business operating under these conditions may be able to draw on reserves in order to keep trading. However, at some point the cash will run out.

Quick Story No. 2 – Beware the Big Contract

It's not just pure sales revenue that should be planned for when building your business. It is the source of the revenue and size of contract that will be as important as the actual revenue itself.

An engineering company with annual sales of £10,000,000 bids for a contract that will be worth an additional £8,000,000 over the next twelve months. Gross margins will be in line with the rest of the business as discounts have not been offered.

> Be careful of dependency upon one or two key customers. A rule I have used in several businesses is that no single customer should represent any more than 10% of my gross profits.

Whilst this 80% increase in sales from one single contract may be a great opportunity, it may also be the one opportunity that shuts the business down. The bidding process alone for a contract of this size may involve investment of time and money, and gearing up for a single order or contract with a new customer can be expensive.

1. Recruitment and Training – New staff will be required to fulfil the new work. There are costs associated with this long before the contract starts, and remember, when the contract ends, you may need to let them go and there may be costs of termination.

2. Operations – Larger premises and new equipment may be required. Whilst it is always possible to find a short-term lease premises and rent equipment, the costs will be higher than those associated with longer-term agreements.

3. Materials – The business will need to buy raw materials before the contract starts and likely pay for them before any money is received from the new customer.

Year	2011			Qtr	1	1st Mon	03-Jan			Company				
		Objective					Goal 1			Goal 2			Goal 3	
Week Commencing Monday	Week 1	Week 2	Week 3	Week 4	Week 5	Week 6	Week 7	Week 8	Week 9	Week 10	Week 11	Week 12	Week 13	Total
	03-Jan	10-Jan	17-Jan	24-Jan	31-Jan	07-Feb	14-Feb	21-Feb	28-Feb	07-Mar	14-Mar	21-Mar	28-Mar	
Holidays	0	0	0	0	0	0	0	0	0	0	0	0	0	0
Activity to Achieve Goal 1														
Proof Read	0	0	0	0	0	0	0	0	0	0	0	0	0	0
Modify and Configure	0	0	0	0	0	0	0	0	0	0	0	0	0	0
Send to Publisher	0	0	0	0	0	0	0	0	0	0	0	0	0	0
	0	0	0	0	0	0	0	0	0	0	0	0	0	0
	0	0	0	0	0	0	0	0	0	0	0	0	0	Total Goal 1
Activity to Achieve Goal 2														
Complete Artistic Review	0	0	0	0	0	0	0	0	0	0	0	0	0	0
Agree Images	0	0	0	0	0	0	0	0	0	0	0	0	0	0
Format Images	0	0	0	0	0	0	0	0	0	0	0	0	0	0
Collate file	0	0	0	0	0	0	0	0	0	0	0	0	0	0
Send to Publisher	0	0	0	0	0	0	0	0	0	0	0	0	0	0
														Total Goal 2
Activity to Achieve Goal 3														
Review Design Options	0	0	0	0	0	0	0	0	0	0	0	0	0	0
Agree Images	0	0	0	0	0	0	0	0	0	0	0	0	0	0
Photo Shoot	0	0	0	0	0	0	0	0	0	0	0	0	0	0
Format Images	0	0	0	0	0	0	0	0	0	0	0	0	0	0
Send to Publisher	0	0	0	0	0	0	0	0	0	0	0	0	0	0
														Total Goal 3
Total	0	0	0	0	0	0	0	0	0	0	0	0	0	0
Hours per Week Available	0	0	0	0	0	0	0	0	0	0	0	0	0	0
Balance	0	0	0	0	0	0	0	0	0	0	0	0	0	0

These factors amongst others will conspire to drain the business of cash especially in the early stages of the contract. I guarantee that there will always be a few unexpected 'surprises' that will add to the costs and excitement of winning the new contract.

All these issues can of course be predicted and included in the terms of contract with the new customer with stage payments and project milestones being included in the agreement. Banks may be sympathetic to funding contracts such as this, and there may even be grants available to help businesses gear up for this type of contract. Planning and close project management can make these types of contracts profitable cash generators for a business. Even so the risks associated with achieving high growth with a single customer should not be underestimated.

Quarterly Plans

Now you have your three-year and one-year business plans with budgets, cash flow, and KPIs. It's time to plan the next quarter. Every member of your team should have a quarterly plan that supports the agreed objectives of the business. The single-page ninety-day plan template identifies the key objective and the supporting goals that come from your twelve-month plan, such that you can allocate actual daily activities in a structured way so you and your team can check on progress on a continuous basis and retain focus.

Where you have teams or departments, the same document can be used. It may be that whilst everyone has the same objective, they have their own individual goals to achieve. There may be dozens of goals spread throughout your business, all contributing to a single objective.

You should allocate time and resources to the goals that support the objective. Where you have routine tasks to carry out that do not directly contribute to the goals, they should be placed in your Default Diary.

Year	2011			Qtr	1	1st Mon	03-Jan					Company		Your Company	
	Objective						Goal 1					Goal 2		Goal 3	
	Complete Book 2						Editing Complete					Images Finalise		Cover Design	
	Week 1	Week 2	Week 3	Week 4	Week 5	Week 6	Week 7	Week 8	Week 9	Week 10	Week 11	Week 12	Week 13		
Week Commencing Monday	03-Jan	10-Jan	17-Jan	24-Jan	31-Jan	07-Feb	14-Feb	21-Feb	28-Feb	07-Mar	14-Mar	21-Mar	28-Mar		Total
Holidays	0	0	0	0	0	0	0	0	0	0	0	0	0		0
Activity to Achieve Goal 1															
Proof Read	5	5	0	0	0	0	0	0	0	0	0	0	0		10
Modify and Configure	0	0	5	6	6	6	0	0	0	0	0	0	0		23
Send to Publisher	0	0	0	0	0	0	2	0	0	0	0	0	0		2
	0	0	0	0	0	0	0	0	0	0	0	0	0		0
	0	0	0	0	0	0	0	0	0	0	0	0	0		0
	0	0	0	0	0	0	0	0	0	0	0	0	0		0
												Total Goal 1			35
Activity to Achieve Goal 2															
Complete Artististic Review	12	12	12	12	12	0	0	0	0	0	0	0	0		60
Agree Images	0	0	0	0	6	8	8	12	0	0	0	0	0		34
Format Images	0	0	0	0	0	0	0	0	15	15	0	0	0		30
Collate file	0	0	0	0	0	0	0	0	0	10	10	0	0		20
Send to Publisher	0	0	0	0	0	0	0	0	0	0	0	10	0		10
	0	0	0	0	0	0	0	0	0	0	0	0	0		0
												Total Goal 2			154
Activity to Achieve Goal 3															
Review Design Options	8	8	8	5	0	0	0	0	0	0	0	0	0		29
Agree Images	0	0	0	2	2	8	0	0	0	0	0	0	0		12
Photo Shoot	0	0	0	0	0	0	8	0	0	0	0	0	0		8
Format Images	0	0	0	0	0	0	0	12	10	10	0	0	0		32
Send to Publisher	0	0	0	0	0	0	0	0	0	0	0	10	0		10
	0	0	0	0	0	0	0	0	0	0	0	0	0		0
												Total Goal 3			91
Total	25	25	25	25	26	22	18	24	25	25	10	20	10		280
Hours per Week Available	25	25	25	25	25	25	25	25	25	25	25	25	25		325
Balance	0	0	0	0	-1	3	7	1	0	0	15	5	15		45

The sample over shows you what a ninety-day plan could look like. Note that you are not allocating all your time to this plan. You will have other activities and day-to-day projects that need to be undertaken during the ninety days, and you have to allocate your time accordingly.

You can see in the sample that I have allocated twenty-five hours of my week to the goals in support of the objectives. I will of course spend more than this in the running of my business, but this is where I know that my primary focus is required. My Default Diary will take care of the rest of my activities; the ninety-day plan and your Default Diary should be completed together so that they complement each other.

There are a number of templates and online tools available for the design of your Default Diary. Check out Google Calendar for example.

The template below shows you the principles of a Default Diary, and along with all the other templates in this book, are available from our web site, www.yourbusinessrulesok.com.

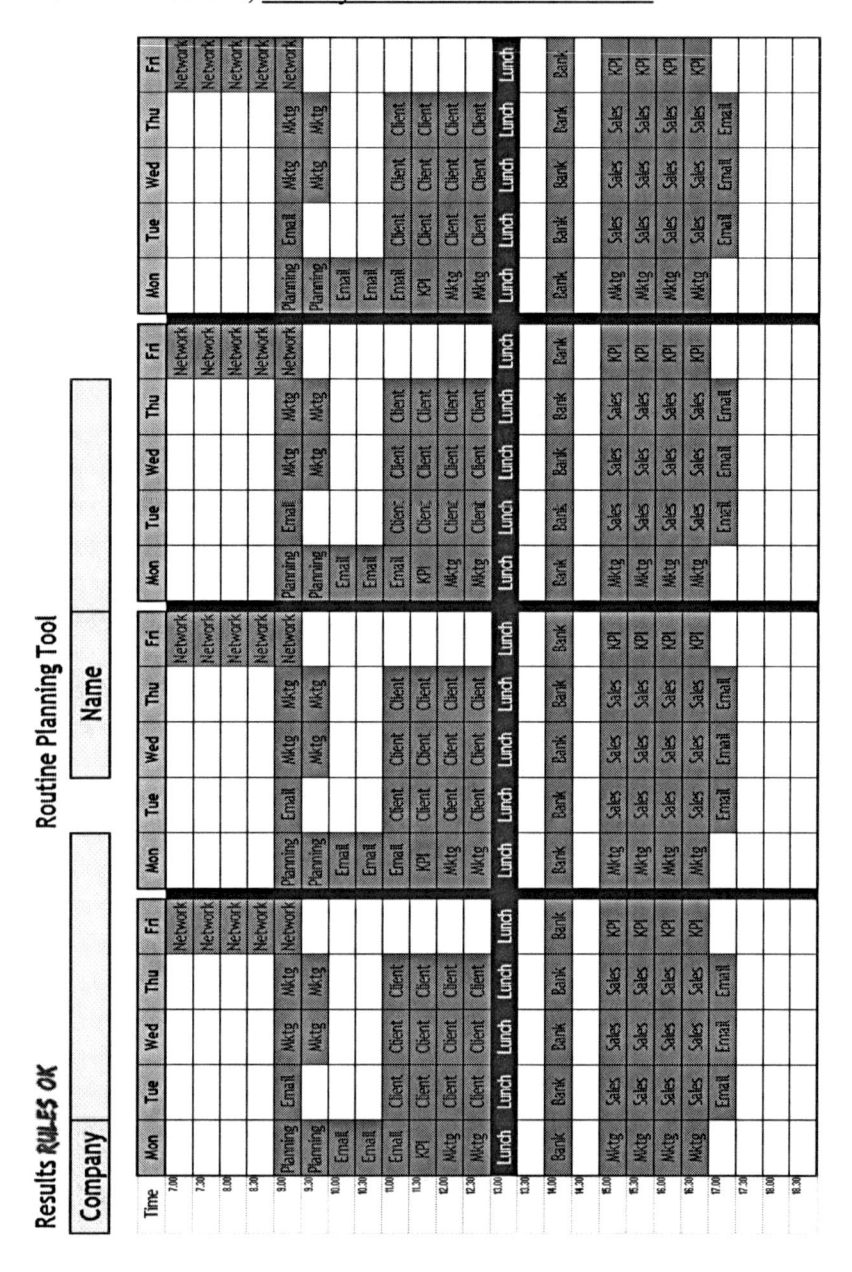

Your Default Diary is not a list of activities you should do if nothing else crops up. It is a schedule of the regular activities that you must carry out in order to sustain your business. It should include reporting, marketing, client work, regular meetings, etc. It shows you what absolutely has to be done on a regular basis. Your ninety-day plans are additional project-based activity in support of developmental goals and objectives.

To make sure that you know what your priorities are on a daily basis, at the end of each day list down all the activities and projects that you know you have to do the following day, and leave it on your work station ready for the following morning. This will allow you to relax after work, safe in the knowledge that tomorrow is already planned. I keep a note book and pen with me at all times so that when I have any bright ideas or flashes of inspiration, I can jot them down for future reference. But then, apparently, I am special!

Get the Product Right

Let's go back to the Mailbox in Birmingham . . .

We had such a great evening that on the way home we decided to book the restaurant and have a birthday celebration there with some friends and clients (they are one and the same really . . .). The table for eight was booked for the Saturday evening two weeks after our first visit.

A minibus was booked, and as we were travelling to the restaurant, Lynn and I were telling stories of our last visit, preparing our guests for a great evening, telling them how good the place was and all about the character of the manager, and so on.

We arrived and were seated; we ordered aperitifs in anticipation of the party atmosphere that was expected to unfold.

But where was 'Kojak'?

All the staff in the restaurant were polite, attentive, and professional, but they weren't Kojak. I asked a member of the team if he was around, and it was explained that he was the trainer. His job was to spend time in each of their restaurants and train the team how to provide excellent service, service that fitted with the vision, mission, and rules of the game of their organisation. He was working at another venue that evening.

The service was good, but it was only as good as you would expect from a mid-range restaurant, nothing outstanding or remarkable, and we were really disappointed that the evening didn't live up to our expectations.

Because the service was 'average' we also noticed that the food was 'average' too; it was good, but neither remarkable nor outstanding.

We have not been back since. I even wrote to them praising the potential I felt they had in their business and the opportunities they were missing. I received no reply.

The lesson here is that it is not good enough to provide a professional and polite service anymore; that is expected as the minimum requirement. To be successful, you have to be extraordinary and remarkable on a consistent basis; it is not the product or service that you provide but the context in which you provide it.

In the SME sector, we do not have a brand that conveys our message or guarantees the experience we will have when we buy from them. McDonald's is a remarkable business, however, their actual products are neither extraordinary nor remarkable, but they have the power of a brand to carry them through which makes the purchasing of any other burger a risk. We don't have that comfort; we have to compensate for our lack of brand with reputation built in being both extraordinary and remarkable.

There are several choices available when it comes to your product or service strategy.

In the classic 1980 book *Competitive Strategy: Techniques for Analysing Industries and Competitors,* Michael Porter suggested that there were three basic strategies that could be selected in business.

1. Cost Leadership – The cheapest in the sector
2. Differentiation – Be different and unique
3. Market Segmentation – Niche player or mass market

In 1996, Cliff Bowman and David Faulkner looked at Porter's model and developed what has become known as Bowman's Strategy Clock.

This defined more variety of strategic choices that can be considered. The eight positions they defined are as follows:

1. Low Price and Low Value – Cheap and not very cheerful. Low customer loyalty and reputation.
2. Low Price – Low margins and high volumes required to make business profitable.
3. Hybrid (moderate price and moderate differentiation) – Good perceived value and lower prices than competitors.
4. Differentiation – Perceived added value and uniqueness (brands in corporations and reputations in SMEs).
5. Focussed Differentiation – Designer products and niche services with defined target markets.
6. High Price / Standard Product – Risky, as the price–value balance needs to be maintained.
7. High Price / Low Value – Monopoly situations allow this, or where scarcity of supply dictates synthetic pricing.
8. Low Value / Standard Price – Short term only and will damage reputation and affect market share.

Some of these strategies are not viable in, and some do not lend themselves well to businesses in the SME arena. To start with, we can probably avoid numbers 1, 2, 6, 7, and 8. This leaves us with 3, 4, and 5, and essentially, what these all lean towards is differentiation.

Whatever your product or service, you have to be positively differentiated from your competition. If there is no differentiation through your product or service, then your customers will simply default to value comparisons, and you will be forced to compete on price. Customers do not buy on price, unless you let them.

The marketing term here is that you need a Unique Sales Proposition or USP. Your USP can be anything you choose, providing it is truly unique to you. Remember this is not just the product or service you provide, but the context in which you provide it and the experience people have when trading with you that matters.

In order to determine what your USP is, or should be, simply work through the following steps:

1. What is the overwhelming frustration or challenge that people have when using the product or service you and your competitors provide? How can you overcome this?

    For example, what is the fear that most people have when going to the dentist? Pain . . .

    When you book a builder or plumber to come round, what is the unfortunate expectation? Not showing up or being late . .

    When you go into a retail store, what do you expect? To be asked if you need any help and then to be ignored when you say that you are just looking round . . .

2. What are the top seven benefits that your customers will derive from working with you or buying your products?

    How will they look better, feel better, be more successful, be happier, wealthier, more knowledgeable, and inspired by working with you. It's not what you do – it's the effect it has that is attractive to your customers.

3. What is it that is truly unique about your product or service? List the top five positive aspects of your business that are truly unique.

   Is it the biggest, brightest, loudest, or the most efficient? Is your location, knowledge, and experience unique? Or is it the results clients get by working with you that is unique? What unique experience and memories will your customers have when they buy from you?

4. How will you get the message out to your prospective customers? What promotional tools will you use?

   The message needs to be truthful and genuine. Don't promise what you can't deliver, and remember to stay true to your vision, mission, and rules of the game. Buyers are complex and need to be persuaded through both logic and emotion. They will generally see through any marketing that appears either desperate or too good to be true. Keep it real . . .

Once you have decided what the product/service actually is and what the experience of buying from you or working with you will be like, you can consider your pricing strategy.

Imagine that you see an advert for Laser Eye Correction that reads 'Corrective Laser Procedures. Just £29.99. Buy one get one free if you book before 3.00 p.m. . . . .'

Personally, I don't want to price shop my medical services. I want to have the reassurance that my eyes are in the hands of experts, so to speak. This price would immediately put me off. Price conveys quality and performance. If I can't judge or compare a service or product directly, I will use price as my guide. Most people when offered a choice of three price points for a service will go for the middle one. They don't want to risk the cheap one, and they are prepared to compromise the expensive one so they go for the middle one. This is the Goldilocks Sales Technique – prices have to not be too hot, not too cold, but just right.

It is very tempting to keep your prices low; it's like an insurance policy that if your marketing and delivery don't work out you can always sell on price if you need to, and if your marketing is really poor – just give the products away for free, and save yourself the expense. Selling low-priced goods and services is a reasonable strategy; however, if you have a truly compelling USP, then price will be only one of the reasons people buy from you. Service, reliability, results, etc. will be much higher on their lists.

You have to have pricing that is congruent with the standards or product or service you deliver. If you appear too cheap, then there is a tendency for you to be perceived as being too good to be true and that there must be a catch somewhere in the small print, or that your goods and services are not up to the standard; not a great way to start the relationship. If you are too expensive, or the perceived value is not in line with the investment required, and without the power of a brand to compensate, then prospects will find the same level of benefits from lower-priced sources. There is a limit to price elasticity.

In the 1994 film *Pulp Fiction*, John Travolta, playing the part of Vincent Vega, is in a restaurant with Mia Wallace played by Uma Thurman. Mia orders the $5 milkshake, and Vincent is so intrigued by this that he simply has to try it and so asks, 'Can I have a sip of that? I'd like to know what a $5 shake tastes like.'

He tastes it and exclaims, 'Goddamn! That's a pretty good &*%$+@ milkshake.'

Price conveys quality, performance, standards as well as value. In the words of the Stella Artois Lager advert – 'reassuringly expensive . . .'

Get the Process Right

The restaurant in Birmingham had a great product – we experienced it the first time we visited. But what they didn't have was consistency of delivery. Every business has the potential to be world class. The challenge and opportunity is not being world class – it's being world class every time.

The process is about systematising your operations so that the promises you make, both perceived and actual, with your marketing are kept. It also means that the differentiated customer experience that gives you your competitive advantage can be delivered with consistency.

Systematised consistency is at the very heart of the franchise methodology. Even mediocrity systematised and delivered regularly will beat occasional excellence delivered randomly. Customers like to have a degree of certainty about your business. When you have certainty of experience, it makes going anywhere else a risk as the experience will be uncertain.

Which brand of toothpaste do you use?

We use Colgate, not because it's the best at cleaning teeth, gives the best value or offers high levels of cavity protection, which it may well do of course. We buy it because we always have. We used it at home when I was a child – toothpaste *is* Colgate.

Chances are that you have used the same brand of toothpaste for years. Same goes with deodorants, shaving gel, hair products, etc. The reason is that we are attracted to consistency. I know exactly what I am going to get when I buy Colgate; the level of comfort I derive from the certainty surrounding the product is more valuable to me than the high risk strategy of actually trying something new; whilst Colgate remains consistent, I'm staying put.

On 23 April 1985, the Coca-Cola Company introduced New Coke to replace their existing Coca-Cola or Coke soft drink. The formulation of the drink was changed with the objective of regaining market share that had fallen from around 60% in 1950 down to around 24% by 1983.

Following the launch, there appeared to be early acceptance of the new formula Coke. New Coke had been designed using focus groups, taste testers, and comparative tests against both 'old' Coke and their biggest rival, Pepsi. There was a tidal wave of negative reaction building, however, with over 400,000 complaint letters and telephone calls received at the company's

Atlanta head office. Even Fidel Castro weighed in against New Coke calling it a sign of 'American capitalist decadence'.

Gay Mullins formed the Old Cola Drinkers of America organisation on 28 May 1985, the intention being to lobby Coca-Cola into reintroducing 'Old Coke'. His organisation received over 60,000 telephone calls and attempted to take out a class action law suit against Coca-Cola. All this in spite of Mullins stating a preference for New Coke over Old Coke in a blind taste test.

On 10 July 1985, Coca-Cola relented and the original recipe Coke drink was reintroduced to the market. Donald Keough, the president and COO of Coca-Cola, said at the time, 'The simple fact is that all the time and money and skill poured into consumer research on the new Coca-Cola could not measure or reveal the deep and abiding emotional attachment to original Coca-Cola felt by so many people.'

So whilst you may not have a brand that is as recognised as Coke, remember, the levels of comfort that your customers experience due to consistent systematised repetition will result in loyalty, retention, and profits for your business.

Systematising your business will enable you to achieve consistent delivery and predictability, for both you and your customers. With systems in place, you can guarantee your products and services because you can predict the outcomes with certainty.

Systems will also allow you to expand with confidence, or simply spend less time working in your business; your business will operate to your standards even when you are not there.

What to Systematise

In your business, systematise everything . . .

As profit is the result of everything that happens within your business, so customer service is the result of the combination of systems and people.

Coming from the UK, living in Las Vegas was like living in a movie set – the cars, the casinos, celebrities, fabulous hotels, stage shows, night clubs, and restaurants. The opening of a new night club is a regular occurrence, and as locals, we would get invited along to several of these events at 'preferred rates', in other words, cheap tickets.

We decided to go to one of these new clubs that was embedded within one of the best hotels on the Las Vegas Strip. At the information desk, I approached the assistant and requested two tickets for entry into the club later in the evening. I was informed that tickets for locals had to be arranged and paid for by calling a telephone number. However, the tickets could be collected from that information desk once payment by credit card had been made.

I stepped away from the desk and called the Ticket Hotline on my mobile phone. The phone was answered by a familiar voice; it was the assistant at the desk I had just left. I asked for two tickets, and I was asked for proof of residency in Nevada. Rather than give her my local rates web site membership number, which I had forgotten anyway, I walked over to the desk and handed her my Nevada driving licence and continued to have a telephone conversation with her although she was only three feet away from me.

When I handed her my credit card, she refused, saying that the details had to be taken over the telephone. So I read out my card information to her. When payment was confirmed, she told me that the tickets would be available for collection from the information desk in the main lobby, which could be found on the left by the white fountain as I entered the hotel, in fact, the very place I was standing and having this bizarre conversation. When the call ended, I stepped up to the desk and asked for my tickets. They were printed and handed over to me immediately, and of course, I was reminded to 'have a nice day . . .'

At the south end of the Strip stands the Mandalay Bay Hotel. Part of this resort is called THE hotel. It is a separate golden tower with amazing views, and it is also quieter than the main

Mandalay Bay resort. There is a piano bar just across from the reception area of THE hotel which is small and relaxed, and best of all, it has a couple of pool tables in a secluded side room that are rarely used. We became regulars here and would drop in for drinks and a game of pool before heading out to dinner to see a show.

Initially, I had to leave my passport with the bar staff in order that they would release the pool balls; there is clearly a market for second-hand pool balls in Vegas.

We would order our drinks, always a glass of champagne for Lynn and Bombay Sapphire Gin and Tonic for me.

After a couple of visits, we got to know the staff, and I wasn't asked for my passport in order to be given the pool balls. When we walked in, our drinks would automatically be prepared for us and placed on the bar. When a new member of the bar staff was there one evening, I approached her and asked for our drinks; they were prepared and as she placed them on the bar, she said, 'Mr and Mrs Holland, welcome back. Would you like the pool balls now or later?'

She had never seen us before, but she had been briefed that if an English couple come in on Saturday and ask for champagne and Bombay Sapphire, it would probably be us and that we would have a game of pool before heading out. How was this possible?

What system could deliver that 'wow' factor to customers? The answer is that systems don't deliver excellence – people do. The bar manager at THE hotel cared enough about his bar that he briefed all the staff about the importance of service, and especially with regulars.

It showed, and I tell that story all over the world in seminars and workshops, and I'm sure that a couple of people have played pool in THEhotel as a result. That is the power of great service. Unfortunately, great service is so unusual that when it shows up, it sparkles really brightly against the drab backdrop of what we are used to.

One Saturday, as we walked in, the bar staff all turned and wished me happy birthday. It turned out that they had checked my passport when we first went there and made a note of my birthday. How cool is that?

You don't have to be world class to be remembered for great service – just 10% better than anywhere else; the average levels are not that high.

There is an unwritten, or maybe it is written, script that retailers use all over the world. I have had the good fortune and opportunity to have travelled extensively, and doing what I do, I notice how businesses interact with their customers.

Here is how the script goes.

Person walks in to a shop. Assistant approaches the person and asks, 'Do you need any help?'

Person replies, 'No thanks. I'm just looking.'

This 'system' is being repeated in shops and stores on every continent. I was once working in Jakarta; however, my bags had ended up in Hong Kong. I explained to my host that I need to go and get some clothes while I waited a couple of days for my bags to catch up with me. He kindly took me to the Taman Anggrek Mall so I could pick up some Polo shirts, jeans, and underwear. Now as all us married men know, we are not qualified to buy underwear ourselves; we need help here. So when I walked into the mall and found a Marks & Spencer, I knew I would be OK.

Entering the shop, I was approached by a young man who asked me if I needed any help; he was using the global script. I said that I did need help and explained exactly what I was looking for and that I didn't have much time. He was so taken aback by this that he didn't know what to do. I hadn't completed my part of the script as predicted, and he didn't know what to do. He called his manager who was really helpful, and I ended up spending over 1 million Indonesian Rupiah. Spending a million on a credit card in a foreign country is always an interesting experience, especially when you're not exactly sure what the exchange rate is. Turns out it was about £70. Phew!

The point with all these stories is that people make systems work, not the systems themselves. At some point you have to allow people to interpret not just the letter of the procedure or process but also the spirit of it.

How to Systematise Your Business

The systems and people within your business is how you translate the vision, mission, and rules of the game into decisions, activities, and actions.

You can start with an operations chart, one that defines the various areas of your business and how they interact and support your product or service USP, vision, and mission. Most operations charts are simply a list of job roles and the names of those team members who fill the roles before you put any people or positions into your organisation, get the structure and process right first. You should find people that support your business, not the other way round. Even if you already have a business, it's a good idea to start with a blank piece of paper, and with your vision and mission in mind, design the structure you know you need to have, rather than simply tolerate the one that may have evolved. You may also find that you are a lot closer to your ideal structure than you thought. Once the operations chart is completed, then you can design your organisation chart around it and include people, positions, and responsibilities.

Design your operations chart using the product, process, and promotions areas of the business; select what support activities you need in each area. Each business will be different; however, providing the primary areas are all covered to an equal extent, and they all support your vision, mission, and USP, the results will follow.

The operations chart is effectively the blueprint for your business; it defines the mechanics of your business that enable it to achieve its objectives. This is the first part of developing your system; you will overlay the rules of the game at every stage such that the culture of your business accurately reflects your defining philosophy and systematically locks it into place, so that achievement of results is not dependent upon you having to be in your business.

Your systems processes and procedures should distil your philosophy and passion such that your team has the knowledge, understanding, and freedom to not only maintain, but develop your business even when you are not there.

Here is an example:

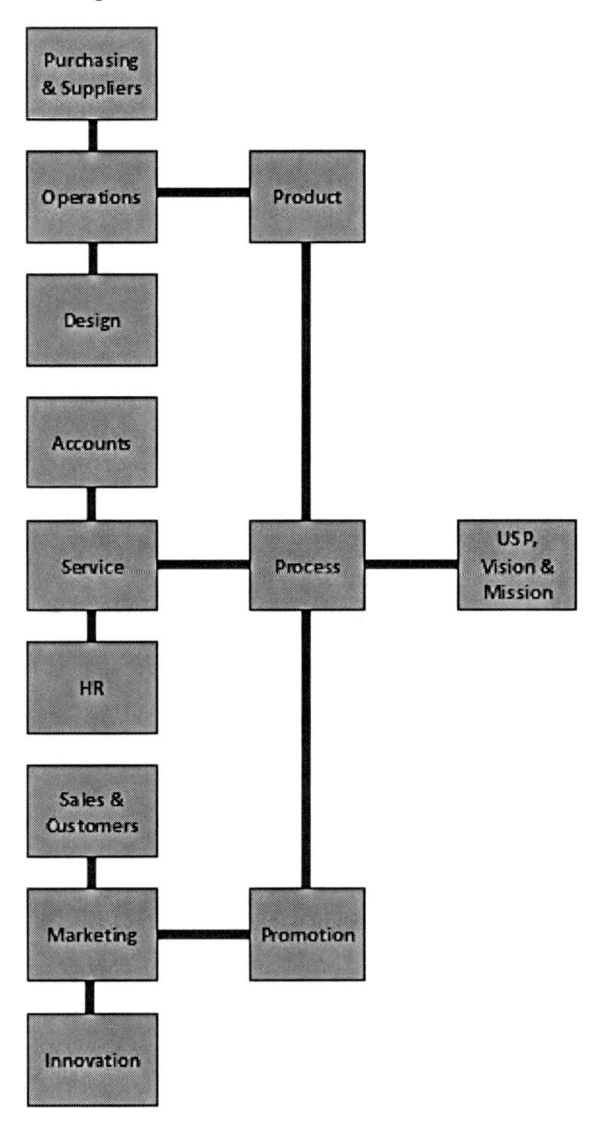

```
Purchasing & Suppliers
    │
Operations ──── Product
    │             │
  Design          │
    │             │
 Accounts         │
    │             │
  Service ──── Process ──── USP, Vision & Mission
    │             │
   HR             │
    │             │
Sales & Customers │
    │             │
Marketing ──── Promotion
    │
Innovation
```

Within each area of the business, select the key objectives that will be the responsibility of one of the team to achieve. For example, the accounts area should produce timely and accurate accounts within five days of month end, or maintain debtors at an average of thirty-four days.

The operations area should ensure that all work is carried out on time and to budget and be measured according to the number of positive testimonials that are received from thrilled customers.

Once you are clear what actual functions you need, how they contribute to the success of your business, and exactly how they are to behave in order to get the results, we can develop the systems that make it happen.

Some years ago, as a very young operations manager, I was responsible for a 100,000 ft^2 warehouse, employing around 150 people just outside of Milton Keynes. The business was involved in the storage, testing, packaging, and distribution of computer hardware and games consoles for the domestic market. I was one of the youngest operations managers in the company, and before I was awarded the promotion, my divisional director and the chairman of the company took Lynn and me out to dinner.

I remember my chairman telling me that we were in the service business and that part of our job was to do whatever it takes to satisfy the needs of our customers. In business, we can make two things, money or excuses; but we can't make both. He told me to look for opportunities to 'wow' our customers and gave me the freedom to use my judgement. He trusted me and made it clear what the expectations were. I still had budgets and forecasts to hit with KPIs for shrinkage, quality, and the usual operational objectives. However, it had to be achieved within the context of customer service.

We had systems for everything. We were an ISO 9000 accredited firm. However, it was the training and 'style' of management and leadership that enabled the philosophy of customer service to become an integral part of the business; it became 'the way we do things round here'.

We would only close the warehouse completely at Christmas, and then only for a couple of days. As you can imagine, being in the business of game consoles meant the December was a busy time for us, and we would be supplying retailers, wholesalers, and the public with systems and equipment right up until Christmas Eve.

At about 17.30 one Christmas Eve – the warehouse and sales teams had left, and I was in my office tidying up loose ends, ready to go home – the security guard took a telephone call. A distraught lady had ordered and paid for a games console, but it had not arrived, and it was a present for her son who really wanted a games console for Christmas; she wanted to know if I could help.

I had two choices.

We had thousands of customers. I could simply say that we were closed for Christmas, and she would have to call back on 27 December when the sales team would be back. After all, with thousands of customers, if we upset one of them, it would make no significant difference to me, my salary, or the profit of the business that quarter.

That thought never even crossed my mind. I remember as a seven-year-old not getting the Scalextric I wanted for Christmas; I got a fire engine instead. It was a good fire engine, but it wasn't a Scalextric. I'm not scarred by it. I'm over it now, and I've moved on and let it go . . .

I remember what my chairman had told me. We are in the service business, and I had found a way of creating a 'wow' for a customer. It absolutely fitted with the philosophy of the business. I remember imagining what my chairman would say that I should do in this situation. I knew what he would have said because I understood the rules of the game, the philosophy, and the culture of the organisation, and I had been empowered to choose how to make them real and true, not to my chairman, but to our Customers.

I took her number and promised to call her back within twenty minutes. She clearly didn't think that I would. I could tell by the tone in her voice. I fired up the sales order processing system and checked if there was an order that was outstanding for her at the address she gave me. It turns out that there was. It had been paid by credit card two weeks earlier and had been cleared for order picking, packing, and despatch. Amongst the thousands of despatches made since the payment was taken, this one had fallen through the net and the system confirmed that despatch had not been made and delivery therefore was still outstanding.

I checked the stock system. All components were available. They needed picking and packing, but they were all showing on the system. I called her back within fifteen minutes and explained what had happened and also told her that our team (that would be me and the security guard) would pick and pack the order straight away and deliver it to her house that evening.

She lived just north of Birmingham, just outside Walsall which is about sixty miles, so even with Christmas traffic I reckoned on about one-and-half-hour journey time. I left the warehouse with the games console and a few extra software titles on cassette (yes, it was that long ago . . .) at around 7.00 p.m.; the components were in stock but located within the pallet storage system, and we needed the order picking fork trucks to help us retrieve them. I arrived at the address at around 9.00 p.m.; the traffic on the M1 and M6 was really heavy. The look on her face when I showed up with the console and extra games programs that Christmas Eve made me understand what a 'wow' factor looks like.

She was genuinely grateful, and I felt great. I had found an opportunity of delivering a 'wow' to a customer. It didn't matter that she was one of thousands; she was the one that needed help.

Customer service is a choice, and sometimes it can't be systematised. When the call came in, I couldn't look up in the manual under 'Distraught Customers on Christmas Eve' to find out what to do. I had to use my instinct.

The reason for this story is that I hope it demonstrates that customer service depends on three key aspects:

1. Leadership – The vision, mission, and rules of the game that encapsulate your Philosophy have to be clear. The gesture of taking Lynn and me out to dinner, the training and development programmes that all the managers undertook, and the way I had seen other people in the business treat each

other, our suppliers, and our customers meant that I knew what should be done.

2. Systems – Whilst it could be argued that if our systems were so great, how could an order have slipped through the net in the first place? It was, however, the systems we had in place that enabled me to check the order on the system, check and locate the stock, pick it, and pack it according to the specification. All managers spent time in every area of the business – sweeping up, order picking, packing on the line – and all managers had to be able to drive a forklift truck. It was this systems approach to the operation of the business that enabled me to sort the problem out.

3. Freedom – In reality, the last thing I wanted to do was drive up the M1 on Christmas Eve. However, I loved my job, customer service is in my blood, and I knew that this was simply the right thing to do. And how I achieved it was up to me. I could have called a courier, got a taxi to deliver it, or invited the lady to drive to Milton Keynes and collect it. Other managers may have made a different choice and achieved the same outcome. I knew that I had the freedom to choose, and having the freedom to make the choice also meant that I had 100% responsibility for the outcome.

The systems you build into your business can only cope with 83% of the issues that will arise. The extra 17% will have to be made up as you and your team go along. It is in the 17% that legends are made. This is where reputations are made and lost.

Your systems should be written down so that everyone can find them and refer to them when needed. You will need to train your team how to use and interpret them. Remember, training is a process, not an event, and continuous learning and development should be a cornerstone of your business. I know that there is a fear amongst business owners that if you train people, they may leave and join the competition or start a competing business. Let's be clear – people don't leave because you train them; they leave because they are not happy and fulfilled in their role.

Training just means that they get more interviews. And anyway, what happens to your business if you don't train them and they decide to stay with you because no one else will employ them?

We use an online wiki for all our systems, documents, and procedures. It is easily updated and can be viewed from anywhere in the world. It contains charts, systems and procedures, work instructions, and documents. It is a living thing that is used daily by the team and means that everyone has access to the same information all the time.

In the Logistics Business we were involved in the storage and despatch of used cars; we recognised that one of the keys to selling cars at the best prices was how they were prepared prior to being put on display. The cars were pre-owned, with an age range of between twenty-four and sixty months. The cars weren't simply cleaned and vacuumed; they were detailed to an extraordinary degree. Lights were removed so that every trace of dirt could be removed; window seals were cleaned and treated so that they were spotless and shiny black just like when they were new; wheels were removed and polished on the inside and out with new tyres fitted all round.

Every car regardless of its age looked like new, in fact better than new. All carpets were shampooed and glass was polished. They even smelled like a new car by the time the team had finished with them. The challenge was that as the business expanded new team members had to be trained. Can you imagine how many words would be required to explain how to detail an entire car?

So we produced a series of videos that showed one of the experienced team members preparing a car for display. The videos covered everything from how to wash the car, the polishing, trim removal and refitting, how to repair small scratches and fabric tears, even how to make sure that when the front wheels were pointing straight ahead, the steering wheel was perfectly centralised and aligned.

The training programme involved several stages, and all team members underwent initial and refresher training on a regular basis. The team would check each other's work to make sure that every car was up to standard.

Video is a great way of teaching people how things should be done. Have videos of you available that explain your vision and philosophy for the business; a picture is indeed worth a thousand words.

With all your systems, be clear how they contribute to the overall objectives of the business. For example, if stock availability is critical to your success, then the systems of stock control, purchasing, and supply need to be designed to support you with associated KPIs and operational targets.

Organisation Chart

Once the blueprint is completed, you can build the organisation that will deliver the desired outcomes. Now you can put names to functions and develop the roles and responsibilities within your business.

Depending on the stage of growth of your business, you may find that when it comes to allocating tasks and responsibilities, your name crops up several times; you are the chief cook and bottle washer. At this stage of the process, that is fine. We will be coming back to the organisation chart when we look at Rule No. 5 – you will need help.

Know Your Numbers

There are critical numbers that every business owner needs to understand; there are those that tend to be common to most businesses; and then there are those that are unique to certain sectors and industries. The key thing is to be able to understand how your business is doing. The KPIs may be financially or operationally based and are great for giving you a running commentary on how well you are performing. However, understanding the finances of your business and what the numbers actually mean is critical to your success.

Efficiency and Productivity

Efficiency

Being responsible for the ground services operations for several airlines at three of the UK's busiest airports – Heathrow, Gatwick, and Stansted – meant that we had around 450 people working shifts that enabled us to operate twenty-four hours a day, seven days a week. Our business was involved with the cleaning, water replenishment, and toilet servicing of commercial passenger aircraft on the ramp where they park the planes during boarding. When you land at an airport and finally park at the terminal gate, you will notice that there are a range of vehicles waiting for the plane; these are the caterers, ground handlers, and cleaners. That is where our teams would have to be on time every time in order that the aircraft can be 'turned' and ready for safe take-off within its allocated time frame. There are two cardinal sins when working airside at an airport – one was compromising safety, and the other is delaying an aircraft.

The pricing was very keen on this type of work. Within the airport facility, only so many companies are licensed to operate and have premises 'airside' where the planes go but the public aren't allowed. So everyone knew which supplier had which contracts and the pricing was extremely competitive. Furthermore, all activities had to be carried out to the required standards of the individual airline, and in accordance with the strict rules and regulations imposed by IATA, the International Air Transport Authority. Any company winning a contract with an airline had to provide essentially an identical service; there was no room for innovation because lives were at risk.

It was only by understanding the numbers in the business and measuring them on a regular basis that enabled the business to prosper.

Utilisation / Capacity = Efficiency

For example, if an accountant has a forty-hour week, but in that week only produces chargeable client work for twenty hours then the efficiency rate is

20 hours Utilisation / 40 hours Capacity = 0.50 or 50%

The same applies in any business; there will be a level of capacity for producing work, and there will also be a level of utilisation. In the example of the accountant, the twenty hours that are being 'wasted' could have been spent opening the post, ordering stationery, making the coffee, filing, surfing the Internet, updating Facebook, etc.

No one is 100% efficient; however, once you measure the efficiency of your business, you can manage it and have targets and objectives around this as a KPI if appropriate. In the case of the accountant, it may be that the maximum efficiency possible is 85%. There will always be a need for some non-chargeable activities such as training, research, meetings, etc.

Other activities either need to be stopped completely or delegated to other more junior members of the team, allowing the high added value, chargeable activity, to be maximised. Accountants are very expensive filing clerks. It doesn't cost what they earn per hour to do the filing; it actually costs what they are charged out to clients at per hour to do the filing.

Different businesses will have different measures of efficiency; this is an example of the type of scenario we

> In the area of Quantum Mechanics, there is a premise that the physical act of observation can affect reality. As reported in Nature - Vol. 391, researchers at the Weizmann Institute have demonstrated that "watching" a beam of electrons affects their behaviour. Take a look at http://www.youtube.com/watch?v=DfPeprQ7oGc for a fun explanation.
>
> So in business, just the act of observation and measurement may affect your results.

encountered at the airports, which will demonstrate how efficiency can be used as a key driver of profit and sales within a business.

Scheduled commercial aircraft have allocated landing and take-off slots at airports. We serviced around seventy airlines and provided a variety of services to a wide range of aircraft types, servicing hundreds of aircraft each week. Clearly, it takes longer to clean and service a Boeing 747 Jumbo than it does small commuter jet, so for each aircraft type we knew when the plane would land, where it would park, how many of our people would be required to service it, and how long it would take.

We plotted all the activities that we needed to perform on a graph so we could see how we need to organise our crews and make sure we had the capacity to meet every plane on time and get it away on time.

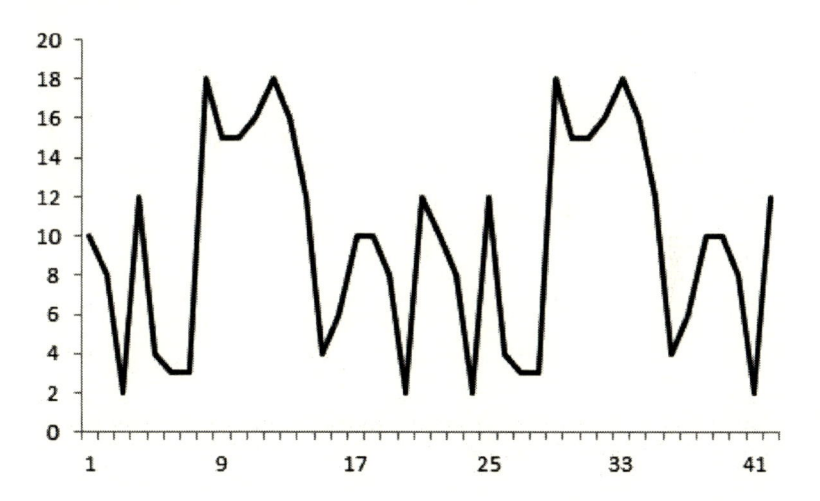

This is how the workload plan looked over a two-week period; the horizontal axis represents the number of eight-hour shifts that make up the two-week cycle. The vertical axis is the number of aircraft to be serviced during the two weeks. The line on the graph shows how busy we would need to be at various times during the two weeks. As you can see, there are very busy times and some relatively quiet times. Our challenge was organising our crews so that they were as efficient as possible when carrying out the activity required.

Imagine if we had a huge team of people sitting around waiting for planes to land. When there were lots of planes, they would be busy, but when there were only a few, many of them would be idle. The challenge we faced was that we had predictable, fluctuating demand with a predictable but consistent workforce.

The next chart shows how simply having a huge team waiting for planes to arrive would look. We would have had to gear up for the busy times in order to cope with peak demand; however, where demand was lower, we would have been highly inefficient.

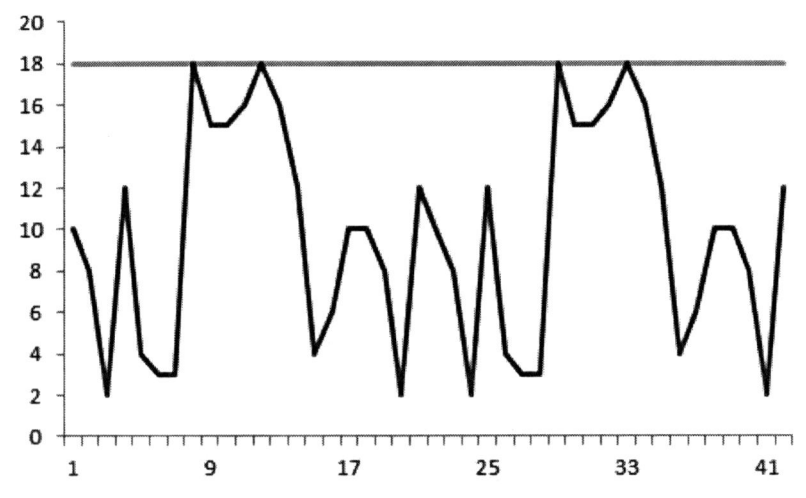

The grey horizontal line denotes the consistent labour capacity that would be generated if we kept a consistent workforce in place twenty-four hours per day. The actual efficiency of the model above is running at just 54%. This means that 46% of our labour resources were being wasted, not due to the servicing crews not doing their jobs well, but there simply wasn't the work for them to do for all the time they were available.

The matching of resources to output requirements was a key determinant of profitability in this business, so increasing the efficiency of our labour schedules was critical to the success of the business.

By understanding exactly what the demand requirements were, we could manage our staff and work patterns accordingly. Through the introduction of a complex array of shift patterns and rosters, we were able to match our labour availability much more closely to the pattern of demand.

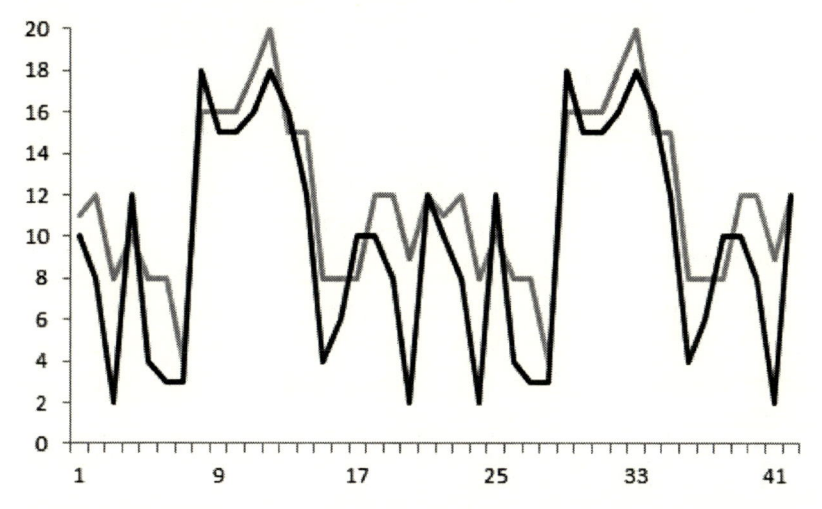

On the chart now you can see that the demand pattern denoted by the black line has not changed; however, the labour capacity pattern denoted by the grey line mimics the demand requirements much more closely. The actual efficiency of this model is 82%.

We would measure our efficiency on a weekly basis; it had such a profound effect on the business. Measuring efficiency in this way meant we were also able to look at commercial opportunities more constructively. On the chart you will notice that we were at our most inefficient during periods of low demand, where the troughs on the black line appear. There is generally a bigger gap between the black and grey lines. What this meant was that we could look at the airline schedules of those carriers we did not service, and find the ones that would essentially fill the gaps for us, raising our demand where we had spare capacity. Conversely, there would be a number of carriers whose schedule conflicted with our capacity plan, and although the increased sales income would have been a positive move, the resulting reduction in the overall efficiency of the business resulting from servicing them made them unprofitable and therefore unattractive to us.

Productivity

Output / Unit of Input = Productivity

For example, if a telemarketer works for five hours and makes 180 phone calls, the productivity rate would be

$$180 \text{ phone calls} / 5 \text{ hours} = 36 \text{ calls per hour.}$$

Productivity is a measure of rate of output and can be used in most businesses to initially measure and then improve performance.

The Dance Sport business covers a variety of products and services. As a young general manager, I worked with a great team of people in London. Our business was the design and manufacture of ballroom dancing dresses for the professional and amateur markets. I affectionately called the business the "frock shop".

All the dresses were unique and designed specifically for a dancer to wear at a specific competition. The colours chosen would have to be complimentary to the colour of the dance floor at specific venues; satin shoes would have to be dyed to match the dress; this was a business driven by passion and emotion. If you think showing up at a party in the same top as someone else is wearing is bad, you should see what happens when two ballroom dancers show up at a competition wearing the same colour and style!

Ballroom dancing dresses are fabulous garments, literally works of art, being 100% hand made from the finest fabrics. Dresses may be spray-dyed in intricate colours or have hundreds of glass rhinestones individually attached.

Productivity in this environment was almost a dirty word. We were producing the world's finest garments, and measuring with something as blunt as mere numbers was always going to be a challenge. Some dresses took a few hours to make whilst others took days. The rate of productivity was erratic; the products were always fabulous. However, my job was to help improve profitability, and it was clear that there was room for improvement.

The answer lay in the underskirts. As one of the directors pointed out at a board meeting, essentially all the dresses were 'simply a chassis with a series of trim options'. Whilst this didn't exactly endear him to the rest of the team, he was right. We had to apply some basic principles to even these most creative of activities.

On average it took twenty-six hours of labour to produce a dress, so we looked at the processes involved and found that although the dresses were truly unique in design and style, they did have some attributes that were common to them all. Most ballroom dancing dresses had full skirts and underskirts that make the dress appear fuller. The degree of 'fullness' is dictated by the grade of fishing line that is sewn into the hem of the underskirt. The thicker the line the more full the skirt will be.

This common 'component' could be made for stock by junior team members and used by the highly skilled dressmakers when they needed them. This somewhat mechanistic approach to what was essentially a unique product enabled the productivity to be increased whilst maintaining the authenticity and uniqueness of the finished garment.

The key to improving both your efficiency and productivity is to have appropriate measures in place. If you can't measure something, you can't manage it. Furthermore, if you don't measure the performance of your business, how will you know when something you do delivers an improvement? Measurement gives us control and control means that we have predictability within the business.

Efficiency and productivity measures should be used together; they are dependent upon each other to a certain extent. They can be applied to any business and to almost any activity. Understanding them is fundamental to the foundations of your business.

Break-Even Point

The break-even point in your business can be described as the point at which your gross profit covers your fixed costs or overheads.

For example, let's assume that a business has monthly overheads of £100,000. The sales income is running at a consistent £300,000 per month with a gross margin of 50% or £150,000 per month.

The total overheads for the twelve-month period will be

£100,000 × 12 = £1,200,000

The gross profit is running at the rate of £150,000 per month and during the year will equal

£150,000 × 12 = £1,800,000

Now we can calculate when during the year the business will have generated enough gross profit to cover all the overheads.

£1,200,000 / £1,800,000 = 66%

Break-even will be achieved after 12 months × 66% = 8 months.

What this means is that all the profit in the business is being used to pay overheads and fixed costs. Only when the twelve months' liability for these costs has been covered by the gross profit, can net profit be taken.

Break-even points can be calculated over a twelve-month period, or you can have quarterly, monthly, weekly, or daily break-even. With the model above, assuming that the sales are evenly spread throughout the year, the daily break-even based on an eight-hour day would be

8hrs × 66% = 5½hrs.

The opportunity with understanding the break-even point in a business is that it can be used as a performance target. I have seen several businesses that break-even half way through the last month of the twelve-month financial year. This is usually way too late as a slight fluctuation in performance during the 11½ months will wipe out any potential for even the slim profits the business could have made.

Knowing what sales have to be made on a daily, weekly, or monthly basis is a great performance measure for the team. If the break-even point is 5½ hours into a working day, set a target to get this down to 5 hours or 4½ hours. The results will be dramatic, and it gives the whole team an instant objective that they have direct influence over.

Margins, Mark-up, and Discounts

Rule No. 1 – Don't discount

The financial performance or your business is dependent on two key drivers – volume of sales and the margins achieved. Having control of these will contribute to your success. The question of volume of sales will be covered in later chapters. What we are looking at here is effectively how efficient your business is with regards to money.

Margin & Mark-up

Margins will be reported in your profit and loss account and predicted in your budgets and forecasts. Continuous monitoring of your margins, especially where pricing of individual jobs or pieces of work is involved is critical.

Just as a refresher, margin and mark-up are not the same. Mark-up is classically how products are priced, whilst margins are the levels of profitability achieved as a result of the sale. I can remember this being really confusing, so I thought I'd spend a few lines explaining them here for clarity. We are looking at gross margins here.

If I buy a TV for £300 and apply a mark-up of 50% to it, the selling price will be £450.

When I sell that TV for £450 the profit margin I achieve will be £150 or 33%.

In both cases, the profit is £150. It is how it is measured that makes the difference.

Mark-up is the profit (in pounds) expressed as a percentage of the cost price (in pounds).

Margin is the profit (in pounds) expressed as percentage of the sales price (in pounds).

When pricing products, plenty of businesses use mark-up. It is a simple and easy rule that is used in manufacturing, retail, and a variety of other sectors. The challenge is that while pricing is set by mark-up, the results of the business are reported as margins. Understanding the relationship between these two elements is important.

If I buy a TV for £300 and apply a mark-up of just 10% to it, the selling price will be £330.

When I sell that TV for £330, the profit margin I achieve will be £30 or 9.1% margin.

Now, if I buy a TV for £300 and apply a mark-up of 200% to it, the selling price will be £900.

When I sell that TV for £900, the profit margin I achieve will be £600 or 66% margin.

Mark-up and margin are more closely aligned at lower levels. 10% mark-up results in 9.1% margin, whereas 200% mark-up results in 66% margin.

The chart shows the relationship between mark-up and margin. There is no limit to the degrees of mark-up you can apply to your products; your customers may have something to say about this of course. However, no matter what the mark-up, margins can never be more than 100%.

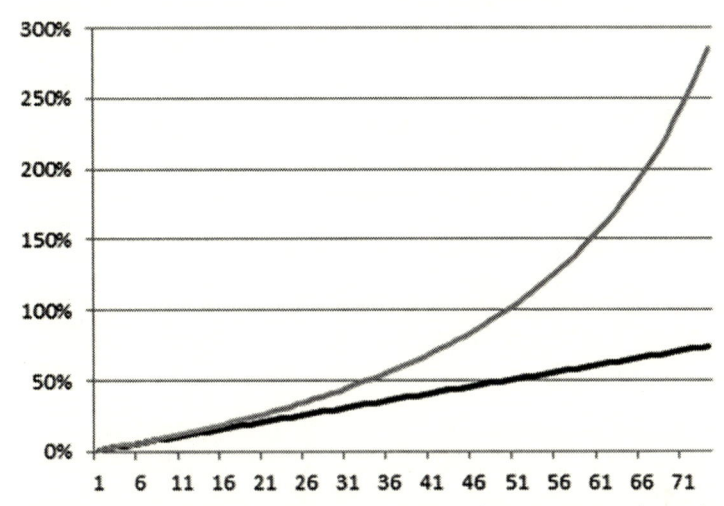

On the chart, the grey line represents the amount of mark-up applied to a product, the percentage being measured on the vertical axis. The black line represents the margin that will be achieved for any given level of mark-up.

If you need to achieve a gross margin of 50% in your business, then simply find 50% on the black line and go up the corresponding point on the grey line and that will tell you what minimum mark-up will have to be applied to your cost prices in order to achieve it.

Discounts

As demonstrated in an earlier chapter, giving discounts can be really damaging to your business if they are applied without understanding the implications.

John runs a business that is involved with the sale of furniture to the public. He operates from a high street shop and has a small range of oak tables and chairs that he imports from the Far East.

John knows that according to his budgets and forecasts, he needs to achieve a gross margin of 50% in his business. This means that he has to apply a 100% mark-up to all his cost prices to achieve this.

In order to improve his business, John decides to evaluate what the sensitivity of his business is when it comes to price variations.

First he evaluates what the effect on the business would be if he offered a 25% discount across the range. This would clearly affect his gross profit and margins, but he figured that he would attract more customers due to the lower price point.

Let's look at the effect of this on his business.

Traditionally, John would buy a table for £100 and sell it for £200 to achieve his target margin. He would make £100 profit on every table he sold.

By applying a 25% discount, the new sales price would be £150, and John would only make £50 profit on every table he sold.

What this means is that in order to achieve the same level of gross profit in pounds as he did before the discount was applied, John would need to sell twice as much furniture.

Second, he evaluates what the effect would be of increasing his prices by 25% across the range.

The effect on John's business would now look like this.

The tables that cost £100 would now be sold for £250 after applying the price increase.

By applying the 25% price increase, he would now make £150 profit on every table sold.

If John did this, he knew he would lose some business as some buyers would be put off by the higher prices. In order to achieve the same levels of gross profit in pounds as he did before the price increase was applied, John could afford to lose 33% of his customers.

The choice is John's; however, discounting will have a disproportionate effect on your margins and in principle should be avoided where possible.

Discounts can be useful to clear out old stock or end-of-line products as it releases cash into the business to invest in newer high-margin products. To make an offer to entice people to buy more and at the same time make the offer attractive in terms of price, consider bundling products together – buy one get one at half the price. These offers will affect your margins, but they systematically increase your sales to more than compensate.

When setting your pricing, remember that your customers don't care about your costs. They care about the added value they will derive from trading with you, associated with the price you charge them.

Profit and Loss Account and Balance Sheet

You should always seek the advice of an accountant when looking at financial statements. Remember, you are a business owner and not an accountant. You need to know how to manage the business based on your interpretation of the accounts and not the actual formulation of them.

Both of my sons, Jonathan and Richard, have been to several of my seminars and workshops and travelled around the world with us, attending events and conferences. When Jonathan was studying business at college, one of the questions he was asked went something like this:

'Given these financial results in a business, what would your first recommendation be to the board of directors?'

His answer, which in my view was absolutely correct, was 'hire an accountant . . .'

As a business owner, you do need to understand the financials of your business. You also need to have appropriate information prepared for you such that you can make informed and timely decisions.

Your accountant will look after the statutory accounts, those accounts that have to be published and filed. For the day-to-day running of the business, you need a solid set of management accounts, usually comprising of a summary profit and loss report and a balance sheet.

The management accounts can be formatted however you like. It is always good practice to have your accounts produced in the same format as your budgets so that direct comparisons between forecast and actual performance can be made.

Management accounts should be systematised such that at the end of each month or trading period, you get a set of accounts within a few days. I usually have them ready within five working days of the end of the month, along with an up-to-date balance sheet.

The management accounts are a record of what has happened in the past. Even if the accounts are ready within a few days after month end, they are still out of date when you get them. Your day-to-day management and use of KPIs and reporting structures should mean that you never get any surprises in your accounts. In fact with good management systems, you should be able to predict them.

The profit and loss account should record the performance of the business in terms of sales, direct costs, and gross profit, as well as overheads and net profits. It should compare the predicted values in each of these areas with the actual result achieved and show variances for the period as well as year-to-date variances and ratios. I have seen so many businesses that run without a regular set of accounts being published during the year, only to find at the end of the year that they have not achieved anything like the results they anticipated. Your business needs constant attention and 'correction making' during the year in order to keep it on track. Waiting for twelve months to see what happens is not a great plan.

The balance sheet gives you a snapshot of the current position of your business in terms of what it owns and what it owes to other people or organisations. The format of the balance sheet is standard and simply records the assets and liabilities of your business; the difference between the two is yours, or owners' equity.

Key information that should be monitored as a minimum and that won't show on the profit and loss account includes the following:

1. **Stock** – There are several types of stock that you may have in your business; it depends on what type of business you have. They can be raw materials, work in progress (WIP), finished goods, or even sales delivered not invoiced (SDNI). Stock equals cash, and in principle, this should be kept to a minimum.

2. **Debtors** – What money is owed to the business? Always have your accountant provide a debtor's ledger report showing the debts by customer and age. Again this is cash in waiting and should be kept to a minimum with debtor days being a key measure. In order to manage the debtors, have a detailed collection policy that is used consistently. This should detail what phone calls are made and what letters are sent to your customers, by whom and when. When starting with a new customer, remember to be cautious while offering credit. Check them out through a reference agency to make sure they can be trusted.

3. **Creditors** – What do you owe to your suppliers? Again, always have a creditor report available and play nice with your suppliers. Treat them as you would like to be treated, and pay them on time.

4. **Cash** – What cash is in the bank? Providing your cash flow forecasting is

> Picking up the reigns of a packaging company just outside Bristol some years ago, one of the first reports I requested was a debtor's analysis. I picked the worst offenders and decided to call each company individually to see what the issues preventing payment were. One director informed me that each month they place all their bills in a bucket and pull them out until they have allocated all the money in their bank at that time, and if I phoned again, our invoice wouldn't even make it to the bucket...

up to scratch, there should be no surprises here. However, always monitor your cash position; cash is the oxygen your business needs to thrive.

Notes

Rule No. 3 – Keep All Your Customers

I've never felt like I was in the cookie business. I've always been in a feel good business. My job is to sell joy. My job is to sell happiness. My job is to sell an experience.

Debbi Fields – founder Mrs Fields Cookies

When growing your business, it is very tempting to start a marketing campaign to attract new customers, and it's a great strategy to employ. However, the most important asset your business may have is your existing customers. We need to have a great system of customer care and service in place for your existing customers before we start attracting new ones.

Now whilst the rule is to keep all your customers - that may not actually be the best policy. We need to bend this rule a little. What you must do is keep all your great customers, and either convert your average or problem customers to great ones, or allow them to go and be challenging somewhere else. To determine which are your great, average, or problem customers, you need to do a GAP analysis.

You may think you know instinctively who your best customers are. What you actually need to be able to do is scientifically measure which ones they are so that you can manage them accordingly.

So, how do you measure how 'great' your customers are?

Initially, we want to define what criteria contribute to making a great customer. The details may be different depending on the business sector you are in, but the process is the same.

First, list down all the attributes that you would assign to your ideal customer. These could include the following:

1. Average Debtor Days – How long on average does it take them to pay their bills?
2. Annual Sales – The total revenue derived from them in a twelve-month period.
3. Average Order Value – When they make a purchase, what is its value on average?
4. Margins – What is the gross margin percentage achieved overall from their activity with your business?
5. Referrals Made – How many referrals and introductions do they make to your business?
6. Product Range – Do they buy the entire range of products or services that you offer?
7. Years of Trading – How long have they been customers of yours? How loyal to you are they?
8. Ease of Servicing – Are they a high maintenance client? Do they complain and query prices or are they more easy going?
9. Growth Potential – Are they growing and likely to expand and develop the business relationship further?
10. Location – Are they in close proximity to your business, making deliveries easy, or are they too far away?

Some of these attributes are specific and measurable. Some are subjective and intangible. However, that is the nature of most relationships, and customers are no different.

Now, based on the criteria you have chosen, decide how your perfect customer would behave in relation to each of them. Now you are effectively defining what your ideal customer looks like, and then we can compare those that you do have against those you would like to have.

Your ideal customer would score 100 out of a target 100 points in each of the attributes you have selected. So now you need to be as specific as you can be in setting the targets in each of the areas, and also how points will be awarded based upon their actual performance. For example

1. Average Debtor Days: 100 points = 25 days average payment terms. Every day over 25 reduce score by 5 points.

2. Annual Sales: 100 points = £25,000. Four points awarded for every £1,000 sales value.

3. Average Order Value: 100 points = £5,000. Four points awarded for every £200 average order value.

4. Margin Percentage: 100 points = 50% Gross Margin. Twenty points awarded for every 10% margin achieved.

5. Referrals Made: 100 points = 10 Referrals. Ten points awarded for every referral made.

6. Product Range: 100 points = Buying 10 different products. Ten points awarded for each product type purchased.

7. Years of Trading: 100 points = 5 years. Twenty points awarded for each year of trading relationship.

8. Ease of Servicing: 100 (subjective, score according to experience.)

9. Growth Potential: 100 (subjective, score according to experience.)

10. Location: 100 = within two-mile radius. Twenty points deducted for every mile in excess of two miles radius from your location.

The perfect customer would score 100 in each of the ten attributes selected, resulting in a 'perfect' total score of 1,000 points. It is possible to score more than 100 points as extremely high sales levels and margins, for example, could earn a customer more points, but your ideal customer would score 1,000. Remember that whilst one or two customers that represent a high proportion of your sales and gross margin may score highly in this ranking system, it may actually represent an inherent weakness and threat to your business.

Now simply measure each of your customers against the criteria you have selected and see how they rank in terms of total points scored.

The chart below shows a sample table based around the criteria set above. A simple spreadsheet is usually good enough to carry out this analysis. You may also need a competent teenager who can design and populate it for you in minutes rather than hours. I am fortunate; I have two sons who are great at this type of work.

Based on the scoring system you adopt, you can decide what level of customer qualifies to be great, average, or poor. For example, any customer scoring 75% and over could be classified as great; between 35% and 74%, average; and anyone below 34%, poor. You will be managing your customers so that they all move towards being great. You will of course have a mix. Some customers will remain average, and some will stay poor. You should nurture the great ones, encourage and incentivise the average ones, and consider getting rid of the poor ones.

Poor customers are a drain in your resources. The margins may not be good. They don't pay on time, or they are just plain awkward to deal with. The best way to promote a poor client to a great one is to increase their prices such that the irritations associated with dealing with them suddenly become worthwhile. If they cannot be promoted, be prepared to let them go, to create space and opportunity for new great clients to be attracted to your business.

The best client you ever had hasn't shown up yet.

Customer		Average Debtor Days	Annual Sales	Ave Order £	Margin %	Referrals Made	Product Range	Years of Trading	Ease of Servicing	Growth Potential	Location	Total	%
Target		25 Days	£25,000	£5,000	50%	10	10	5	100 pts	100 pts	2 m		
John Brown	Result	25	22,000	4,400	52%	4	8	6			4		
	Points	100	88	88	104	40	80	120	75	50	60	805	81%
Tim Green	Result	27	20,000	10,000	40%	2	5	2			2		
	Points	90	80	200	80	20	50	40	85	10	100	755	76%
Helen White	Result	45	30,000	2000	35%	5	10	4			6		
	Points	0	120	40	70	50	100	80	50	50	20	580	58%
Richard Black	Result	25	18,000	3,000	35%	0	2	3			6		
	Points	100	72	60	70	0	20	60	20	10	20	432	43%
Karen LeBlanc	Result	35	18,000	2,000	25%	2	3	5			8		
	Points	50	72	40	50	20	30	100	35	25	-20	402	40%
Sarah Gray	Result	45	24,000	4,000	30%	1	2	2			10		
	Points	0	96	80	60	10	20	40	50	50	-60	346	35%
Jade Smith	Result	40	24,000	1,000	35%	2	5	2			11		
	Points	25	96	20	70	20	50	40	75	10	-80	326	33%
Coral Jones	Result	45	15,000	3,000	30%	4	3	1			7		
	Points	0	60	60	60	40	30	20	20	10	0	300	30%
Steven Gold	Result	45	12,000	2,000	35%	2	4	2			8		
	Points	0	48	40	70	20	40	40	25	25	-20	288	29%
Kenny Silvers	Result	60	50,000	2,000	20%	0	1	3			12		
	Points	-75	200	40	40	0	10	60	10	10	-100	195	20%

So now we have this information we can put strategies in place to build the business with our existing customers, rather than simply go out and get new ones.

What this information enables you to do is to manage your customer relationships on the basis of evidence. The way forward is not to get rid of your poor customers but to manage them and the average ones so that they all become great. Of course, this may not be possible with every customer you have, but based on the ideal criteria you have selected, specific strategies and tactics can be introduced that will help improve performance.

The principles apply whether your customers are wholesalers, retailers, distributors, or members of the public, major corporations, public sector or small businesses.

Taking each of the criteria in turn, we can introduce targeted strategies that will enable you to manage your customers such that they all, or at least the majority, move towards your 'perfect customer' model. The criteria I have chosen in the example are generic to plenty of business. There may be some additional specific ones that will be helpful to your business, and a couple of them may not fit your needs. The basic ratios can be measured and improved in almost any business.

1. Average Debtor Days – First of all, consider what agreements have been made with each customer. If you have agreed to sixty-day terms, then you may be stuck with it, unless you offer incentives, usually cash, for early settlement. Make it easy too for your customers to pay you. Accept credit cards, online payments, direct debits, not only cheques.

Make sure your terms of trading are clear. They should be discussed and agreed as part of the sales process, incorporated into agreements, and included on every invoice raised.

Always carry out credit checks before offering credit to any customer, and take up references from other suppliers to make sure that they are credit worthy. If you feel that a customer should pay upfront for goods or services, then so be it.

To keep all your customers paying on time, either according to the individual agreements you have made, or simply in line with your standard terms and conditions of trading, you need a system of cash collection. The process you use may be different depending on your business sector; however, these are the basic steps:

1. Make sure all invoices are accurate and sent out on time. Sounds obvious, but I have seen plenty of businesses where

poor invoicing is the cause of most of the problems with cash collection. Be clear when the debt is actually incurred, and the agreed credit period starts from. It is usually the date on which the goods or services are provided, or the date when the customer receives the invoice, whichever is the later.

2. Send out statements of account to all your customers every month to remind them that they owe you money; the statement should show the value of the debt, the due date, and also how many days overdue the payment is, if applicable.

3. If the money doesn't arrive on or before the due date, within twenty-four hours send a standard, gentle reminder email requesting information regarding the payment of the debt and when you would expect them to respond.

4. If still no payment, send out standard letters at seven days, fourteen days, and twenty-eight days after the debt became due. Each letter should be polite and factual, each one steadily escalating the pressure placed on the customer for continued non-payment. The second two letters can suggest that the debt will be passed to a debt collection agency if it remains unpaid.

5. If after twenty-eight days the debt remains unpaid, pass it over to the debt collection agency. If you threaten to do this, you must follow through. Not pleasant, but if they don't pay you, they are not your customers.

This process should be fully systematised and documented within your accounts function. You should have visibility of exactly what is being done to which customer and only you or your nominated representative should have the authority to approve credit notes and debt collection agency instructions. The reason for this is that credit notes are like writing a cheque, and you need that to be under your control, and if debt collection agencies have to be engaged, something has gone wrong with your system or the customer relationship. You may decide that commercially a telephone call from you to your customer may be an option prior to sending the boys around.

By applying a systematised approach to the raising and sending of invoices and collection of the debts that they impose, you may well find that some customers with traditionally poor track records improve and come into line with your expectations of your ideal customer. They may promote themselves up the league from poor to average.

Working in the licensed trade, a colleague was involved in the collection of money from licensed premises in London. His cash collection process involved a few gentle reminder calls and a couple of letters. If no payment was received, he would invoke 'dog day Friday'. This involved a couple of big lads going to the offending establishment on a Friday with a big dog to politely but firmly ask for payment. Although it did seem to get results, please do not try this strategy.

Accounts clerks involved with the management of purchase ledgers carry out a thankless task. They may get plenty of letters and phone calls requesting payment, or even threatening legal action, but they very rarely get recognition for the work that they do. In our business, we decided that we would not only have a process for collecting debts but also have a process for rewarding and thanking our customers when they paid on time or early.

Every invoice we sent out had a chocolate bar included inside the envelope. We actually had several accounts team members call us and thank us for the invoice and say that they were looking forward to the next one; how often does that happen? As we progressed, we built a relationship with the accounts team at all of our customers so that after a while we were sending specific types of chocolate bars to different customers depending upon the preference of each individual. My teenage son, Richard, had the job of buying all the appropriate chocolate and sending out the invoices; he was on our organisation chart as our director of chocolate.

Why would we do this?

Because if there was ever a payment that didn't arrive when expected, we would make a phone call and speak with our friends in the accounts department. They would always take the call and always gave us the true reason for non-payment. If they said that the cheque was in the post, we knew for once that was true. If they said they needed to wait a couple of days for a big cheque to clear into their account and then the payment would be sent, that was true too. We never had to send out any letters or involve debt collectors.

Finally, plenty of businesses rightly have systems and procedures that control the collection of debts. How many businesses have a system for thanking and rewarding customers for on-time or early payment?

If a payment doesn't arrive, you will send out the email, then the letters at seven, fourteen, and twenty-eight days, and eventually advise the debt collection agency. What happens when a customer pays on time or even early? Usually nothing. We decided that if customer paid on time, although they were contractually obliged to, we would thank them with a phone call, a letter, or a card. If a customer paid early or immediately upon receipt of invoice, we would thank them and send round a thank you with a gift, more chocolate, flowers, or a bottle of champagne, depending on the size of the payment.

If you reward people for great performance, not only penalise them for poor performance, you will find that you will get more positive results.

We did this, and continue to do it, because our mission and rules of the game state that if we are in the relationship business, this is one way we achieve congruency with our own standards.

2 & 3. Annual Sales & Average Order Value.

There are two variables that dictate the level of sales derived from your customers – average order value and the number of orders made.

Annual sales = Average order value × Annual Number of orders.

In order to increase the annual sales from an existing customer, you have to adjust one of the other two variables. In an ideal world, we would have strategies in place that would increase both the variables and result in higher sales being achieved. In reality, we may find that as we increase one of the variables, the other reduces, and vice versa. It really depends on the type of business you have and the product and services you provide.

Lynn and I will eat out in a restaurant once or twice a week. We have a number of restaurants within our local town to choose from, and we go to the same one maybe two or three times a year.

There is huge potential for the local restaurants to encourage us to go back and increase the number of orders we place with them, because we use a variety of restaurants on a regular basis. There is also potential for the restaurants we frequent to increase the average value of the orders we place while we are there.

With this scenario where a business is providing a product or service that is purchased on a regular basis by a variety of customers, strategies to increase both the frequency and value of the orders will be effective. What we are doing in this situation is increasing the proportion of 'spending share' with each customer.

Let's say that we spend around £4,000 a year in restaurants. It is up to each individual restaurant owner to encourage us to give them a larger share of that spending.

In France, the bread doesn't contain preservatives like it does in other countries (in the USA, a loaf of sliced bread could last for a week before going stale). For this reason, it is usual to buy fresh bread every day from the local bakery. Each morning, we will walk or ride to the bakery and pick up a couple of baguettes.

In this situation, it is unlikely that we can be encouraged to go to the bakery any more than once a day; they already get 100% on our bakery attendance activity. Where there is scope for development will be with the amount of money we spend while we are there. They sell a lot more than just bread, and yet we rarely buy anything else from them.

The local fitness centre charges around £5 for entry. Once in there, we have access to all the equipment and facilities for as long as we like. My attendance at the fitness centre is erratic. I probably only go about eight times a year. There is huge scope for my attendance to be improved. I may still only pay the fixed fee for entry so my average order value will be constant. However, the number of times I spend that £5 with them could be easily doubled.

So the choice of appropriate strategy between increasing the average order value or raising the number of orders that are placed, or both, will depend upon the business you are in and the customers who buy from you.

What franchised businesses do very well is systematise their tactics to maximise their sales income through one or both of these strategies. It is an opportunity that is regularly missed by the independent business owner because their product emphasis dominates the process and promotion activities, which is where these strategies have their roots.

Before we look at individual strategies that can be employed to increase your average order value and/or the average number of orders placed, there is one strategy that works in just about any business.

The number one strategy that is guaranteed to help you keep your customers and encourage them to spend more money with you is to simply provide a remarkable service on a consistent basis, and that is consistent with the USP, vision, and mission of the business.

In 1996, Harlan K. Ullman and James P. Wade from the National Defence University in the USA wrote a paper describing the military tactics that would be the most effective in battle. As others have in the past, from the Romans and Sun Tzu, they confirmed that 'shock and awe' was the most effective strategy to overwhelm the enemy and destroy its will to fight.

In business, we can use the same tactics, not against our competitors, but in a positive sense with our customers. If your customers feel a sense of shock, or a better term may be 'surprise', and awe with the product and service you offer, then they will keep coming back for more. The best way to beat your competitors is simply provide products and services that are so remarkable and unique that they become overwhelmingly attractive to your customers. They will pay more for them and keep coming back to buy more.

Average Order Value

In order to increase the average order value, there a number of generic strategies that can be tailored to suit your individual business.

1. **Price Increase** – If you truly provide an amazingly unique product or service experience, then you may be justified in raising your prices. It may be that if you put your prices up by 5%, no one would actually notice. If you have ranked your customers, you will probably find that the great customers and even the average ones are not too price sensitive. If you put your prices up, you will increase your sales and margins with your best customers and maybe dissuade some of the problem customers from staying with you. Fewer customers with a higher margin may be a better proposition than more customers with lower margins.

2. **Bundling** – Rather than have a range of individual products and services, bundle your products together in kits or sets. The increased order value will allow you to offer a discount to the customer, whilst maintaining or increasing your gross profit income. By doing this, you may of course reduce your margin percentage. So watch the results of these strategies carefully to make sure that you are better off overall as a result. Food franchisers have recognised how powerful this can be; you don't buy a burger – you buy a 'meal deal'.

   This approach can be applied to any product or service; undertakers should tread carefully here. The way to create a range of bundles in your business is to list down all the services and products you sell, and maybe some more that you should, and then group them together in a way that makes sense to your business and adds value to the customer. There are a number of ways that you can then construct your bundles, and name them. The table gives an example of how an accounting practice could bundle all their services into one of four groups, each bundle being appropriate for a different size of business. Before the accounting practice starts bundling, it should look at all the range of products that are purchased on average by its existing customers, the analysis carried out when identifying the perfect customer will be useful here. If for example the average customer buys two products, then the lowest grade bundle available should be for three or four products. You need to ensure that the bundling gives you a benefit and that you are not simply selling what you always did, giving it a name and reducing your margins.

	Bronze Program	Silver Program	Gold Pogram	Platinum Program
Year End Accounts	■	■	■	■
Personal Tax Returns	■	■	■	■
Bookeeping		■	■	■
Management Accounts		■	■	■
Business Planning			■	■
Payroll Services			■	■
Tax Planning			■	■
Company Secretarial			■	■
Sales Ledger Management			■	■
Auditing				■
Estate Planning				■
Consultancy				■

If all your products or services do not easily fit onto a neat list that can be summarised in a neat table, choose those which you think could be reasonably grouped together. Allocate names to them and promote them. A DIY business could have a wallpapering kit, plumbing kit, and a shelf-fitting kit. Restaurants in France regularly have a number of fixed price 'menus' available at different price points. There is usually a ten euro, fifteen euro, and twenty euro 'menu'. Each one includes an increasing array of courses and dishes; this is bundling in the same way as the DIY store.

In our business of selling fruit and vegetables, we would put together, say, £10 of fruit, place it in a £2 wicker basket, cover with cellophane with a bow on it, and sell it for £20. The bundling and packaging added value to the goods that individually they didn't have.

There is an alternative to bundling that doesn't really fit anywhere else, so I will explain it here. It is almost the reverse of bundling – the perceived value of the solitary product. We used to sell flowers at some of our shops. Today, a bunch of twelve red roses ordered on the Internet and delivered to your home will cost around £45; a single red rose will cost about £10.

We would sell some of our roses in individual gift boxes, with a gift card and a red ribbon attached. The box had a plastic window so the rose could be seen inside; the box was lined with white tissue paper, was printed in colour on the outside, and looked exclusive and expensive. About 15% of all the roses we sold were sold in the individual boxes rather than in bunches, or bundles. Every four individual roses we sold, we made as much profit as we did on a bunch of twelve.

As a bit of fun, I used to sell potatoes in individual boxes lined with tissue paper and having a red bow attached, and I sold quite a few of these; I even did the same with an onion, tomato, and a banana.

The point is that sometimes in certain businesses there is an opportunity to reduce revenue and increase margin by adding actual or perceived value to small quantities. Turnover is vanity; profit is sanity.

The bundles should represent your preferred purchasing decision for your customers and should be constructed in such a way that you get the benefit of increased sales income whilst the customer gets a great value deal, perceived or otherwise.

Don't bundle together items that always get purchased together anyway. You will not increase your overall sales revenue, and if you discount the bundle, you will lose margin and be worse off than you were in the first place. If, for example, in your business you notice that you have a top ten fast moving and popular products, don't bundle these together. Bundle the top selling products with some of the slower moving stock so you can increase the pace of your stock turns.

Finally, whilst bundles are attractive to some customers, remember to leave scope for those customers who need or want something different. In my business, I will bundle together training workshops, programmes, and support services in a variety of ways that enables any business to be able to work with us. I also recognise that businesses are unique and have individual needs that may not be best served by one of our standard programmes, so we also have the custom programme, where we will design an approach that suits the exact needs of an individual business. Same with all businesses, whilst bundles are a great way of building sales revenue, remember to leave scope for the customer who needs something a little different.

3. **Offers** – Making specific offers, not discounts, if done well, can generate good results. Here's a selection with some of the pros and cons for you to consider. Remember, these strategies are to incentivise your customers to buy more when they buy from you; revenue will go up whilst actual margin percentage may go down, be sure that the net result is more cash margin with any strategy employed.

   BOGOF – Buy One Get One Free. Great for clearing out stock as you come to the end of line. Marginally better than discounting as you are holding the price point of your product and simply giving away a second product with it. The beauty of the BOGOF offer is that you are giving away high perceived value at little cost to yourself. The perception in the mind of the customer is that they are getting two for the price of one and effectively getting a 50% discount. In reality what you are giving them is a marginal benefit equivalent to the cost price of the second product. Good where there are high mark-up products as the perceived value compared to the marginal cost of the offer is good. Doesn't improve your sales income or improve average order values unless several purchases are made, and it reduces your margins; not great as a long-term strategy. Good as an alternative to discounting and may attract customers into the business, giving you the opportunity to sell them additional products, and hence increase sales.

   BOGO ½ Price – Better than the above as, providing you sell more volume under the conditions of the offer, your revenue will increase. Your gross margin percentage will reduce with this offer. When putting any offer together, it's important to look at the underlying buying patterns of your existing customers. If you find that on average, your customers already buy two products at a time, for example, then the offer should be to buy two and get one for half price. Incentivise only where there is resultant improvement in the averages.

Buy Two Products for £XX – Same effect as the BOGOF but may look more appealing to the customer as the perception is that both products, not just one, are discounted. Works well where there is a range of different products at a similar price point, such as books, DVDs, etc. This strategy may encourage a number of similar purchases to be made and therefore achieve an increase in order value.

Conditional Free Gifts – Giving away a product that is of low value to you but has high perceived value to the customer that is contingent upon the making a significant purchase is a great strategy. First, measure average order value of your business; then choose a product or number of products that when purchased will increase the average results. Then, select low-cost incentive that will encourage the customer to spend more than the average and still feel they have got a great deal.

Let's use a clothing business to demonstrate the effect. The average order value in the business is £200. The offer is that if a customer buys a suit from the £300 range, they will get a free dress shirt valued at £60. The shirt actually costs the retailer only £20. So again the customer's gift is perceived value and not actual money value. The increased margin realised on the sale of the £300 suit compared to the average £200 order value more than covers the £20 cost of the shirt. This only works when customers are incentivised to spend more than the average and when the extra margin fully funds the 'free gift'.

The customer perception is one of good value; they are getting a great suit and a new shirt for just £40 more than they would have paid for a basic suit anyway. You can always do the double whammy here of 'restricting' supply of these suits to a maximum of two per customer. Scarcity is a great motivator in sales and will dramatically increase your average order values.

4. **Offer Biggest First** – When helping customers make purchasing decisions, should you offer the basic or smallest product first in the hope of getting an early decision, or offer the luxury or biggest product first and risk rejection?

   The answer is always offering the high price product first. There are a number of reasons for this:

   a. They might say yes – The best way to increase the average order value of your business is simply to allow your customers to buy more by offering them the more expensive items. Build this process into your sales systems, and make sure your team knows to offer the high-price products first all the time.

   b. Reciprocation – If they say no, that is great, because it now allows you to make a concession to them by offering an alternative product or service at a lower price point. We are programmed to reciprocate. If I buy you a drink, you are obliged to buy me one. If I ask you £500 for a product and you offer me £400, I am almost obliged to come back with a concessionary offer of £475, to which you will offer £450, and we will shake hands on the deal. The fact that you have made a concession and offered an alternative places a burden of reciprocity on your customer. They have to enter the negotiation you started. This is not a simple 'yes or no' conversation anymore; it's a question of what will the order value be at the end of it.

   c. Down is easier than up – If you offer the smallest or cheapest product or service first, and make sale, it is really difficult to go back and sell them on the bigger more expensive product afterwards. Selling down the range is a lot easier than selling up after the decision has been made.

5. **Offer Trade-In's** – A web development company did this and got great results. This is the way it worked: They knew that the average order value of the business was around £5,000, so they made an offer that on any new web site valued at over £7,500 we would give them £1,000 trade-in on their old web

site. What this actually meant was that we were selling web sites for £6,500. The customers had a high perception of value as they were being 'given' £1,000, and the business owners increased their average order value. It is also a great way of generating new business as well as encouraging existing customers to buy more products.

Trade-in or part exchange offers have been used in the car trade since car trading began. It's not that the car dealers actually want your old car; it's that if they take away from the customer the pain associated with selling a car privately and give them money for it, it makes the process easier.

These offers can be made in any business, and can be a fun way of building your business. Be creative and unique in order to build the order values.

6. **Upsell** – Similar to offering the biggest first. Where the upsell can work really well is when the customer has a product or service in mind, but through incentives and added value, however, they are persuaded to buy the bigger, brighter, or the more powerful one.

This happened to me when we moved to France, and I fell for it hook, line, and sinker, I even saw it coming, and I was helpless to resist. I was given some very solid advice by a friend who lives about 50 km south of us in Nancy. The advice was that in order to 'fit in' we should have at least one sensible vehicle in the fleet, and it should be small, French-made, and diesel.

I went to the Renault dealer in Nancy and looked around for a car that would allow us to 'fit in', and sure enough I found a Renault Megane 1.9 Diesel in blue that seemed to tick all the boxes. Speaking to the car salesman in somewhat broken French, I said I'd like to test drive the car, which we did, and we returned to the dealership to complete the purchase.

Then, in a stroke of either brilliance or sheer luck on his behalf, the car salesman told me that this would be great car for my wife and enquired what car I would be driving.

So now in my mind, the Renault Megane 1.9 Diesel was a ladies car. There was a moment of opportunity here for him, and he seized it straight away. Sensing my disappointment at the thought of buying a ladies car rather than a man's car, he simply leaned across the desk and said, 'Come with me. I have something to show you'. Miraculously, he had learned to speak fluent English in the last fifteen minutes.

I followed him to the sports section of the showroom, where parked in the corner was a Renault Megane 2.0 Sport. This was still a small diesel hatchback, and it was made in France, so it complied with my specification. However, this was the man's version, with bigger wheels, thinner tyres, two exhausts not one, and it was a dark metallic inky grey. It just so happened to be another 5,000 euros up on the other Megane too, but the offer of a full set of new car mats and a full tank of fuel sealed the deal.

When you can demonstrate that the product your customer wants is not the one they really need, you can sell them a bigger more expensive alternative, providing they perceive value in the other product over and above their initial choice. If you can sow the seeds of doubt in their mind regarding the suitability of their initial choice, as my Renault Salesman did with me, then you are on your way to a great upsell.

7. **Cross Sell** – Selling complimentary products along with a primary purchase. Can be similar to bundling in some cases, but it is really where, through expert knowledge, you advise a customer that they should consider purchasing product B as a direct consequence of purchasing product A.

Always works best with the 'assumptive cross sell'. It works like this.

In a restaurant when ordering a steak, you have the option of adding a sauce to accompany your food order, peppercorn, béarnaise, etc. If I am asked, 'Would you like a sauce with your steak?' by the waiter, I have the option of saying yes or no. If the waiter makes me assume that I should have a sauce with my steak by making an 'assumptive cross sell' then my choice is narrowed from a yes or a no answer to a pepper or béarnaise choice answer. To do this, the waiter changes his question to 'Would you prefer the pepper or béarnaise sauce to accompany your steak tonight?'

The cross sell is easiest to introduce when the complimentary products are of lower value than the primary purchase, although there are cases when the cross sell can double or treble the order value. 'Would you like a filet steak with your pepper sauce?' is unlikely to be as effective in building the order value.

Again, this technique works in any business or sector. When my father passed away, and we were arranging the funeral, the undertakers smoothly asked us if we wanted flowers from their natural or colourful range. Not, 'did we want flowers?', but assuming that we did, simply from which range would we be making our selection.

8. **Training and Review** – With any strategy that is introduced, there are two key aspects to bear in mind, in order to maximise the returns.

    Your team will need to be trained on how to introduce the strategy to customers and be incentivised to measure and manage the average order value results. The daily or weekly monitoring of the results achieved will help maintain the focus, and feedback to the team regarding the responses received from customers will be critical. The use of scripts can help your team with the process, however, simply repeating a couple of glib sentences to every customer in every situation will become dehumanising for the team and repetitive and predictable for your customers. Train your team in the principles of selling and allow them to apply them as they see fit given the individual situation they find themselves in (the Nordstrom effect).

    Any strategy must be measured and the results checked to make sure they are in line with expectations. The offers you make and the strategies you employ will be dependent upon your business and the customers you serve, but regardless of the sector you are in, it is the results that are critical. Be prepared to adapt strategies and tactics regularly based on the results. Also be prepared for some strategies not to work from time to time. The method of managing your strategies should follow the MOIRA process.

```
          Analyse  →  Measure

                M.O.I.R.A

          Report       Objective

                Introduce
```

Measure – Measure the performance of the process or system before you make any changes to the method of working. This gives you a fixed start point against which future results can be compared.

Objective – Agree to an objective for the future performance of the process or system. Consider the consequences of not only the improvement in one aspect of the business but the potential for reductions elsewhere and make sure the net effect is positive. For example, sales values vs gross margins.

Introduction – Introduce the strategy to your business with training and consultation with the team. Consider limited time offers, introducing the strategy in one small part of the business first before rolling out to the whole company.

Reporting – Measure the results achieved as frequently as possible and within the shortest reasonable timescales. Daily and weekly reporting will enable adjustments to be made to any strategy introduced. Share the results with the team, whether they are positive or negative.

Analyse – Look at the results and consider what changes, if any, need to be made. This analysis should include the raw data for the strategy being considered – in this case average order value – and also the consequential effects that the strategy has on margins, customer experience, and the number of times the customer comes back to order again. Remember that any strategy you introduce must be consistent with your philosophy and the vision and mission of the business. If customers sense that they are not congruent, they will lose trust in your motives.

Number of Orders

This is where we need to encourage your customers to come back and buy from you more frequently. The challenge and opportunity of course is to increase the number of orders, whilst maintaining or increasing the average order value as described above.

There are two ways of measuring this activity in your business. The first is to simply count the number of times a customer orders or buys from you over a twelve-month period; then the averages can be worked out and appropriate strategies selected accordingly. The second is to calculate the average time between the orders being placed.

Both of these statistics have their merits. The first one because it allows direct calculations to be made from annual sales and the average order value results, and it gives an easy to understand KPI that can easily be measured and reported. The challenge with measuring the number of orders is that, by definition, you will have to wait twelve months to find out what the results are in response to any strategy you introduce. It is a 'rear view' KPI, similar to a set of accounts, and whilst useful, doesn't lend itself easily to proactive management.

Measuring the average time between orders placed, whilst essentially measuring the same data, allows for a more proactive stance to be taken. If we know that the average time between placing orders in your business is thirty-eight days, for example, we can put strategies in place to improve this, and we will know whether or not the strategy is working much more quickly. Knowing the information for individual customers allows predictions to be made regarding their future purchases, and specific strategies can be introduced to improve their buying pattern. The results here will be evident almost immediately.

Regardless of which measure is used – using both is probably best – the same strategies can be introduced.

1. **Ask Them to Come Back** – Sounds obvious, but by simply inviting people to come back and visit your business or thanking them for buying from you in the first place will encourage them to come back more often.

    When we are born, we have three inherent, built-in fears – falling over, loud noises, and abandonment. There is not much a business can do to prevent a customer falling over or encountering loud noises. We can, however, make sure that they don't feel abandoned by us by keeping in touch with them and letting them know that they are part of a group of customers whose business and continued support is appreciated and respected.

    Build a database of all your customers, and find an excuse to keep in touch with them. If you produce a newsletter, make it interesting and unique. Send them cards at Christmas, for their birthday, or any event that seems appropriate. I really don't want to get a birthday card from the undertakers; it looks like a countdown clock coming from them. So choose your medium with care.

    Joe Girard was born in Detroit, Michigan, on 1 November 1928. He went on to become recognised in the Guinness book of records as the world's greatest salesman. From 1963 to 1978, he sold 13,001 new vehicles at a Chevrolet dealership. Joe has a great philosophy towards selling, and his thirteen rules for success underpin his great attitude and approach to the business of sales.

One of his most famous strategies, also one of the most simple, was he would send everyone who bought a car from him thirteen cards every year – one every month and one for Christmas. He made sure that he was in people's minds so when they thought about buying a car, they thought of him.

He would sell six new cars every day; he even employed himself a team to work for him within the dealership to handle all the paperwork. He became so effective that he only saw people by appointment and had his team pre-screen prospects before he met with them.

Inviting recent customers to come back on a regular basis is important. Make sure to keep in touch with those customers who haven't bought from you for a while, or if you have the data, from those prospects that never bought from you at all. Keep giving them the opportunity to.

2. **Future Bookings** – Most of us go to the hairdressers on a regular basis. I have been going to the same barber's shop since 1967 when my dad took me as a toddler. I don't always go there as it is a long way from Las Vegas, Metz, or wherever in the world I find myself, but when I'm in the UK, if I can, I go back to Harold's in Quinton, Birmingham. I have had my haircut all over the world and had some interesting experiences and challenging outcomes. There is one strategy that barbers and salons should always use – with every customer, all the time – and that is to arrange the next appointment with the customer before they leave the premises.

Being new to Las Vegas, I decided to find myself a new barber's, and in one of the many faceless strip malls that seem to simply be a duplicate of each other, I found a shiny new barber shop. The whole experience consisted of a process of attempting to sell me colouring and tinting, a head massage, hair oil, waxing, and shaving. I could buy eight haircuts and get one free, introduce a friend and get a free massage, join their well-groomed men's club, and even buy merchandise from key rings to baseball caps. It was upselling and cross-selling gone mad!

The haircut was second rate. They were in the marketing business, not the barbershop business, and it showed. When it came time to leave, I was asked if I would like to make a future appointment; I declined.

That was an extreme case of promotion taking precedence over product, and was unfortunate.

I eventually found a more 'traditional' barber's shop in Sumerlin on the northeast side of town. These guys were good, so good that the mayor had his hair cut there. The police were regulars, as were the soldiers and airmen based over at the Nellis Air Force base. There were badges and emblems from the different squadrons, police departments, and even the fire department pinned on the walls. There were a few people waiting in front of me, but fresh coffee and cookies were provided in the waiting area with a selection of new magazines and newspapers. The place had vibrancy

> In April 2011, I actually got to my Barbers in Birmingham. As I was sat in the chair, I saw in the mirror that someone turned up and was escorted into a separate room – jumping the queue. I asked what the room was, and was told that if people booked and paid a small premium they could walk in and go straight into the private room to avoid waiting. It has taken them 42 years to explain that service to me – if only I had known...

about it. The team was attentive and skilled; the product was good.

It was so good that when it came time for me to leave, I asked to be booked in again in four weeks' time. As I said this, Joe, my barber, looked at me and said that in order to keep my hair looking good, he would like to see me again in three weeks' time, not four. I agreed and the appointment was set. He gave me a card with the appointment date on it, and I gave him my mobile phone number so he could call or text me if he needed to change the appointment.

The lesson here for all of us is that whilst in any business, we should be confirming the date of the next order. If our product and service is attractive enough, and delivered consistently, people will want to book in for next time to make sure they can get in.

Joe did another couple of clever tactics as well. First, he suggested that instead of coming back in four weeks, I should go back in three in order to keep my hair looking good, which sounded good to me. Joe knew, because I asked him on subsequent visits, that on average, his customers have their hair cut once a month, or every 4.33 weeks. If he got me to come back every three weeks, over a year I would spend around 45% more with him than if I went there every month.

Second, he took my mobile number so that he could call or text me if he needed to change the appointment. What this also meant was that he would call me a couple of days before the appointment just as a reminder and to make sure that I showed up. I also got a text the day before the appointment.

If your customers buy your products or services on a regular basis, make sure that your systems and procedures encourage them to return firstly through excellence of delivery, and secondly, by agreeing with them the date of their next order.

Taking this strategy one step further would involve entering into contracts with customers. This may well be the case for several business to business arrangements anyway; contracts are a great way of ensuring repeat business. They can also be used with the private buyer as well in some situations. Health clubs and fitness centres use this approach. They don't actually care whether you turn up or not. You are on direct debit for twelve months anyway. Their challenge is to get you to join in the first place, probably in January!

If you have contracts with your customers, whilst these are great for predictability and long-term income, watch out for complacency setting in within the team. For example, if you have a three-year agreement with someone, and they can't buy from anywhere else, make sure that the contract is managed really well, with service and quality KPIs introduced. Treat every contract as a one-month booking from a service perspective to ensure the standards will be maintained throughout, and renewal will be more likely.

3. **Loyalty Schemes** – The supermarkets are great at this. We have a loyalty card for every supermarket in the area. Wherever we go, we are loyal customers, so the strategy with these businesses has lost its novelty and significance. In fact, if a supermarket doesn't have a loyalty programme, it is unusual now. A loyalty scheme in this sector is not a USP anymore – it is an essential.

The principle of rewarding your loyal customers is a great way of building long-term relationships and demonstrating that you value their business and appreciate them continuing to work with you.

Remember that you are building a long-term relationship. I have been with Lynn for over thirty years. We first met at high school, and she doesn't have a loyalty card with my name on it. So whilst you are not getting married to your customers, treat them like people, not commodities. The relationship that is based on continued 'shock and awe' will keep them coming back on a regular basis.

The best way of encouraging and rewarding loyalty is, therefore, to simply do a great job every time. As a business coach, all my clients would appear on my team chart; as a client, they became part of a group. When we run planning workshops, they would get together, compare notes, and socialise; in 2011, we are going to Le Mans as the guest of one of our clients, and they have invited other clients of ours to come along.

The essence here is to build a community spirit, a sense of belonging that binds people together and keeps them coming back for more.

After a period of time of working together, my clients would qualify to give me referrals. The reason they had to qualify to do this was because I wanted them to know that I took the community of my clients very seriously. It was an elite club of entrepreneurs, business owners, and executives, and I was careful about who was brought into the team.

We would run quarterly planning workshops for all our clients. We still do, and providing they had been with us for at least six months and demonstrated solid performance in their business, they would be invited to join our international events programme.

Our standard quarterly planning workshops would be held in hotels or offices in the UK. Our international events programme is held in locations such as Monaco or Cannes. This year we are planning them in the Bahamas and the Far East.

The reason we did this is that, first, we were genuinely careful of who joined our team of clients. When at events and seminars, I would invite prospective clients to speak with some of my existing ones. This did two things. First it enabled the prospective client to see what it was like working with us; second, it involved my clients in the process of bringing new clients to their team. On a couple of occasions, based on the feedback from my clients, I have not offered programmes.

My client results and client retention statistics were amongst the best in the world.

There are plenty of schemes that can be introduced to both encourage and reward loyalty, depending on your business sector.

In the USA, Starbucks have a loyalty programme where customers register online for a card, and every time the card is used to make a purchase you will get a star; thirty stars take you to 'gold member' status and, providing you get thirty stars every twelve months, your status will be maintained.

Before you achieve 'gold', you will pass 'green' level at five stars, with free syrups and refills on brewed coffee and tea. At gold status, you will get a free drink of your choice for every fifteen stars you earn, a personalised gold card that recognises you as one of their favourite customers, and personalised offers and coupons.

The key here is technology. Starbucks know that loyalty is personal, and that if we are to be encouraged to go there more frequently, the incentive message needs to be personalised to our own tastes and buying patterns. By using the card with every purchase, Starbucks will know what we buy when we buy it and how frequently we repeat. They can then individualise the offers and incentives that we receive such that they are more attractive to us.

On the Starbucks web site, you can even buy your own loyalty card, having it custom designed to your own specifications, and if you really want to, you now have the ability to buy your coffee by using an app. on your mobile device.

When loyalty is combined with technology, personalised offers, and rewards, the process becomes compelling to customers. Of course, the product and process needs to be consistently good. However, this is where promotional activity can lock your customers in.

Harrah's is one of the big four casino operators in the USA. They have a loyalty programme called Total Rewards, which uses intuitive technology to encourage their customers to play longer and spend more money. The loyalty cards are like credit cards. Players swipe the card at slot machines, and the card registers wins and losses, accruing points that can be traded in for gifts.

What Harrah's have also done is recognise the point at which individual customers walk away from the machines; how much are they prepared to lose before they stop playing. When they approach this limit, which is different for every customer, a member of staff will receive an alert. The customer will be approached and offered a free meal, complimentary points to add to their card, or some other 'feel good' experience that mitigates the predicted negative experience that was about to happen when they reached their 'limit'. This positive stroke resets the emotions of the player, and they return to the machines and continue to play beyond what would have been their initial 'walk away' point.

Now, it may be that you are not a huge casino operator with 48,000 employees, or a global drinks franchise with around 17,000 locations in fifty countries. The principles regarding encouraging loyalty are the same regardless of your business. The following model demonstrates the key areas that need to be systematically maintained:

```
     Purchasing  →    Customer
     Decision         Experience

           Length of
           Relationship

     Personalised
     Rewards          Community
```

Customer Experience – The best way to build loyalty is to deliver excellence with consistency. If the product is not up to scratch, no amount of promotion will compensate.

Community – Your customers need to feel that they belong to a group, a collective of like-minded people with whom they share similar tastes and preferences.

Personalised Rewards – One size does not fit all. For a rewards programme to be effective, it needs to be bespoke and designed around individual behaviour and patterns.

Purchasing Decision – Your customers always have a choice; your programme must be designed to encourage them to choose your business over anyone else's more of the time.

4. **Increase Range** – There are a number of ways that you can adapt your range of products and services to improve your number of orders.

Before you go ahead and increase your range of products and services to your customers, make sure that they are aware of what you currently sell first. You will be surprised when you send them a full list or brochure of what your business actually does, the responses you get. Simply educating your customers regarding your full range is a simple first step.

Increasing your product range to suit the needs of your customers will encourage them to spend money with you that they may be spending elsewhere right now. The supermarkets do this when they attempt to introduce their own insurance policies, credit cards, loans, and even mobile phone agreements. Probably best here to expand the range with complementary products or services, rather than start a completely new business, at least to start with.

A landscape garden design and installation business had a great reputation for fabulous water features and the use of contemporary materials and colours as part of their schemes. What they realised was that the more adventurous the designs, the more the installations tended to deteriorate over time. The installations began to look tired within about six months of them being completed. This was not good for their reputation or levels of customer satisfaction; referrals were being affected.

The introduction of a maintenance programme was the solution. This strategy worked on a number of levels. First, the installation was kept in good order as it would be visited every three months and cleaned, tidied, and put back as good as new. Second, the customers remained happy with their purchase, and as there was now an on-going relationship with the company, the opportunities for additional sales and referrals was increased.

Third, the number of transactions was increased as additional work was forthcoming from the customers. The average order value also increased because the maintenance contract was paid full twelve months in advance and added to the initial price of the installation.

When increasing your range, remember you are selling to a consistent range of customers; the alternative products that you add to your collection need to be attractive to them.

5. **Exclusivity and Product Leadership** – If you are selling products and services that are available from a number of sources, or there is no differentiation between what your business provides when compared to other suppliers, customer loyalty can be a challenge. When you can develop exclusive lines, or introduce products that are only available from you, there is scope to increase number of orders, average order values, and margins in one go. Brands operate in this way. It is why brands exist, such that products can be positively differentiated from others through recognition, and the associated standards of quality and performance can be conveyed consistently. This is really an extension of the differentiation strategy already discussed.

Being known as an innovator in your sector will appeal to a number of your customers who want to be the early adopters of new ideas, technology, design, or capacity. The early adopters may only form a small percentage of your customer base, so make sure that you keep traditional lines in stock for the rest of them. Building obsolescence into your range will encourage early adopters to replace their purchases with you more frequently.

Computers are a great example of built-in obsolescence, the pace of innovation, and technical advances. In 1965, the co-founder of Intel, Gordon E. Moore, described a trend concerning the number of transistors that can be placed on an integrated circuit, that the numbers will double every two years. This trend became known as 'Moore's Law'.

This law has been complied with over the last forty years and is now used as a predictor of future capacities and as an objective for development. Of course, there is the notion that if Moore's Law is used as the target for development then compliance with the law will become a self-fulfilling prophecy.

What Moore's law shows us is that things change exponentially. Therefore, obsolescence is virtually guaranteed with any IT purchase.

Your suppliers can be really helpful here. That is one reason you should treat them well, as if they were part of your team. They can have a dramatic effect here in bringing you the newest products as soon as possible, if that is your chosen strategy.

4. Margins

First let's take a look at gross margins, either as a percentage ration based on the sales value, or as a cash value contribution to the fixed costs or overheads in the business. Management of your margins is critical to the success of your business; however, even these two measures can be misleading sometimes.

Project managing the manufacture of specialist weapon system for the British army, my role was to initially support the commercial department in the submission of tenders and quotations for submission to Ministry of Defence (MoD) contracts branch. The manufacture and supply of the weapon system was put out to competitive tender, and we were one of eight subcontractors invited to provide quotations.

When quoting the MoD, submissions have to be delivered to the specified address by a certain time on a fixed date. Late submissions are not accepted, and no discussion will be entered into regarding the submissions prior to them undergoing initial evaluation. It is a rigid system designed to be fair to all subcontractors.

The first stage of putting a price together is to take all the engineering drawings and assess the materials required to make the products and also estimate how many labour hours will be required to assemble them into the finished product. The MoD usually arrange for collection of such systems by their own secure transport so all prices were requested as ex-works, or excluding delivery.

For obvious reasons, weapons systems are built to exacting standards and specifications. Every component must me made according to the design in terms of not only dimensional accuracy, but material content, hardness or toughness, and surface finish. There is no room for creativity when it comes to weapons; that way they only kill the person in front of them, not the people behind them.

In the company I was working for, as many companies do, there was a pricing policy that had to be maintained in order that all quotations would achieve the budgeted percentage margin on sales.

The pricing policy was to charge all labour at a fixed rate and to add a percentage to all material costs associated with the product in question. Because our labour to material content ratios were similar across the range of products we manufactured, by sticking to these rules ensured that we achieved our target margins.

The pricing was based on the following:

Materials would be charged at cost plus 50%.

Labour charged at £30 per hour.

When priced according this method, we knew that for our 'average' manufactured products, the material content was about 35% of the price and labour made up the other 65%, and we would make around 55% gross margin on all sales.

This method of calculation meant that we made around £25 added value for each man hour of production. Added value is simply the profit made on the labour added to the profit made on the materials divided by the hours required to complete the manufacturing process.

To manufacture this particular weapon system, it required a specific piece of material that was very expensive. It was so rare that only one supplier in the UK had the material in stock, and further production of the material had been terminated some years earlier. What was in stock was all there was, and whilst there was enough to complete the production run of the weapon system, and provide spares support, that was about it.

We knew that as there was only one source of supply, all the subcontractors would be asking for the same quotation from the same supplier; they were onto a very good thing, and their prices reflected that.

We also knew that the pricing policies of all the competing businesses were roughly the same. We had been competing with them for years, and we all knew how each other worked.

The labour hours to manufacture the system came out to 275, which meant that we would be putting in 275hrs × £30 = £8,250 as our price of labour for the job. The actual cost of labour was £10 per hour, so we made £20 profit on each charged hour.

On that basis if material content was 35% and labour 65%, the material content, after mark-up, should have been around £4,500 which in turn should have meant we would have paid a cost price of £3,000 for the purchase of the raw materials from our suppliers.

Including the 'inflated' prices that came through from the sole supplier of the rare material, the total cost of the materials came to £8,000; the material content was way higher than the average.

With that cost, we would have included £8,000 + 50% − £12,000, material costs to the job, and then added the £8,250 labour charge, giving us a selling price of £20,250.

This selling price would have resulted in us achieving a gross margin of £9,500 or 47%.

47% was below our target of 55% margin, so really we should have increased our prices to £23,500 in order to comply with the company policy.

However, because the material content was so high, it skewed the figures. If we had raised our prices to £23,500, our gross profit would have been approximately £12,750 which when divided by the number of hours taken to produce the system, would have given us this:

£12,750 / 275hrs = £46.36 added value per hour.

Our target for added value per hour was £25 per hour, so this result would be great if we could achieve it, but effectively the pricing policy would have made us too expensive.

When we worked out the prices based on the added value per hour target, the prices came out like this:

Actual coast of labour	275hrs × £10/hr.	£2,750
Actual cost of material	£8,000 from suppliers	£8,000
Added value	275hrs × £25	£6,875
	Total	£17,625

The gross margin when calculating by this method was only 39%, way below our targeted levels; however, we were recovering our added value per hour so in money terms it was a good deal. What at first appeared like discounting actually showed up a weakness in the rigid pricing policies of the company.

We assumed that the competitors would ruin with prices at around the £20,250 mark. The margin at this level as shown above was 47%, and we could see from their published accounts that they were achieving 55% margins, like we were, so we took a commercial decision to throw out the constraints placed on us by gross margin policy and quoted the price at £18,950, and won the contract.

The reason for all this detail is to demonstrate that commercial decisions have to be applied to your pricing and margins. The margin percentage reported in the accounts on the basis of the contract above were lower than we were targeted to make, and notes to accompany the accounts were sent to the board for the monthly meeting.

I was called to attend the meeting and explain why the margins had dropped so significantly in the accounts; I did. And because our gross cash margin was stronger than target, and the corresponding net profits were stronger than budget, I came out alive, with a promotion that followed shortly afterwards.

Sometimes, reducing gross margins can be done without affecting the profitability of the overall business, and whilst the usual strategy is to increase them wherever possible, this tactic can be useful in some situations.

So back to normality. What are the ways in which we can increase your gross margins?

The answer, unfortunately, is that it depends on the type of business you are in; however, the following strategies are a great place to start and can be adapted to suit a variety of businesses:

Gross Margins

1. **Price Increase** – Already covered this, but if you can raise your prices, even just a couple of percentage your gross margin will increase, but the effect on the net margins will usually be dramatic. If you are making 10% net profit in your business, and you increase your prices by just 2%, your net profits will jump by 20%.

2. **Sales Training** – Your gross margins are a reflection of quality of your sales activity. Train your whole team in the art, science, and process of negotiating and sales skills. This will have a dramatic effect. See next chapter.

3. **Efficiency and Productivity** – How you measure the productivity and efficiency of your business will dictate the strategies that will generate improvements. As we saw earlier with the airports, matching capacity to demand is critical in driving your gross margin.

    Plastic injection moulding involves squirting hot, molten plastic into a mould, waiting for the plastic to set, opening the mould to remove the product, and then closing the mould so the process can be carried out again. Production machines are automatic, with robots removing the products from the moulds and hoppers continually feeding plastic granules into the moulding machine where they are heated and turned in to liquid plastic ready for the squirting process.

The limiting factors with this process is the length of time it takes to inject or squirt the plastic into the mould, and the amount of time it takes for the plastic to cool sufficiently so that it sets and can be removed from the mould without damage. In order to increase productivity from what was already a very efficient system, we had to improve one or both of the limiting factors.

The injection process has to be carried out at specific temperatures and pressures such that the viscosity of the liquid plastic allows the mould to be completely filled, so there was not much room for improvement there. The cooling process, however, simply depended on the time required to cool the mould to the point where the moulded product could be removed and passed to the next production process.

The moulds were water cooled, so the cooling time taken to cool the mould depended on the amount and temperature of water that could be passed through waterways within the mould. If we could increase the pressure of the water, put additives in it, and reduce its temperature as it entered the mould, we could reduce the cycle time and increase our productivity. We decided to invest in a new chiller unit to achieve this and subsequently increased both our output and our margins.

Once this limiting factor had been eliminated, and as production increased, other 'pinch points' became apparent and subsequently improved on an on-going basis.

Productivity and efficiency improvement should be a continuous process. It doesn't have to be the case that your team has to work harder or even smarter, although that is a good place to start. Look for the structural inefficiencies that may be in your business due to process, procedure, or mechanical processes. As a tip, when looking to improve the operational aspects of a business, ask the people actually doing the work what, in their view, has to be done or changed to improve things. You will be surprised at how insightful their answers will be. Also, watch out for the 'always done it that way' responses; a red light should flash in your head when you hear that statement.

4. **Buy Better** – Where raw materials are a cost of delivering your product or service, always review the costs associated with them. Renegotiate with your suppliers, or ask them how they can help. If the relationship with them is good, they may have some tactics that will maintain the business for them and enable savings to be passed to you. This is not simply an excuse to hammer your suppliers into giving you discounts but working with them as partners in the process. They will want you to be really successful, so you keep buying from them and they are guaranteed to talk to you; you are paying the bills after all.

The consequences of your terms and conditions of trading can have a dramatic effect upon your gross margins. The transport industry, for example, has the challenge of having high direct costs associated with fluctuating commodity markets, mainly the cost of crude oil. Where there are costs which are genuinely outside of your control, have clauses in your agreements that allow for the introduction of surcharges to cope with the variations in your costs. Don't use them as a way to profiteer during inflationary times as you will lose your customers when they find out. Be open and fair.

For anyone involved in transport in the UK, this will make sense to you. Don't use red diesel – you will get caught.

5. **Reduce Wastage** – The Royal Small Arms Factory was a sprawling establishment of machine shops, ranges, and administration buildings. The gun barrels were made in the barrels shop, alongside which there was a canal. When after a number of years the canal was drained for maintenance, there were dozens of gun barrels found in the mud. If a barrel didn't meet specifications, the machine operator rather than report the defect, would simply throw the barrel over the fence into the canal.

Wastage of materials or wastage of labour due to poor efficiency and productivity can be very costly to your business. The cost of all waste comes straight off your margins. Any savings go direct to the bottom line.

If your products are perishable, then your purchasing, stock control, and sales systems need to be geared around ensuring that waste is kept to a minimum.

If waste materials are produced, then have policies in place to dispose or recycle the waste in an environmentally sustainable way.

In 2009, Tesco, the UK supermarket chain announced that the 5,000 tons of leftover meat were being incinerated to produce electricity for the National Grid, and enough power was being generated to power 600 homes.

Even more creative was the 2011 decision by the council in Redditch near Birmingham in the UK, to allow the waste heat from a crematorium to be diverted to heat a public swimming pool.

Both of these schemes, whilst logical, attracted opposition from pressure groups; so being creative is not the only solution when it comes to managing your waste.

6. **Incentivise** – Your team can be incentivised to maximise your gross margins. In one commercial department, we changed the name of the team from the sales team to the margin team. This change of focus meant that discounts were eradicated, and sales were made on value and quality, not price and cost. The sales engineers were transferred to the profit department and called profit engineers. Prospects didn't want to see a salesman anyway, but they were intrigued to meet a profit engineer however. When your team incentives are in accordance with the KPIs of your business, then you will get the results you predicted.

The company accountant was given a 'royal crest' to attach to his office door – he was now the 'cash king'. His biggest contribution was not reporting what happened in the past but managing our cash and keeping the debts down. He wanted to call his team 'the debt dogs', but we didn't think that would work too well. Make the incentives fun, and people will buy in.

Net Margins

Everything you do to improve your gross margins will also improve your net margins. There are, however, some specific strategies that can be introduced that will keep your fixed costs or overheads under control. These may have no effect on your gross profits, but again every pound gained will be added to your bottom line. The best way to reduce the effects of your overheads on your profits in your growing business is to keep them at the same level, regardless of the increases in sales revenue. This is not to simply get people to work harder and longer, but there will be hidden inefficiencies in your business that will be eradicated when the pressure is on. The application of pressure produces both heat and light.

1. **Cut Costs** – Set a challenge to all your managers to reduce every line of cost in the business by 8%, and see what they come back with. Doesn't include reducing headcount; that is something that should be on the basis of added value, not costs alone.

2. **Reduce Absenteeism** – Usually, where you have a direct labour element to your business, the holidays and sick pay that are paid by the company will appear as overheads, not direct costs. Minimising absenteeism will achieve two objectives: first, it will cut the actual costs of paying staff that are not at work, and second, it will increase the capacity of the business to produce more added value work.

3. **Expand** – Opening a second branch will dilute the overheads over a larger operation. Centralised accounting, administration, HR, marketing, and purchasing will mean that your overheads will be used more efficiently, and as a percentage of sales, be reduced.

If your business can accommodate it, expand and stay put through the introduction of shift working. A production facility that is only operational eight hours a day is idle for sixteen hours. Shift work doesn't reduce you overheads in terms of total expenditure, but it allows you to be much more efficient and productive with every pound you spend on them.

4. **Budgets and Reporting** – Make sure that the accounts are produced on a regular basis, with overhead variances both for the individual period and year to date being identified and investigated. When your team's attention is on the accounts on a regular basis, and they know that they are both responsible and accountable for the results, they will make sure that all costs are tightly managed.

5. **Purchase Orders** – Introduce a method of controlling all the purchases that are made within the company. Take a look in your stationery store to find out how much you could save. If all purchases have to be signed off by a manager, then that extra pack of pens, Post-it notes, or desk tidies will not be bought.

5. Referrals

Referrals will be covered in the next chapter when we consider the best ways of attracting new customers to your business. The main reason that referrals are included here is that whilst they are a key criteria that you can choose when working through your GAP analysis, they are also a barometer for the perception you customers have about your business. If the relationship is strong, and the customer is continuously impressed with the products and services you are providing, they will provide referrals. If they are not, then they won't.

If the referrals dry up, then ask yourself what is happening to the relationship between you and your customers, and how it can be improved. In terms of keeping all your customers, referrals are a great prediction mechanism or early warning signal that will allow you to be proactive in managing the relationship, rather than wondering why they left you after all those years. As in life, don't take your long-term relationships for granted.

6. Product Range

Again, the degree to which your customers buy your whole range is both an indication of the strength of the relationship and a guide to where the relationship can be improved or extended. For example, if a customer is only buying five services out of the twenty you offer, it is likely that they are buying the others from somewhere else. This gives you the opportunity to build your business with that customer and have specific strategies, see bundling, in place to encourage more of your range to be purchased by them.

Conversely, if you notice that the number of products your customers are purchasing from your range is reducing, then this is an early warning sign that there may be challenges with the relationship. By managing this KPI, a proactive approach to managing the relationships with your customers is possible.

7. Years of Trading

In my business, I want to have long-term relationships with my customers. Six years ago, in 2005, I first met Neil Hillman. He was a client of mine, became a friend, and now his business has grown to the extent that I am privileged to be a non-executive director on the board of his company, The Audio Suite in Birmingham, UK. Several of my customers have been with

> Attending a regular networking event, one of the members would always show up in a dark suit with a tailor's tape measure draped around his shoulders.
>
> He was an undertaker and would simply go up to people, ask them how they were feeling, and start to measure their shoulders and height – great way to break the ice.

me for a number of years. They are friends, colleagues, and supporters now, and I am grateful for that.

Whilst the relationship and services provided may change and evolve over time, customer retention is one of the acid tests of a great business. Long-term customers should be rewarded, thanked, and congratulated.

8. Ease of Servicing

This is a subjective measure and should be treated carefully. You do not have to like all your customers; it is a bonus if you do, unless you are an undertaker.

What we are looking for here is the overall relationship they have with your business – are they polite to the team, do they continually change their minds, complain, threaten to take the business away from you, say good things or negative things about you, etc. Are they flexible? Do they understand that you are in business to make a profit at the same time as providing great added value to them? Do they believe that they are the only customer you have?

Allocating points on the GAP analysis is based on your perception and feelings, or the feelings of the team towards then. It may not be tangible, but it is worth registering how the relationship is perceived by you team. I once had an otherwise great customer, whose buyer continually changed specifications without notice, became abusive to members of my team, and even tried to date one of the married girls in my office. Everything else about the GAP analysis was great, with this exception.

I approached my client and explained what was happening; he was grateful for the feedback. He had had it from other suppliers, and it was damaging his company's reputation in the industry. The buyer in question was assigned alternative duties, with another company.

9. Growth Potential

This is subjective but a key attribute to build into your customer profiling. Sometimes your smallest customer may have the greatest potential; there is a real opportunity that when you support your customers as they get started and grow, they will remain loyal to you in the future. If you maintain this as a measurement, it will also mean that you monitor and check on progress as the relationship develops and are able to proactively help them.

10. Location

The location of your customers may or may not be important to you. However, if you are delivering your products on a routine basis, then having customers that neatly fit into your existing delivery routes is ideal. Your marketing can be directed accordingly, and your pricing can be adjusted to attract those customers who are in your preferred location.

Alternatively, you may actually want customers in every continent and can attribute points, not on the basis of proximity but on the basis of geographic diversity.

Notes

Rule No. 4 – Attract New Customers

I know that half my advertising doesn't work; trouble is I don't know which half.

John Wanamaker

This statement is unfortunately true for the majority of businesses; indeed for some, it is wildly optimistic. It doesn't have to be true for yours, providing you follow the rules.

In the previous chapter, we defined what your great, average, and problem customers looked like; we have defined and systematised your USP, and your foundations are in place. By now your business will be showing improved sales and margins from existing customers. The order values will be increasing and so will the frequency of the orders being placed.

With the ground work completed, when new customers are attracted, instead of kicking them in the teeth, you will provide great service and products to them in the long term. Your strategies for customer retention and order values will look after your customers when you get them; this section is concerned with getting more of them.

Your business will grow when the rate at which customers leave you is lower than the rate at which you attract new ones. Reduce the one and maximise the other, and you will grow. The greater the differential, the greater the growth. That is why customer retention and 'years of trading' is such an important measure in any business. It is a lot cheaper to retain a customer than get a new one.

In the same way that the annual sales is dependent upon the two variables of average order value and number of orders placed (or time between orders), the number of new customers you attract is dependent upon another two key variables.

New customers = No. of enquiries × Percentage of enquiries converted

So, as with sales income, you can't just get more customers – you have to manage the two variables. If you get a new customer, then something must have happened to encourage them to come to you in the first place, and then convince them that buying from you was the best choice.

The effectiveness of your sales and marketing will dictate the levels of growth your business achieves. Marketing is the process through which enquiries are generated; sales is the process through which they are converted into customers.

It is likely that you are getting enquiries into your business already so the first variable to look at is your conversion rate from enquiry to order. There are a couple of reasons that you should work on your selling process and conversion rate first:

1. You already have the enquiries coming in, so you may as well convert them. The investment required to increase the conversion rate is minimal and may simply involve training or adapting your processes, procedures, and offers. It will make your existing marketing more effective.

2. There is no point in investing in generating more enquiries if your conversion strategy is not effective. Your conversion rate is one of the most significant limiting factors in business. Getting this right before new enquiries are generated will ensure that you get the best return on your marketing investments.

Conversion Rate

Your conversion rate will be dependent upon the quality and calibre of the enquiry you receive as well as your ability to close the deal at the sales meeting. How your enquiries are converted into customers will depend upon the type of business you are in. The conversion could be over the phone, on the Internet, at a face to face meeting, or simply while the prospect is looking around your store or showroom. Sometimes, in order to convert a prospect, you will have to go and meet them to close the deal.

Other times, you will need to rely on your advertising and offers to close the deal for you.

There will be a number of conversion rates that may be applicable to your business, including online conversions from page visits to requests for information, from direct mail or telesales activities. All these rates need to be measured and managed.

There is always a process, a series of filters that your prospects go through in order to become your customer. They may not know it, and you may not know it, but whether by design or default, there is a process. Our opportunity is that we can take control of the process by designing our own systems of marketing and sales activity and manage the filtration process.

Imagine your marketing activity to be like a hopper with a series of filters at different levels. In business, we pour our marketing activity into the top of our hopper, and out of the bottom of the hopper, a number of customers appear. This is your sales and marketing system. The efficiency of your system will define how many prospects have to go into the hopper in order to get a customer to drop out of the bottom.

All your prospects will come to you armed with their own set of filters that they will fit into your hopper. The filters in your process are the points at which they decide not to proceed to become a customer. There are three main types of filters, excuses, or objections that we have to manage:

1. The 'buy an alternative' filter
2. The 'think about it' filter
3. The 'do nothing' filter

Whether or not your prospects use these filters depends on you, the quality of your product or service, the offer you make, and the added value you provide. We can choose to blame our prospects when they don't buy, we can blame the recession, blame the competitors, or blame them for being an idiot and not seeing the value. Alternatively, we can take full responsibility for our business and recognise that we generate every objection we get, and that through our activities we actually encourage our prospects to use one of their filters. In fact sometimes we hand them a filter to use the first time we meet them. In business, you can make money or you can make excuses, but you can't do both.

Taking responsibility for your results is the first step to taking control of them. Your business offer needs to be so compelling that the filters are bypassed; when your offer and added value is stronger than the best filter your prospect has, you will win the sale.

The process is of course dependent upon how attractive your offer is and to whom the offer is attractive. You may have a truly compelling product or service that is presented well with a strong USP that is congruent with your philosophy and vision. If you offer it to the 'wrong' people, they will not buy. Targeting is the key to improving your conversion rate. When the target is right, the filters are not as strong, and there is an increased likelihood that people within your target market will buy from you.

> When a Salesman was complaining that the filter his prospects used on a regular basis was the 'think about it' filter, he blamed them for being indecisive.
>
> When he started to get to all his meetings on time instead of 10 minutes late, he found that the filter had been removed.

For example, when we run our international retreats and workshops, if we knew exactly which people wanted and were ready to go to the Bahamas for two days in September, we would simply send them an invitation, and they would all show up. Of course, we don't know exactly who these people are; we know broadly the type of people, who are most likely to want to attend, and if we invite enough of those people, we know we will find enough of the ones who are ready to come to the Bahamas with us. The people who don't come along will choose to use one of the filters in order to exclude themselves from the event, because we either selected the wrong target, or through our offer and their perception of added value which didn't get through their filter.

Every prospect has these filters; it will depend on the quality of the marketing and sale strategies, tactics, and systems that are implemented, whether they are used and are effective.

Here is how the conversion rate hopper looks. For now we are looking to refine our strategies and improve the conversion rate result we achieve from your existing prospects before we add new prospects to the process.

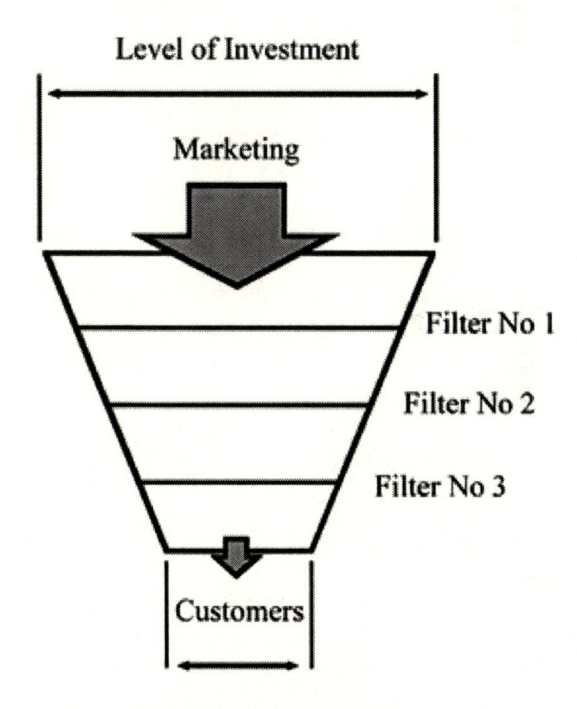

Level of Investment

Marketing

Filter No 1

Filter No 2

Filter No 3

Customers

Return on Investment

The filters may of course be in a different sequence to those listed earlier, but they all have to be passed through in order to get the sale, and we will need separate strategies to tackle each one. The single most powerful strategy that gets through just about the best filtration system that any of your prospects have is to deliver great products, services, and added value to your existing clients all the time. This will build your reputation and attract prospects to you. When someone comes to you because they have either been referred or because they know you do great work, their filters are almost turned off, and your conversion rate from these types of prospects will be the highest you have.

On the model, the width of the hopper is dependent upon the amount of activity or levels of investment associated with your marketing; the width at the base of the hopper represents the number of customers that are converted as a result of your process. The relationship between these two values represents your customer acquisition cost, or how much does it cost you to 'buy' a new customer.

If you invest £1,000 in marketing and from that activity you get two customers, then your acquisition cost for each customer is

Marketing investment / No. of new customers = Acquisition cost

£1,000 / 2 = £500 per new customer.

The closer the width of the base of the hopper is to the top of the hopper the better and the less the acquisition cost will become. The measure of the efficiency of your conversion rate process will be defined by two key ratios:

1. Conversion rate percentage – how many new customers are converted for every 100 prospects you generate.

2. Acquisition Cost – what does it cost to attract a new customer.

The acquisition cost is important as it will help with budgeting and planning your marketing activity and providing a KPI by which your marketing can be measured and monitored. It should be measured along with the conversion rates at each stage of the process; measuring only one can be misleading. If, for example, one of your strategies has a very high conversion rate, it may look attractive and effective compared to others you are using. If, however, each new customer is costing you £10,000 to acquire, whilst other strategies are lower conversion rate but only costing you £1,000 to acquire new customers, then the lower conversion rate strategy is likely to be the best one for you to continue with. Conversion rate measures the efficiency of your strategies; acquisition cost measures the productivity.

Understanding what an acceptable acquisition cost is for a new customer to your business will help refine your activities and allow you to plan your activities and investments accordingly.

First, we need to know what a customer is worth to you when you get them; this can be calculated by the following formula, using data we have already calculated.

Sales Value = No. of orders annually × Ave. order value × Ave. years trading

Gross margin value = Sales value × Gross profit percentage

For example, in a business the following results are known:

1. Number of orders placed per year – 6

2. Average Order value – £750

3. Average Years Trading – 2.5

4. Gross profit – 50%

So each order that is placed with that business will make, on average;

$$£750 \times 50\% \text{ gross profit} = £375$$

Each year the customer places an average of six orders, so the annual gross profit value of a customer to this business is

$$£375 \times 6 \text{ orders} = £2,250$$

On average the business retains its customers for 2.5 years, so the lifetime gross profit value of a customer to this business is

$$£2,250 \times 2.5 \text{ years} = £5,625$$

First, obvious rule – do not spend more money on acquiring clients than you will make from them during their lifetime with you!

What this does enable you to do is realise the actual return on investment that you will get from your marketing and customer retention activities.

How much would you pay in order to 'buy' a customer from which you will earn £5,625 gross profit?

The answer, of course, is as little as possible, and that is why taking a systematised approach to your conversion strategies is so important. It gives you control.

In the example, let's assume that as a board of directors we decide that the target for acquisition cost in the example business is to be no more than 20% of the lifetime gross profit value, giving us

$$£5,625 \text{ lifetime gross profit value} \times 20\% = £1,125$$

Even if this target is achieved, there is a 'profit path' that the customer will take as the trading relationship progresses.

When the first order is placed, and assuming that the value of the order is the £750 average value anticipated, the gross profit on the order will be

$$£750 \text{ order value} \times 50\% \text{ gross profit} = £375$$

What this means is that this business loses money on the first orders placed, and when the subsequent orders are placed over time, accounting for the losses from the first order, the cumulative gross profit over the first few orders will be

Order 1 – £375 Gross profit – £1,125 Acquisition cost = £750

Order 2 – £375 Gross profit + £750 = £375

Order 3 – £375 Gross profit + £375 = £0

Order 4 – £375 Gross profit + £0 = £375

Order 5 – £375 Gross profit + £375 = £750

The 'profit path' the customer will take under these conditions, providing that the averages are maintained over the two and a half years, can be charted.

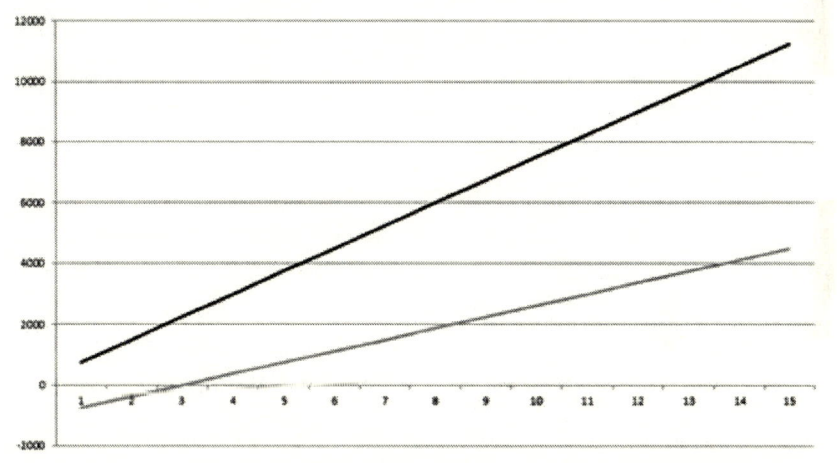

On the chart, the vertical axis represents the value of sales over time, and the horizontal axis, the number of orders placed over the anticipated two and a half years.

The black line shows the sales income to the business, and the grey line, the 'profit path' that the gross profit contributions take under these circumstances. As you can see, it is not until the fourth order that any money is made. The first three simply recover the acquisition cost expended in getting the customer to buy in the first place.

From this information, we can calculate the break-even point in terms of sales value and also timing of the orders.

The break-even point in terms of sales value is

Acquisition Cost / Gross Profit % = Break-even Sales Value.

£1,125.00 / 50% = £2,250 or three product sales.

The break-even point in terms of timing is

(Break-even sales value / Average order value) −1 × Average time between orders.

(£2,250 / £750) − 1 × 2 months = 4 months.

Note: The −1 in the formula is required as there is no time allocated for the initial order.

From this information, you can see how critical customer retention is. Lots of businesses attract new customers, only to 'kick them in the teeth' with poor service or delivery, and this is how they lose money. That's why we looked at retention before we looked at conversion rates.

There are ways to mitigate this of course. It may be that as part of the marketing process, there is a bulk purchase offer included that will recover the acquisition cost completely on the first order. In the case of the example above, if 10% discount was offered, providing the first order was worth at least four times the average order value, then the gross profit would look like this:

Sales income − Cost of goods sold = Gross profit

If the sales value was initially £750 and the gross margin 50%, we know that the cost of goods sold will be £375.

Sales income = (£750 × 4) − 10% = £2,700

Cost of goods sold = £375 × 4 = £1,500

The gross profit from the first order under these conditions is

£2,700 (Sales) − £1,500 (Cost of goods) = £1,200 (Gross profit)

Now taking into consideration the initial acquisition cost of £1,125, the actual profit from this first order is

Gross profit − Acquisition cost = Profit

£1,200 (Gross profit) − £1,125 (Acquisition cost) = £75 (Profit)

By doing this, this business is guaranteeing that there is at least a marginal profit from the start, even on the first order. They may well have to wait eight months before they get another order as the customer may keep them in stock and use them over time of course. This offer works really well where the degree of perishability of the goods, or shelf life, is shorter than the combined number of days between the orders that would be anticipated by the bundling of the products. They will perish before they use them and will have to buy more stock accordingly.

This is why the supermarkets bundle together perishable goods and discount them. They know that we will buy the produce because it looks good value, only to find we have to consume it more quickly than usual. Otherwise it will go off, only to then return to the supermarket again and buy the next bulk deal. It's why we have Turkey curry, sandwiches, and stew at Christmas . .

Unblocking the Filters

The way to unblock the filters, or at least reduce their effectiveness, is to build a process around you conversion process. Imagine that I am in the business of selling jet skis. I walk into your office, unannounced, with a sexy brochure in my case, interrupt your day, and ask if you'd like to buy a jet ski for £6,000. What would you say?

'No' is probably the shortened version of the answer, maybe followed by explicit instructions concerning travel and multiplication.

This is how so many companies do their marketing and selling. This is not only random targeting, but cold and disengaging. Even if I happen to walk into the office of someone who wants a jet ski, I may get thrown out because my process of selling was so abrupt. It is called cold calling for a reason.

This represents an extreme situation, but in reality it is what happens on a regular basis. It is how time share selling got a bad name, why door-to-door salesmen disappeared, and why we avoid street traders. People like to buy, but they don't like being sold to. The challenge is to guide them on a path towards your product or service, at the end of which they choose to buy.

In any business, there are several levels of sale that may have to be completed; you are not just selling your product or service. The levels will be different from business to business. However, recognising, managing, and controlling them will improve your conversion rate.

Let's take the example of selling a jet ski; before I can sell a jet ski to anyone, I have to sell them on several other levels.

1. I have to convince them that water sports are good.
2. Then I have to demonstrate that using powered craft is better and more fun than rowing or sailing.
3. From the range of power craft available, I then need to prove to them that a jet ski is the best for them rather than a speed boat.
4. Once I have positioned that jet skis are the right product for my prospect, I need to convince them that my particular company and brand is the best for them.
5. With my brand being accepted, I need to propose the actual model of jet ski from our range that would suit their requirements the best. This may include offering finance if applicable.
6. Once the model is selected, I can sell safety equipment, trailers, spares, and accessories to go with the jet ski. I may even add it to the finance deal.

7. With all the equipment in place, I can now sell the maintenance programme that will keep their machine in top condition so that it can be resold or traded in the future.

8. Throughout all of this, I have to sell myself. People will buy from people they like, and people they are like. If at any stage trust is lost, then the deal will be lost with it.

So just to sell a jet ski, there are eight levels of sale required. That is why I couldn't just walk in cold and sell you my jet ski. I had missed out steps one to four, and I had failed number eight automatically. For your business, there may be more steps, or there may be less, but they need to be identified. Otherwise, if a step gets missed, the filters will be used by our prospects, and the process will stop. Let's assume that the process above is the one we need to build a systematised conversion process around.

First, we will look at this in more detail in the chapter when we consider the generation of new enquiries. Targeted marketing only gets you past steps one or two. Just because you are targeting your marketing, you still need to go through the following stages in sequence. Depending what business it is that you are in, this process may be done from start to finish while they are in the showroom with you, or it may take weeks of communication, letters, and questionnaires, or phone calls. It doesn't matter how the stages are covered, but they have to be covered.

Before we start to add new prospects to your hopper, you will need to consider how your current prospects are being handled; your conversion process can be 'retro fitted' to your current contacts.

This is a suggestion for how the process could look for the jet ski business; the same logic can be applied to any business, although clearly the tactics will be different. Please remember, this is very basic and is designed to give you an idea of the principles involved.

In the example, the process has been applied to the strategy of attending an exhibition. Other processes may be required when handling enquiries from the web, via advertising, or referrals.

Step 1 – Convincing that water sports are good

Renting a stand at a leisure exhibition will at least get the company in front of people who are interested in leisure activities in general. The questions that the exhibition team need to ask of the people approaching them need to start with questions that follow the steps in the process. It's no good simply asking what colour jet ski a person wants when they approach the stand. They are not ready for that yet. Step one is to simply find out if they currently engage in leisure activities on or in the water.

It doesn't matter whether they do or not, but depending upon what they say will give the team the information they need to continue the conversation. If they haven't been involved in water-based leisure activities, then the conversation needs to one of exploring the possibilities to see if it is something they might consider; if they have been involved, then they can progress straight to step 2.

Unless the prospect agrees that water-based leisure activities are good, there is no point in going to the next stage. They can be disqualified from the process, and the sales team can move on to the next prospect.

Step 2 – Powered craft are better

When the team has confirmed that the prospect likes water-based sports and leisure activities, then the question of powered craft as opposed to sail or oar-powered craft has to be explored. If the prospect loves sailing and abhors the noise and disruption that jet skis make, then although he passes step 1, he will need to be disqualified at step 2.

Step 3 – Jet skis are better than boats

When it has been confirmed or proven that power craft are the best option, then the conversation can move on to convince the prospect that of all the power craft available, jet skis are the best in terms of speed, versatility, value for money, etc.

Not selling any jet skis yet, just the concept of a jet ski for now.

Step 4 – Our company and jet skis are the best

Only when the prospect agrees and actually realises that in fact jet skis are the best powered craft to go for, should the range of jet skis available from the company be explained. The background of the business, the vision and philosophy of the owners, and the track record and the USP of the products on offer can all now be discussed.

Step 5 – Which product specifically is the right one?

The top of the range is the right one to offer, at least the right one to offer first. Let the prospect have the opportunity of buying. If the offer isn't taken up, then other products in the range can be explored, offering finance or other incentives to overcome any objections that may arise.

I have seen plenty of sales people get to this or a similar stage of the process and lose the deal, simply because they didn't close the deal. They just kept talking until the prospect got bored and put a solid 'I'll think about it' filter in the middle of the hopper and the deal was lost. At our workshops and seminars, closing and overcoming objections are the most popular areas for people to work on.

Close the deal with a great question, and then shut up. Let them think, and let them choose to buy. If they don't buy, then simply go back up the steps and go over the features and benefits that get you through the filter.

Step 6 – Cross-selling other products

Only when the major purchase has been confirmed should additional items be sold. They may have already been bundled into the deal at step 5, but there is always room for a pair of gloves, wet suit, helmet, matching key ring, etc.

Step 7 – The final offer

Those who have seen the TV series *Columbo*, with Peter Falk, will remember that he would have a conversation with a suspect that appeared to be of no real consequence, and then as he was leaving, he would turn around and ask a great question that caught the suspect off guard. This is how you handle the final offer. It is almost a throwaway comment at the end of the process.

So with the jet ski, the offer of a maintenance programme should be made as a final necessity, to keep the machine in good condition.

Step 8 – Selling themselves

Not so much a step, rather a continuous process that has to be interwoven through the rest of the process. Selling is about the relationship that a prospect has with the company, the product, and person they are dealing with. If any one of these three aspects falls down, the deal will be off.

All stages of the process need to be systematised with the appropriated brochures, facts and figures, scripts, and questions all lined up and ready to go. If at the end of the process, an order isn't forthcoming, then a system of following up must be put in place.

I once had a prospect come to a seminar of mine; he didn't become a client that evening. We kept in touch with a newsletter and invites to other events, and it was twelve months almost to the day, that he came to another seminar of mine. After the seminar, he said that he had been thinking about what I said the year before, and that he was ready to get started on a programme.

Now that we have a system, we can measure the conversion rates of each stage. The table below shows how the numbers could look.

Total Enquiries	Total Prospects In	Number Converted	% of Prospects In	% of Total Prospects
Step 1	175	142	81%	81%
Step 2	142	35	25%	20%
Step 3	35	24	69%	14%
Step 4	24	18	75%	10%
Step 5	18	4	22%	2%
Step 6	4	3	75%	2%
Step 7	3	1	33%	1%

The table shows that a total of 175 people showed an interest in the company during the exhibition. These are the number of prospects. Then at each stage we can see the conversion rate compared to the total number of prospects, and the prospects that progressed to each individual stage.

So the conversion rate from step 1 to step 2 was 81%, which meant that the people at the exhibition were open to considering leisure activities on the water. The conversion rate from step 2 to step 3 was only 25%, suggesting that only one in four were convinced that powered craft were better than sail or oar-propelled craft.

The lowest conversion rates were the ones between step 2 and step 3, and step 5 and 6, so this is where attention needs to be focussed initially. Providing the sales team are following a pre-determined process, the process itself can be adapted and then the results reviewed, obviously looking for improvements. Without this sort of detail, all that could have been said about the exhibition was that it generated four sales of jet skis.

The challenge is that without the information regarding the stages of the process, we wouldn't know why some people bought and others didn't. Your marketing activity is like any other activity. It needs to be measured, the return on investment analysed, and strategies put in place to improve the results.

The same type of data can be produced for a variety of sales environments. In the management consultancy sector where telemarketers are used to book appointments for sales people to attend and sell consulting contracts, the sales process looks like this:

Step 1 – Initial telephone call

Step 2 – Appointment booked

Step 3 – Brochure sent by post, and receipt confirmed by telephone

Step 4 – Questionnaire sent to prospect and received by office

Step 5 – Consultation by phone and confirmation of meeting

Step 6 – Sales meeting

Step 7 – Client starts programme

This process may take two weeks to complete, and at each stage, there will be a conversion rate that can be measured and managed accordingly. Most sales people will know their conversion rate from sales meeting to customer, even allowing for following up and delayed decisions. Their conversion rate is critical. However, the processes that precede the actual meeting require the same levels of attention; every prospect costs money. And in business we need to know exactly where the money is going.

What Strategies to Get Through the Filters?

Let's look at each of the primary filters in turn and the strategies that can be employed at the different stages of your process in order to get through them. All the strategies we looked at earlier to improve average order values and number of orders placed will have an effect here. Remember, the filters are just the excuses that a prospect will use to stop your sales process, however, also remember that you hand the excuses to each and every prospect through your activity, behaviour and process.

The 'buy an alternative' filter: If this filter or objection is used against you, then the value proposition of your product or service has not been established in the mind of the prospect. The prospect will have a number of reasons that will be used to justify the decision, but whatever they are, they are all symptoms of the same condition – low perceived added value when compared to the alternative. To get through this filter, consider the following strategies:

Clarity around USP – If you haven't got a USP, then get one. Even if the competition is more expensive than you, if their perceived value and differentiation is higher than yours, they will get the business.

Sales Training – Train your team how to use a progressive system of selling as shown above and to close the deal professionally during the process.

Provide new customer incentives – At the risk of upsetting your existing customers, consider offers of finance or special bundles of products or gifts to encourage them to sign up.

The 'think about it' filter: This usually means that the prospect thinks you are too expensive or that your product or service is not up to standard. They won't tell you this, of course; they are too polite, so they will tell you that they need to think about it, or speak to their wife, husband, or partner before making a decision. The decision has nearly always been made of course, and the decision is no. To get through this filter consider the following strategies:

Positioning – Make sure ahead of the meetings or discussion that all parties to the decision will be in attendance. If at the meeting they say they need to speak to their partners, then for them this is true, and the best you will do is book a follow-up meeting with them at a later date when the partner is available.

I am not allowed to buy socks by myself, so if any decision has to be taken, Lynn and I make them together. At one meeting, before we started discussions, the salesman was talking to me while Lynn was finishing a call. When she came into the room, he looked at her and immediately asked if she would make him a coffee, white with one sugar, assuming she was an office junior and not a shareholder director of the business. When you come to our events and meet Lynn, you will understand that this was not a smart move on his behalf. Surprisingly, he didn't get the business. I did tell him why, but he blamed Lynn for being so sensitive. Interesting!

Needs and Wants – Customers do not know what they need, but they know what they want. The job of anyone in sales is to establish the needs and fulfil them. Wants are optional, needs are critical; I want chocolate, but I need oxygen. I will fight you for both, but the oxygen is non-negotiable. If we only identify wants, then being optional, the prospect will choose to think about it. If we identify needs, then there is no thinking to do – it has to happen.

Process – The progressive process has not been followed. At every stage of the process, the prospect has to qualify to go to the next stage. If at the end of the process, they still want to think, it suggests that either a step has been missed, or that one needs adding in.

The 'do nothing' filter: Doing nothing can be our biggest competitors. It's the easiest lowest risk choice a prospect can make; it is guaranteed to be safe. This filter may be added at any time during the process. It maybe that the budget has been cut, the strategy has changed, circumstances have evolved, etc. To get through this filter, consider the following strategies:

Targeting – Make sure that the prospects are qualified to progress to the next stage, such that you are sure that they will be buying something.

Offer – Change the offer. It may be that the filter is not true and that they just have a smaller budget than originally. Reposition your offer to suit their budget and keep a deal on track.

Speed – Time kills deals. Agreements are like bread – they are best when fresh – and not like wine; they don't get better with age. Sometimes a deal will evaporate because the moment is lost, so consider the timescales for your process, and don't drag it out.

Not now or not ever – The process of converting prospects into customers can take a long time. Your selling process needs to match the buying process of you customers, not the other way round. Systematised follow-up us critical.

With any of the filters, the objection of money can be used. The 'can't afford it' or 'too expensive' objections are usually not true. What they show is that the targeting, value proposition, and relationship with the sales team was not up to standard. If a prospect thinks your sales team is untrustworthy or lacks knowledge, a prospect will very rarely tell them that, unless you are in New York. They will use a money excuse to delay or avoid the decision to buy.

When a prospect uses their filter at any stage of the process, you will have to assess if they are right, or your process needs adapting. Sometimes your product will not be right for a prospect. They don't need it. A competitor's product is better for them, or doing nothing at that moment in time is in their best interests. Remember that you are in the business of adding value, not in the business of simply selling at all costs. Your conversion strategies should be designed to help your prospects choose to become customers, not trick them into it.

Number of Enquiries

So now we are ready to generate new enquiries and attract new customers to your business. It is time to do your marketing.

There are fundamentally two types of marketing to consider:

1. Above the Line (ATL): This type of activity is associated with broad advertising and brand awareness campaigns using media such as TV, billboards, newspaper adverts, etc. This approach tends to be difficult to measure in terms of responses and acquisition cost.

2. Below the Line (BTL): These activities are specific and targeted towards a specific group or niche, sometimes requiring direct contact through email, direct mail, or telephone. Direct measurement is more straightforward, as campaigns and offers are narrower.

In your business, the focus needs to be BTL – the more targeted and specific your marketing, the better. Whilst global brands will use the ATL approach while looking to maintain their products in the minds of people, maximise market share and extend the brand into new products. In the small- and medium-sized enterprise (SME), we are building a reputation, not a brand. We operate in selected niches and differentiate ourselves in terms of quality, service, and relationships. Our marketing needs to be designed accordingly. You will have to cover some ATL strategies as well, as we shall see later.

Enquiries are the method by which we feed our hopper. Once contact has been established, then your conversion strategies will take over and take the enquiry through to a sale and on to be a long-term customer.

Earlier, we described your customers through GAP analysis. When marketing, you are looking to attract more great customers, maybe a few average ones, and no poor ones.

Understanding what your great customer looks like enables you to be really specific and targeted with your marketing. First we need to define the characteristics that are common to all your great customers. A pulse and a cheque book is a great start but is hardly a niche, unless we go back to the undertakers of course, when just the cheque book is required and a pulse is not so good.

Helen runs a marketing consulting business; she has defined her great customer as having the following attributes:

1. Owner managed businesses
2. Been in business for at least three years
3. Sales revenue of between £2m and £5m
4. Selling in the B2C – business to consumer market
5. Within five miles radius of her office

With this information, Helen can build a database of all the businesses that fit her criteria. Let's assume that this database consists of 4,000 businesses. Now, plenty of companies will call this a niche and direct emails, direct mail, or telephone campaigns at this list, but it is way too broad yet.

Within these 4,000 businesses, there are thirty-four further business categories listed. For example, there will be salons, hotels, restaurants, insurance companies, etc. Now we can break the list into business categories depending upon type. The list will include dozens of business types and allow us to get more specific.

Helen finds that in the list there are a total of 178 restaurants, so the restaurant sector could be a good niche for her to start marketing to. Within the list of 178 restaurants, there are a variety of types. There are Italian, French, and Indian; there are pubs and high street cafes. The list now looks like this:

1. Italian restaurants – 29
2. Chinese restaurants – 35
3. French restaurants – 19
4. Indian restaurants – 33
5. Pub restaurants – 35
6. Cafes – 26
7. German restaurants – 1

Helen also notices that within the list, there is a further subgroup of twelve restaurants that are vegetarian.

This chunking down of a database based upon your criteria of your great customers allows you to send messages to your prospects that are specifically aimed at them. The message will speak their language, and they will be more likely to respond.

It doesn't matter whether your target is consumers, business owners, or corporations. The more you refine and identify your target, the better. In BTL marketing, you need to use a sniper rifle, not a machine gun.

So, Helen's database now has 4,000 businesses, with thirty-four separate business categories, 178 restaurants with eight sub-niches if we include the twelve vegetarian restaurants.

Whilst Helen's niche is the 4,000 businesses that she knows she can provide services to. From a marketing message perspective that is not specific enough. Your customers are not interested in your niche; they are interested in what you can do for them. Helen has a number of niches, and the message to each one must be tailored to suit them specifically.

First, we need to know the biggest challenge facing the restaurant business, so Helen calls the British Hospitality Association and does some research and discovers that the single biggest challenge facing restaurants are numbers of covers on weekdays, especially Monday to Wednesday, and people not showing up after reservations have been made.

Now we have an issue to discuss, a challenge we can help our prospects overcome. No one wants to hire a marketing consultant or an accountant, lawyer, coach, or adviser – they want to hire a result. If you can solve a problem for a customer so that they make more money, work less hours, feel better, look better, or have a better lifestyle, you will be hired – if you call yourself a consultant, coach, accountant, or lawyer, they don't care. It's not what we call ourselves in business – it's the benefits we deliver that are of interest. We don't have brands; we have reputations.

Helen decides to write a flyer and send it to each of the owners of the restaurants in her defined niche. The letters are all similar but adapted to suit the interests of each specific niche, one for the owners of Italian restaurants, Chinese, etc. The content of the documents are the same, and the message is consistent.

The flyer should suggest that Helen can fix two key issues in their business: bookings on week nights and no shows for reservations made – solve these and she will get a client. She will call her services marketing; her customers will call her a problem solver. That is what your marketing needs to focus on – benefits of your product or service, not the features of it.

Helen chose to use direct mail as the medium because it almost has a novelty factor now. Everyone gets emails. But direct mail that is specifically targeted includes the person's name (don't send out anything starting dear sir or madam) and offers to solve an issue that they actually have. This is much more attractive. Helen printed the addresses on the white envelopes, stuck a stamp on, rather than using a franking machine, and included a foam stress ball inside; an envelope with a lump in it is more attractive than a flat one, and it can't be put at the bottom of a pile of post. The pile will fall off. It has to go at the top.

'Working with us, this will be the last stress ball you ever need . . '

Direct mail at best will get a 1% response rate; from every 100 letters you send out, you will get one phone call. The response rates go up depending upon the quality of the letter or flyer, the offer, and the specific nature of the contents. When they are followed up by a telephone call, the rates increase again.

Helen decided that she would send a series of letters to each niche she had identified. The first suggested that she could help with weekday bookings, the second with 'reservation no shows', and the third reminded them of the first two. Then one of the team would follow up with a telephone call with the intention of booking appointments for Helen to go and visit the owner.

This is where you must have your ATL marketing in place. When a letter arrives on the desk of a prospect, if they show any interest at all, they will check you out on the Internet. You must have a great web page that includes testimonials, details of your vision and mission, the services you provide, and the benefits your customers derive from working with you. I was with a client once who told me that he wasn't sure that the Internet was going to 'catch on' and that he would wait and see how it developed before he got a web site. I think the Internet has now 'caught on' whether we like it or not.

In Helen's niche market, there was a single German restaurant. We live about forty-five minutes from the German border, so when it comes to evenings out, we are really fortunate – we can eat in France, Belgium, Luxembourg, or Germany. Of course, the French food is generally excellent; however, whilst Germany is not widely known for the quality of its cuisine, there are a couple of fabulous restaurants over towards Saarburg that are worth the drive.

If you decide to go there, travel through Luxembourg to Remich, head north along the Moselle, and take the small ferry across to Germany. Fabulous! I didn't realise that Luxembourg had so many vineyards.

Anyway, the single German restaurant is perhaps as small as a niche can get, so rather than writing to the owner, Helen has dinner there on a Tuesday evening. The place is so quiet that the chef, who also owns the restaurant, is able to come and talk to the customers, both of them, so Helen gets a great meal and a sales meeting all rolled into one.

Strategic Choices

The number and type of strategies you choose will be dependent upon the business you are in. Some of the best strategies for me include writing a book and running seminars, so if you are reading this, please come to one of my seminars to keep my numbers looking good.

Whatever business you have, don't have just one strategy running. Have a broad range. It may be that your prospects need to be touched by your business several times before they respond. With more than one strategy running, when one goes quiet, the others may compensate and continue to generate a steady stream of prospects into your hopper.

There are hundreds of ways to generate enquiries to your business, from TV advertising to business cards, web sites to telemarketing. The choice of which ones to select will depend on which ones allow you to target you prospects with the most accuracy. The following list is not exhaustive but will give some ideas of what is available to you. With all these strategies, remember to measure the results. With each strategy, we can measure the number of prospects that go into our hopper, the conversion rates at each stage, the acquisition cost, and the length of time taken. Over time, there will be a series of statistics available for each strategy you use that will enable you to plan your activities with certainty, because you will know what works and what doesn't.

For every £100 you invest in marketing, you should get £500 back in profit, not just revenue. When we can do that with your marketing through targeting, messaging, and systematised follow through, you will know that some of your marketing doesn't work, but you will know that most of it does. And your budget is now unlimited because for every £100 in you put in, you get £500 back – that is what owning a business is all about. It's not the hours you work – it's the systematised and predictable return on investment of your knowledge and cash.

Referrals – Being introduced to a prospect by an existing customer is probably as good as it gets. You will attract referrals by being consistently excellent at what you do. Systematise you referral programme so that you have a select team of customers who know that they are your ambassadors, and they get benefits accordingly. Your existing great customers will know people who are like them and will fit the profile you have selected. With referrals and introductions, the easiest way to get them is the most overlooked – asking for them.

Alliances – If another company works with customers that are in your target market, and they provide complimentary services, form an alliance. We do this with banks, accountants, lawyers, and networking groups; we all provide services to the same market, and by putting on events and making offers specifically tailored to the needs of the customers of the alliance partner, it becomes a win-win situation.

For example, when I run a planning workshop that is exclusively for the customers of one of my alliance partners, we co-brand the event. I design package deals and special offers that are available to them only as a consequence of them being customers of my alliance partner. I tailor the programme to suit the customers, and my alliance partner will attend all the events and participate in the presentation of the workshop. This is great added value for their customers; I get to meet with new people who may choose to work with us on an ongoing basis, and the alliance partner is building a great relationship with their customers by world-class training and planning opportunities at great value.

Advertising – Providing your advertising is as targeted as it can be through insertion in trade magazines, specialist publications, or local press, then this can be very powerful. You advert must include an offer, not just your telephone number and your business name. Offers need to be specifically aimed at getting the prospect to call or visit within a certain timeframe, so limited-duration offers are good. Including coupons can help with response rates.

Telemarketing – Scripted telemarketing to a specific niche will get results. Your telemarketing team need to be trained, and understand that politeness and patience are the two key attributes of using the telephone effectively. Make sure that any database you use can be contacted by telephone as there is opt out and opt in rules that need to be complied with. The response rates will vary here, depending on the offer and the business. If we use telemarketers, for every thirty handset movements that are made, an appointment is made, for example.

Direct Mail and Email – Again make sure that your lists are opted in for being sent email and direct mail. These should be targeted as previously described and sent out in a series or sequence with specific offers attached. Make them informative, funny, and unique to get the best response and combine with telemarketing to increase the contact rates.

Web site – This is a must. Your web site should be easy to navigate, identify you, your business, and the benefits that your customers will experience as a result of working with you. Testimonials, free resources, and events calendars should be kept up to date, and new content should be added in a systematised way. You will be checked out online so make sure that your web site is consistent with your other marketing activities and congruent with your vision, mission, rules of the game, and philosophy. Consider taking expert advice regarding search engine optimisation and web marketing. These are 'dark arts' and require specific specialist attention to get the best results.

Social Media – Increasingly, the world is becoming connected through social media web sites. There are more than 200 of these sites, from the well-known to the obscure. Facebook is perhaps one of the best known with around 500,000,000 members; Twitter has 175,000,000; Bebo has 117,000,000; MySpace, 100,000,000; and LinkedIn, 80,000,000. In business, you and your company need to be connected. This is how people will find you and your products. Remember people buy from people, and the easier it is to find you the better.

Networking – This is an underutilised resource. Attending events run by your local chamber of commerce where you can meet and mix with other business people is a good way of building you professional network. There are a number of early morning breakfast clubs that through membership and exclusivity meet on a regular basis specifically to pass business introductions to each other.

Exhibitions and Events – Being seen is important if you want to become recognised in your sector. Where you can, get on stage and present or promote your business. Being on stage makes you the expert, and people are attracted to experts.

Location and Overheads – The rent you pay should be judged as a marketing expense. Depending on your business, if you need people to come to you, then your location is important. I treat every expense as a marketing expense. What I mean is that if I am placing my business with a range of suppliers such as banks, insurance agents, etc., I will expect them to work with me in the development of my business. I will help them, and they will help me – that way I get free insurance and services because the business they send to me pays for the services I buy from them.

Follow-up – Whatever strategy you choose, make sure it includes a systematised way of keeping in touch and following up all prospects. There are a number of CRM systems available that will help you do this in a planned and structured way.

Summary

Understanding your process of both generating and converting enquiries from a variety of sources into new customers will allow you to plan the expansion of your business with certainty. You will understand what it costs to attract a new customer, what they spend, and how long they stay with you; your business can be modelled in the boardroom before it engages with the market. Your marketing will never be 100% successful. If it is, then you are probably selling something illegal, or you are too cheap. Either way you should stop, but by applying simple rules of MOIRA to your new customer acquisition process, you will have taken control of your business.

Notes

Rule No. 5 – You Will Need Help

No institution can possibly survive if it needs geniuses or supermen to manage it. It must be organised in such a way as to be able to get along under a leadership composed of average human beings.

Peter Drucker

Your people are your best assets, or your greatest liabilities – the choice is yours . . .

Your philosophy, vision, mission, and rules of the game inputs will be interpreted by your team and translated into standards of service, quality, and behavioural outputs. That will define the results your business achieves. You can't do it all by yourself. At some point you have to move from the monarchy to the hierarchy; and that needs process and control.

The next model shows how the results of your business are dependent upon the outputs from your team, which are in turn dependent upon their interpretation and application of the leadership they are given.

The quality of the results will be a direct reflection of the quality of leadership and the quality of the people you engage to help you. If you don't get the results you want, then either the leadership inputs or the team's interpretation of them need to be addressed. Customers are either satisfied or not, depending upon how your business treats them. Customers are neither happy nor unhappy before they come into contact with your business. How they feel after contact depends on how they are treated while they are with you. The responsibility for the customer experience lies within the business.

I remember being sat in a management meeting at a large electronics company, which shall remain nameless. There were about twelve of us managers representing the operations, finance, sales, and marketing departments. I was from one of the subcontract logistics providers, and whilst not employees of the company, we were involved in the distribution of the products; so we had to be represented at the meetings. We were all armed with our reports and recommendations for the managing director who was due at any time.

After about fifteen minutes of waiting, we heard a sports car race into the car park, mount the kerb, and slide to a halt under the glass atrium that covered our main entrance to the building.

He burst into the meeting room, threw his keys onto the table, and demanded that someone go and park his car while he went to freshen up before the meeting commenced. Everyone took a step back, and I got the job of moving the car.

When finally the meeting started, he stood up and said five words to us all that I have remembered to this day: 'All our customers are b@*&$#ds . . .' He had decided that his philosophy and leadership were correct, and that it was up to the customers to comply with the company, not the other way round. The company closed for trading shortly afterwards; a business reflects its leaders.

Your business will attract team members and customers to it depending upon the leadership you deliver and the philosophy you embody. If we want to attract world-class people and customers, then we need to have a world-class business for them to be attracted to. The model below shows how the results are dependent upon the leadership of the owner, interpreted through the people in the team.

Leadership → Inputs

- Vision
- Mission
- Rules
- Training
- Engagement
- Trust

Interpretation

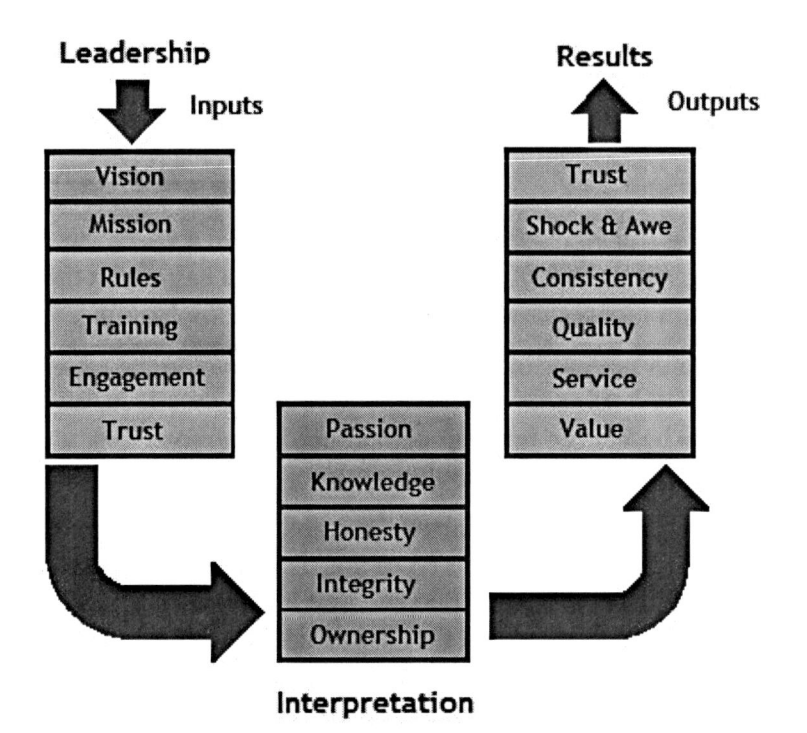

- Passion
- Knowledge
- Honesty
- Integrity
- Ownership

Results ← Outputs

- Trust
- Shock & Awe
- Consistency
- Quality
- Service
- Value

In order to grow your business, you have to build a model of leadership that guides, inspires, and enables your team to deliver the standards of service and product that you define, even while you are not there.

Your business will reflect you because you are in control of the inputs to the system. This is where your philosophy becomes tangible and defines the culture of the business. Having the right people, who will respond to the environment that you have developed, will be fundamental to your success. You will know how the process is working when you compare the anticipated outputs and results from your leadership inputs, with the actual outputs and results achieved.

There are two key areas to focus on when developing your team:

1. The quality of the leadership inputs.
2. The interpretation and product or service delivery.

The standards of the output depend on these two variables.

Leadership – the input into the system

A leader is a person who has followers. Leadership has been studied and analysed since organised groups were first recognised as being more productive than individuals. The first 'civilisation' was arguably in Sumer in what we now call the Middle East, around 6,000 years ago, and even before that, nomadic tribes had leaders and followers.

In the book *On Heroes, Hero Worship, and the Heroic in History*, first published in 1841, Thomas Carlyle proposed that great leaders shared common traits and that there were common talents, skills, and physical characteristics of people, predominantly men, who rose to positions of power, influence, and leadership. The trait theory of leadership, as it became known, suggests that history is made by the intervention of great men, and that leaders are born rather than historic situations supplying the environment for leadership to emerge.

'Cometh the hour, cometh the man.'

Criticism of the trait theory led researchers to evaluate the behaviours displayed by leaders. David McClelland defined leadership as a pattern of motives, including the need for power, low need for affiliation, or self-control. In 1939, Ralph White, Ronald Lipitt, and Kurt Lewin researched the performance of groups of eleven-year-old boys under three different styles of leadership – authoritarian, democratic, and laissez-faire – with the results suggesting that the democratic approach was the most productive. Earlier, in 1936, Lewin had published 'Principles of Topological Psychology' and proposed an equation stating that behaviour is a function of both the person and their environment. This contradicted popular theories of the day and gave significance to a specific situation when explaining a behaviour, rather than simply relating them to a person's history or track record.

$$B = f(P, E)$$

In essence, this means that a person's past does not necessarily dictate their future, as the environment and indeed the person may have changed. Also interesting is when looking to recruit someone, how much emphasis is placed on their past performance and CV, neither of which are guaranteed indicators of future achievement.

Situational Leadership Theory was developed by Paul Hersey and Ken Blanchard and was introduced as 'Life Cycle Theory of Leadership', in the 1970s, being renamed later. Reassuringly, this theory suggests that there is no ideal leadership style that suits all situations, rather that there are a range of leadership styles that will be effective depending upon the situation. The choice of leadership style will be contingent upon the maturity of the environment in which the leadership takes place.

Hersey and Blanchard defined the different leadership styles in terms of the degrees of task and relationship behaviour displayed to their followers, ranging from S1 to S4.

S1 – Telling: The leader directs the individuals and gives specific instructions regarding the task, how it should be performed, by when and by whom.

S2 – Selling: The individuals or group is given clear direction. However, their consent and support towards the task or process is elicited through discussion and reasoning.

S3 – Participating: The way to achieve agreed objectives is decided through shared decision making. The leader maintains the relationship with the group but reduces the involvement in the actual task.

S4 – Delegating: The majority of the responsibility has been given to the individual or team. The leader monitors performance and results, while enabling the team to decide on the process employed.

What this means is that as your business matures, or depending upon the situation, a different leadership strategy will be required. A good leader knows what strategy to use in any given situation. Furthermore, the people you have in your team may be situational as well. Some people are better in a small entrepreneurial company, whilst others are better in a more structured and stable environment. As your business grows through its stages of development, you will need help from different people at different times, and whilst you will need to attract new skills and personalities to your business, you may equally need to let some go. One of the reasons that jobs for life are disappearing in commerce and industry doesn't have so much to do with the people employed, rather the pace of change of the environment in which they operate; they will be changing at different speeds, with one eventually becoming literally redundant from the other.

The pace of change in your business will be amplified, when you choose to grow. The environment in which even a stable business operates is changing and developing at an exponential rate, once you start to change your business as well. It can be destabilising for the team, and that is why they need leadership. No one needs a leader to inspire them to stand still and do nothing; leadership is about inspiring people to take action towards a shared objective.

When you consider great leaders, they are usually in the world of politics, military, or religion. Pick any of the great leaders you can think of and consider the attributes that made them great. The words drive, determination, charisma, values, and passion may all spring to mind; our challenge is that whilst all of these may be true, regardless of whether you agree with the results of their leadership, leadership in business cannot be dependent upon the personality of the owner, manager, or CEO. Once that person leaves, the leadership leaves with them.

There is a difference between a person being the leader of a company or team and providing leadership to a company or team. The first requires the leader to be present, the second doesn't. Being a leader involves being on stage, rallying the troops, and inspiring through thought and action. Whilst providing leadership means that we have to distil the essence of the leader into models, artefacts, belief systems, processes, and procedures that enables people to understand the essence of the message without having to be personally invigorated by the leader to comply with it.

Leadership is built into your business, not bolted on as an afterthought. Franchises can expand globally because they are in the business of providing leadership, and yet very few people would be able to tell you who the CEO of McDonald's or Yum Brands actually is. Come to think of it – who has heard of Yum Brands? Now Jim Skinner of McDonald's and David Novak of Yum Brands are of course great leaders of their people and their businesses, however, what they recognise is that the provision of structural leadership through systems, brands, and the culture of reward and recognition enables them to manage and grow their global businesses.

David Novak's book *Accidental CEO* is definitely worth a read.

Training

Training is a process, not an event. The training that people were given ten or even five years ago may not be applicable today; the environment has changed. If you want people to keep up with the market, then the knowledge they apply needs to be refreshed on a continuous basis. Training can take many forms, from the formal academic to specific skills and on-the-job instruction. It depends what the needs of the business are.

Training that supports understanding of the company vision, mission, and rules of the game is critical and should be updated and refreshed regularly with both existing staff and newcomers. Induction training is perhaps some of the most important training that you can do.

With the ten-year and three-year plans in place, we can predict the skills and attributes of the team that will help you to achieve the objectives, and a training and development programme can be designed accordingly. This plan may include simple skill analysis and training or technology updates through to product innovation and research and development. In order to get the correct output from your business, the correct input in terms of knowledge and skills is fundamental.

If customer service is important to your business, then don't assume that people will use what you may regard as common sense, and serve your customers how you would – they won't. First, there is no such thing as common sense, just a reference to own unique experiences and patterns that happens to be common to us only; second, you set the rules, and in order for people to deliver the service, you design. They need to know what is expected.

Engagement Through Models, Artefacts, and Rituals

In order to organise a group of people, whether they be in your business, a sports team, a platoon of soldiers, or street gang, there are some fundamentals that are required. We already have the vision, mission, and rules of the game in place in your business. Now we need to lock that in with models, artefacts, and rituals. Relax; I'm not suggesting that you a have company song here or group hugs in the car park before work, but leadership has to be present in the business whilst the leader is not there, and the models, artefacts, and rituals that you introduce, serve as your leadership surrogates. People will create their own models, artefacts, and rituals if as leaders we do not give them ones of our own. Belonging and loyalty to a cause are powerful motivators; as leaders we need to ensure the cause chosen, is the success of our business.

The models in our business will include the processes, procedures, jargon, and culture of the organisation. Every business sector has its own sayings, jargon, and acronyms, understanding of which is restricted to those in the 'know'. Your business will have these by virtues of the business you are in, and through publication and reinforcement of your vision, mission, and rules of the game. Others will emerge that are specific to your organisation. These sayings and protocols allows the individual to identify with the group, feel a sense of belonging, and have a structured comfort zone in which to operate.

Packing military spares for long-term storage requires the designing of packages according to specific military standards. The packing process including the preparation and protection of products must be carried out in a controlled environment using approved materials and suitably trained staff. The language of the business revolved around the terminology associated with the processes. People would hold entire conversations by simply using recognised military specifications, abbreviations of materials, and acronyms for processes.

In 1986, as a shiny new designer, new to this industry, I walked into the production area with my head full of a different set of specifications, abbreviations, and acronyms. Mine came from the world of weapons design and manufacture and didn't fit with their world of packaging and preparation. I was tested by the people. If someone talked about an 81-15 lined with 1253, an 81-14, or even simply 1763 or 9313, and I didn't know what they meant, I was excluded from the group, even ridiculed for my apparent lack of knowledge – I didn't qualify to be part of the 'gang'. As I learned the jargon, I became accepted in to the team. If you really want to find out more about military packaging or are having trouble getting to sleep, simply type 'Def Stan 81-41' into Google and see what turns up – happy reading . . .

People want to belong and have the pride and satisfaction of being associated with a credible group that has language sayings and protocols that are unique. In the extreme, this is how gangs and cults operate, all having their own language and models that not only differentiate them from other groups but give clear and definitive guidance around the requirements of compliance with the group. On a much less severe basis, the same is true in business.

Anyone who is a follower of sport and chooses a particular team to follow will understand the power of uniforms or team colours. The Manchester United football kit is one of the most recognised uniforms on the planet; I am amazed that even in the tea rooms of Indonesia, there will be images and pictures of Manchester United, revered by people who don't even know where

Manchester is. A uniform is a demonstration of allegiance and belonging. Doctors, nurses, and firemen as well as the military all have them, as do the servers in your local McDonald's. Consider having company polo shirts, badges, scarves, and other artefacts that will enable your team to identify with the business. When a person wears the colours of the group, they will identify with them more strongly and even defend the group to 'outsiders'.

In the USA, prisoners wear orange jumpsuits as their prison uniform. In Lincoln County, Tennessee, the prison authorities were concerned that no one reported a prisoner that had escaped to the police. The reason was that the local university in Knoxville has a football team, the 'Vols', who wear orange shirts, so no one notice someone else in the same colours. The colour of the prisoner's uniform was changed to pink – which I'm sure went down well in with the prisoners. The moral of this story is to let your team design the uniform and choose the style and design. They will wear something that they design rather than something you impose.

Cults are well known for their rituals of initiation and operation. The Masons, the Church, and all organised groups have rituals and ceremonies that define them and give structure and meaning to the belief system or value set of the group. So whilst in business we really don't need to start sacrificing goats at the regional conference or hold daggers to the hearts of the new recruits in the accounts team, we do need recognised patterns of behaviour that define belonging to the team.

The New Zealand All Blacks Rugby team perform a ritual before every match they play. They perform the Haka, a traditional Maori dance that lets the opposition know in no uncertain terms what they are in for. The Papa o Pango Haka was introduced in 2005 and is used as an alternative with the more traditional Ka Mate Haka. This ritual is part of what it means to be an All Black. Other teams know it, and all round the world, this ritual defines them. In 2007, the Italian Rugby team decided to ignore the Haka and were then beaten 76–14.

Another ritual of the All Blacks is that they tend to go on and win on a regular basis; out of thirty-four games against England, they have won twenty-seven and drawn one, so there must be something to this . . .

Rituals can include the simple introductions made at the start of every meeting, a regular pattern of events and meetings and reviews, newsletters, celebrations, etc. Rituals become 'the way we do things around here' and can be structured such that anywhere in the world the same rituals are followed.

In the UK, I would attend networking events that were held in the early morning. These events are run by BNI – Business Networking and Referrals and BoB – Business over Breakfast, among others. Whilst working in Budapest, I was invited to go to one of these events, and although the language was foreign to me, I knew exactly what to do and when, because the ritual and process was the same as it was in the UK. I even knew what was being said because the same scripts were used. When it came to specify what referrals I was looking for, I simply asked for introductions to business people called David – as this is a very popular name in Hungary, and I got four referrals.

Having procedures, processes, and rituals mean that your team will carry your philosophy, vision, and mission with them all the time, without you having to be there with them.

Trust

At some point, with all the training, engagement, rules, mission, and vision in place, you have to let your people go and deliver, trusting that with the leadership and guidance you have given to them, they will interpret your philosophy into reality. Trust is an exercise in reciprocation. If I am trusted by someone, I am obliged to repay that trust by respecting and complying with the conditions it places upon me. Tell your team that you trust them – when you are sure that you do, the S4 stage of leadership has been achieved. Don't place trust in people who aren't ready. My belief is that all people are trustworthy in principle. However, I am not going to trust my business to people who aren't trained and ready; it is not fair to them and not fair to me or the other members of the team. Trust is conditional upon the training provided and the attitude displayed.

Trust has to be earned as well as given. Consistency of behaviour and compliance with the rules of the game by you as the owner will be important here; you can buy compliance, but you have to earn trust.

Your vision, mission, rules of the game combined with the objectives that are agreed give your team a framework within which they can operate. Within that framework, they can use their best judgement, and you will have to allow them to do it. The degree of freedom they have will depend on the clarity, significance, and understanding they have regarding the boundaries you set.

The more freedom you allow the more trust you will have to give. Freedom to make decision and act must have constraints. Within the constraints or boundaries, discretion can be used. If

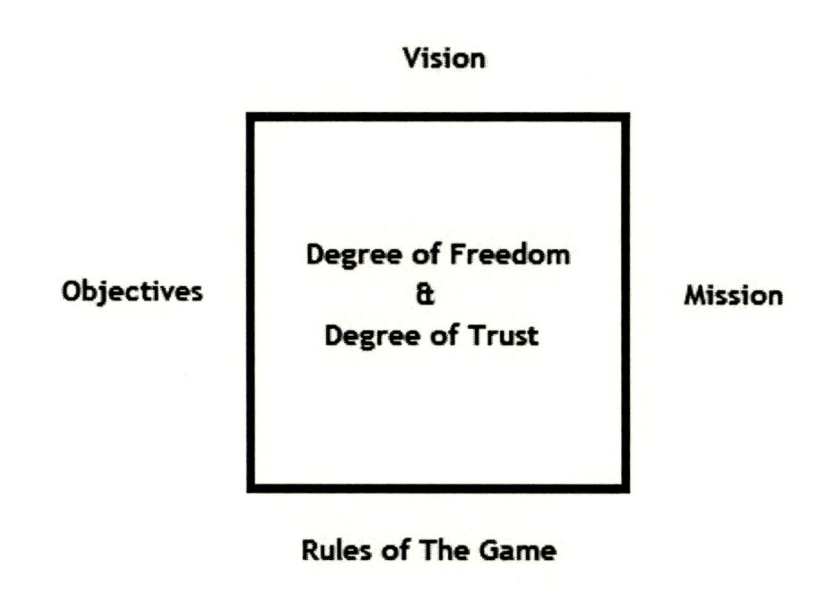

Vision

Objectives **Degree of Freedom & Degree of Trust** **Mission**

Rules of The Game

decisions need to be made that are outside the boundaries, then everyone should know who to go to.

Different members of your team will have different degrees of freedom and trust placed upon them. Your role is to establish and control the boundaries.

Interpretation

How well your leadership is translated into actions and decisions will depend on the calibre, aptitude, motivation of your team, and of course, the quality of leadership and definition of the boundaries that they receive from you.

On the assumption that the inputs and leadership have been structured well from the previous chapter, we can now look at your ideal team members.

The organisation chart we referred to earlier in the book now needs to be refined and completed. Whilst you have the roles and positions designed and structured, you now need to define the profiles of the individuals who would be best at filling the positions.

Before you start deciding what attributes your ideal employees have, remember that it can be easy to make them discriminatory, even without intending to. So take advice from your local chamber of commerce, council, trade association, or professional institutes and get guidance to ensure you comply with the letter and spirit of relevant codes of conduct and legislation.

Developing job descriptions and performance standards for each position within the business will help you to understand the type of person that would perform best in the framework you have designed. We are profiling the role to be performed, not the person that will carry out the role. Ignore the people you may have already employed, and start with a blank sheet of paper; what would your ideal blueprint for your business look like, what functions would there be, and what type of people would you employ?

Defining the requirements of the positions first will enable us to define the type of people that will fit into them the best. There are a number of profiling tools that will enable you to describe both the job functions and the working environment. That in turn will describe the profile of the type of person that would be suitable for the role.

The DISC profiling system, for example, is a quadrant-based behavioural model based on the work of William Moulton Marston and classifies behaviour under four headings:

1. Dominance – Control, power, and authority
2. Influence – Sociability and interpersonal skills
3. Steadiness – Patience, persistence, and reliability
4. Compliance – Structure, patterns, processes, and procedures

A person can take the DISC test by answering twenty-four simple adjective-based questions and rating answers depending whether the statements made are least like or most like them. The report will give a profile of the individual with accompanying text to explain how the traits defined may manifest themselves in certain situations.

For example, my profile, according to the system is shown on the chart below. My profile would be described as a High Dominance High Influence, or simply 'DI', as you can see my scores in terms of stability and compliance are much lower. This would suggest that whilst I am good when being in control and also good at influencing others, I don't value stability, and I follow the rules providing that I design them! This makes me sound like an unstable maverick.

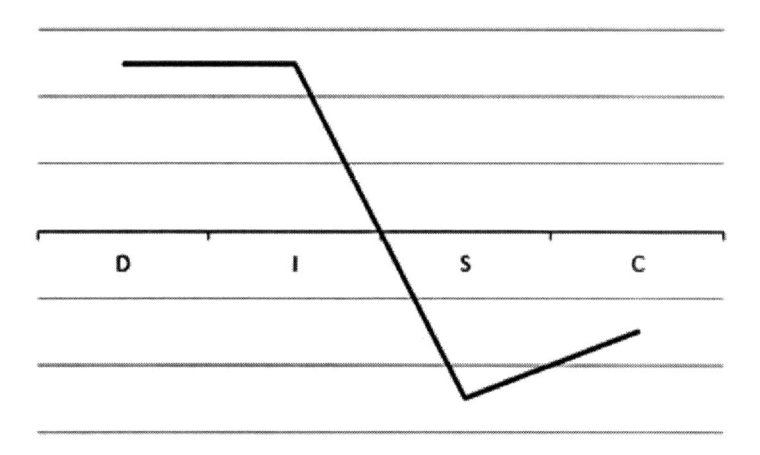

Now, if someone else has their profile completed, and their D is higher on their chart than mine is on mine, does it mean that they are more D than I am? Not necessarily, because this type of profiling can be situational. What I mean by that is that the four attributes are being compared relative to each other. My D is much higher than my S, for example, whereas there are areas of my life that are very stable – Lynn and I have been together for over thirty years. I don't have many memories without her. This would suggest a high S.

So my profile demonstrates the relationship between the four characteristics that are personal to me and should not be used as anything more than a guide. I may have very strong S and C characteristics, for example. It just so happens that my D and I are higher still. Using these tools to compare people with each other can be difficult.

The DISC profile process can be used to describe the person that would fit a defined role. By answering adjective-based questions about the job function, a DISC profile can be produced that will predict the profile of the ideal candidate for the position. Now my sons have distinct DISC profiles. One would be great as a CEO and the other great as an entrepreneur, which I'm sure they will be in time if they choose to. The missing ingredients are of course knowledge and experience.

The ideal candidate to fill a position will need to have the personality traits that will enable them to operate successfully and also the appropriate knowledge and experience. Your person profile should therefore include the following:

1. Knowledge – Specific industry knowledge and experience, academic qualifications, or relationships within the industry.
2. Skills – Specific skills relating to processes, programmes, or environments that would be helpful in the position.
3. Personality – DISC or similar, when compared to the requirements of the role.

Now we have defined the roles within the business and the profiles of the people who would be ideal working within them. It is time to compare the current reality to the predicted structure and look for the gaps.

This process should be used for designing development, training, and support policies that will enable people to adapt to the disciplines and requirements of the future organisation. Everyone should be given the opportunity of learning and embracing the new roles. This is not an excuse to simply fire everyone and start again. You may of course find that you are closer to the plan than you think and the people you have fit well into the new organisation chart you have developed.

As the business grows or positions require filling, the job and person profiling that you have done will enable best people to be hired. The traits of the individuals that apply for the jobs can be assessed before they start work with you, such that you can be more confident of a good fit with the team and also within the framework of trust and freedom.

Las Vegas is home to a company called Zappos. They are a very successful online retailer of shoes and other consumer products. When a new employee is hired, they must be trained in all areas of the business. This four-week induction process includes working in a variety of areas in the business and specific training regarding the company strategy and culture. Everyone is paid during this time, and at the end of the four weeks, the intention is that they will take up their posts within the company.

After two weeks of the initial four, 'the offer' is made to all the new trainees. The offer is that they will be paid for the time they have spent with the business so far and will be given $1,000 if they quit the programme and leave the company. This is done to test a trainee's commitment to the business, the culture, and the strategy. Better to spend $1,000 dollars now than have damage done to the company in the long term by hiring the wrong person.

When you are clear about your philosophy, vision, mission, and rules of the game, you need to be equally clear that these points are to be taken seriously, and they should be built into everything that the company does.

Summary

The outputs that you want from your team will dictate the success of your business. By managing the inputs through leadership and systems and ensuring that you have the right people in the right places in your business, the interpretation of your philosophy can be controlled through your team.

Being specific about what structure and profile of people you need is necessary if an effective business is to be constructed, one in which leadership is provided through systems, processes, and procedures, not simply the charisma of the leader themselves.

Notes

Rule No. 6 – Systems Rules OK

If you can't describe what you are doing as a process, you don't know what you're doing.

W. Edwards Deming

Your business is a system. It may be complex, but it is a system of inputs, processes, and outputs. So far we have looked at the processes involved in building a great business. Now we need to consider how to capture those processes such that they can be understood by everyone in the business.

This could be a very short chapter, because the answer to the question, how to systematise a business is simple – write the systems down.

The intention of systematising your business is that the dependency on you in the monarchy structure is reduced and the dependency upon the structure within the hierarchy is increased.

'The king is dead, long live the king . . .'

Using the operations chart described earlier in the book – now that we know what actually works well inside your business – we can systematise it so that the performance will be locked in.

Many businesses will systematise too early if they are not careful. They simply describe the procedures and systems that deliver average performance. This was a criticism, somewhat unfairly, of the BS5750 and ISO 9000 accreditations. They didn't improve the business, and they simply documented what happened within it.

I remember introducing a Quality System to the AQAP1 (military version and forerunner of ISO 9000). The assessment team found zero defects or non-compliances during the three-day inspection, which was unheard of. So I was asked to create a minor non-compliance so that it would validate the inspection process; fun times.

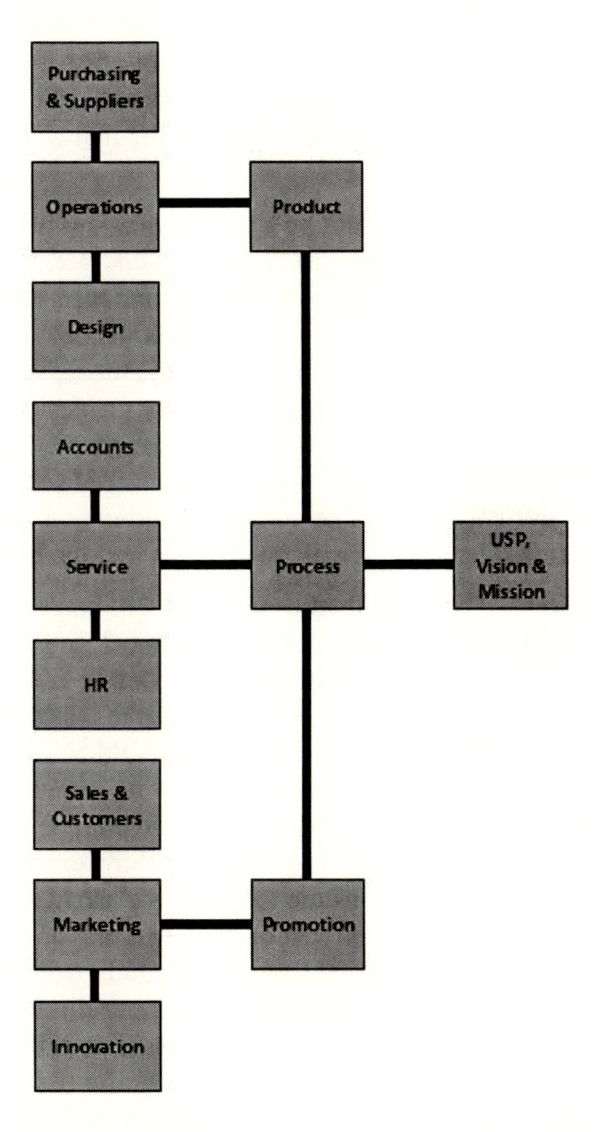

```
Purchasing
& Suppliers
    |
Operations ——— Product
    |             |
  Design          |
    |             |
 Accounts         |
    |             |
 Service ——— Process ——— USP, Vision & Mission
    |             |
   HR             |
    |             |
Sales &           |
Customers         |
    |             |
Marketing ——— Promotion
    |
Innovation
```

Within each area of the chart, systems should be documented and maintained. The actual systems should include the following categories of information:

1. **Process Overview** – What is the primary function and objective of the department or division? How does each part actually contribute towards the objectives of the business as a whole? Each area needs to be defined not only in isolation, but in relation to the other areas of the business, the people who have responsibility for it, and the KPIs that will be used to measure the performance.

2. **Process Flow** – This should be a simple diagram that details the inputs and outputs from each department. Decide what format the inputs need to be, and then define the same for the outputs. The timeline of the process should be detailed here, for example, when a request for a design is made, what is the turnaround time that will be guaranteed by the design department. Your departments need to treat each other as customers and suppliers and provide guaranteed services accordingly. These can be printed large and put on the wall of the office. The more visual the systems are, the better.

3. **Procedures** – The individual procedures that make up the process should be written down and put into a flow chart or similar visual record. Procedures need to define who does what to whom, with what by when – if that makes sense! These are the 'how to' instructions and should be as simple as possible. Running an engineering drawing retrieval contract on behalf of the Royal Navy, we would be audited on a regular basis. Our job was to maintain the drawings of all the underwater weapons the Royal Navy had at its disposal, and it was critical that our systems and procedures were 100% fool proof. One afternoon, an audit team turned up and asked me to accompany them on the audit. Feeling confident, I escorted them to the drawing office and showed them in. The procedures were kept in a specific file that was colour coded and located in a unique and predefined position so they could find them easily.

   The lead auditor walked in to the drawing office and announced that this was a drill and that she would be conducting an 'all areas' audit. Then she requested that every electronic device, computer, printer, and copier was tuned off and unplugged from the wall; all lights were to be turned off as well. With her team, they were going to go away for thirty minutes and read the procedures, then come back, and using only the guidance they had from the manuals, attempt to retrieve print and copy a series of drawings.

So we waited, and thirty minutes later the audit team returned to a darkened drawing office. The forty staff were all taken outside, and I was invited to participate in the audit.

'Where is the light switch?' I was asked. They were not detailed in the procedures, neither, it was noted, were the instructions regarding the storage and replacement of the bulbs on a pre-planned basis.

'How do I operate the computer?' Whilst the procedures were clear and specific about how to access the correct programs, passwords, and files, how to plug the computer into the wall and turn it on were missing, so the procedures were useless.

And so it went on. By the time the audit had finished, we knew we had a lot of work to do. The reason that the audit was so thorough was that in the event of war, if we were all wiped out and someone new had to come and run the department, they had to be able to do everything on the basis of the procedures. There had to be a copy of every key, disk, document, and procedure kept in a fireproof building, remote from the main building so that if we got burned down or bombed, the procedures would be in tact – I was going to mention that if all the drawing were destroyed in an attack, the procedures wouldn't help much, but I didn't.

I learned more from that single audit than I had in my career to that date; that's why when I put a quality system in place in the future we had to actually fabricate a non-compliance to validate the assessment and prove that the audit team had actually been there.

In the military, if a procedure fails, then someone may get killed, and whilst this may not be the case in your business, applying the same basic criteria to the development of your procedures as the military, or as the best franchisers do, will ensure that your systems are fool proof.

4. **Work Instructions** – Where specific details are required to perform a task, then specific detailed instructions may be required. These can be videos, audio, written or photographed, providing they are clear and concise. Make sure that any instructions make the operators aware of any safety issues and licensing or specialised training required – for example, the driving of forklift trucks requires current vehicle specific licenses for each operator.

5. **Person Profiles** – What are the attributes of the person that would be deemed qualified to carry out the functions. Here, the DISC, academic, or experience profiles can be identified for reference so that anyone can recruit the right person for the job.

You may think that the manufacture of wiring harnesses for trucks may not sound like the most exciting business in the world, and you'd be right. But the procedures and processes that have to be put in place to ensure that when it gets plugged in, it works right first time are very detailed. When it came to the person profile for those who were involved in the actual assembly, we had to make sure that everyone had an eye examination every six months, not just for their sight, but colour recognition. Where yellow, red, green, and blue wires are involved, the eyesight of the operator was important.

The person profile helps with recruitment and also the development of training programmes to either maintain skills at the appropriate levels or fill the gaps in someone's experience so that they can progress within the business.

The days of quality manuals kept in huge lever arch folders with issue numbers and dates on them have gone – thank goodness. The key aspects of the systems in your business are as follows:

1. Ease of use and understanding for the team.

2. They must support the vision, mission, and rules of the game, and not be contradictory.

3. Detailed enough that anyone can understand them, and that they know not just how to operate the computer, but how to plug it in in the first place.

4. Be kept up to date at all times, so that new policies and procedures are introduced with the appropriate training as soon as possible.

5. There must be a feedback loop from all areas of the business. If customer service is suffering because the buying process means that stock is not available when required, then corrective action must be taken; complaints are results of a break in the system somewhere. Equally, good news needs to travel around the business as well.

6. Your systems must be audited and tested. Imagine the Royal Navy turning up in your office; would they be able to run the business without you? This may sound a little extreme, but this is exactly what the franchises do, they build a system such that anyone with the appropriate training can make the same burger, in the same box anywhere in the world.

Occasionally, it is a good idea to create a crisis, not an actual one but a 'pretend' one. Assume there has been a fire, and all your computers have gone up in smoke. Where are the backup disks? Or assume a key member of staff goes off sick. Who knows the passwords and processes to do their job? Post-it notes on the front of the monitors don't count as systems either.

Electronic recording and retrieval of your systems documentation is the key. As stated before, we use a wiki-based system that means we can access our documents from anywhere in the world.

They are instantly updated for everyone as soon as we change them and the whole system is backed-up every day.

As a final thought, your systems processes and procedures will define how to build and run your business. This is your secret sauce. Protect it well. It has value. The more specific your systems are, the more you need to protect them, unless you intend to sell a copy to someone; and that's what we call franchising.

There are some things, situations, and occurrences that cannot be systematised. These unexpected events are where your trust in your team comes in to play. It's how Nordstrom allow their teams to use their best judgement at all times. At some point, you will have to allow your team to do the same. Sometimes they will get it right, and sometimes they will get it wrong. That's why it's called judgement, not certainty.

Given the same situation that was probably outside of the systems and procedures, two people in the same organisation can make different judgement calls. To demonstrate this, I will tell you a true story about my mom, synchronicity, and the power of making someone's day.

Some background first.

My dad did his National Service in the RAF. When he was due to be de-mobbed, he decided to have his palm read so he could look into his future in civilian life. The fortune-teller told him that he would die when he was abroad – which was a pretty safe guess for someone in a military uniform. So he decided never to go abroad, and from then on, the farthest that he went overseas was the Isle of Wight, which hardly counts.

My mom was only a child when the Second World War broke out, and it wasn't until 1948 as a teenager, that she was allowed to go on an overseas school trip to Switzerland. Travelling by train and ferry, the trip took thirty hours in total. My mom and dad got married in 1952, and from then until when my dad died in 2010, she never went abroad. So Mom's only trip overseas was the 1948 journey to the Alps with her school, returning to the UK on 19 September 1948.

After Dad died, and to give Mom a welcome diversion, we invited her to come and stay in France with us for a few weeks. So with her shiny new passport in hand, we picked her up from Shropshire and headed south. For three weeks we took Mom all over France, visiting Reims, Bordeaux, and Paris. We drove to Warsaw via Berlin and came back via the Czech Republic. We travelled through Luxembourg and Belgium, and she even had a blast on the back of the Harley along the Moselle to Pont a Mousson.

When it came time to head back to the UK, we drove to Calais to meet the ferry. We crossed the channel on a regular basis, and out of habit, we use P&O from Calais which takes about ninety minutes to reach Dover, just enough time for a coffee and lunch.

Having been out of the UK for the first time in over sixty years, Mom requested that lunch should be fish and chips from the on board restaurant. Anyone who travels with P&O will know that fish and chips on their ships is served on a plate, but with greaseproof paper printed to look like newsprint, placed on the plate first. So it looks like the meal is being eaten out of newspaper.

As we ate the meal, Mom was saying how it was over sixty years ago since she had made the same journey with her school, and what a great time she had, when from under the mushy peas, she saw the date of the newspaper that had been printed onto the greaseproof paper – 19 September 1948. It was a reprint of *The Times* that was used to mimic newsprint, the same date as she would have been on the ferry over sixty years ago.

This was an amazing coincidence or act of synchronicity, but whatever it was, it was one of those moments when the hairs on the back of my neck stood up, and I suddenly felt cold.

And here is where the judgement calls come in . . .

To mark this coincidence, we thought it would be great to get a fresh piece of the grease proof paper showing the date of publication, and put it into the album that Lynn had made that chronicled Mom's European tour of six countries in three weeks – what a great end to the journey.

I approached the restaurant supervisor, explained what had happened, and requested a single piece of the grease proof paper so that we could have it as a souvenir. His response was that it was more than his job was worth to go giving away company property, and that someone had been sacked the week before for giving away a plastic bag to a customer – so the answer was no.

Taken aback, I had to tell Mom that P&O company regulations meant that we weren't allowed to have a single piece of grease proof paper with the date printed on it. Amazing . . .

We went to another deck and did some duty-free shopping; there was an information desk, with a lady with a customer service badge on. So I thought I'd try again. I explained about Mom and 1948 and the fish and chips – before I'd finished, she jumped in and said, 'And you'd like a few sheets of greaseproof paper, right?'

She disappeared and within minutes returned with two pieces of greaseproof paper, which when joined together, clearly showed the date of publication as 19 September 1948. Brilliant! She said it was her pleasure, and she hoped that my mom enjoyed her trip and would come back and see them again on board.

Here is a copy of the joined pieces of P&O Greaseproof paper so you can see the detail.

So the question is how did two people from the same organisation, given the same scenario, within ten minutes of each other arrive at different conclusions?

The difference is management, training, and degrees of freedom; systems are great but at the margins where legends are made is where freedom, trust, and judgement based around your philosophy will make the difference between average systems-compliant service and remarkable 'shock and awe' – or simply making someone's day.

Systems Rules OK – but the mavericks get remembered.

Your systems need to be designed such that you and your business are not the subject of on-going "errorist" attacks – human errors cost you money.

Notes

Rule No. 7 – You Have to Innovate

Innovation distinguishes between a leader and a follower.

Steve Jobs

Lewin's Rule of B= f(P, E) applies to your business as well as the individuals within it.

The environment in the future will be different than it is now, and therefore, if the profitable growth behaviour is to be maintained, then the products and processes of the business need to proactively stay ahead of the changes. Reacting to change is an option. Proactively anticipating and creating the changes is of course preferred.

All your systems, methods, and practices need to be open to change, so do your people – the degree to which a business accepts and embraces change will be a defining factor in its long-term success. However, just to be radical, one strategic choice is to do nothing. If everybody is innovating and changing all the time, there just may be a case for staying as you are. This carries inherent risks, but don't innovate just for the sake of it. Innovate because you need to, not just because you think you should.

The classic product life cycle model applies to products, services, and businesses. The chart below plots the stages of growth of a business from birth to adulthood; what happens after this is dependent upon how the business and the business owners behave in the medium term. Following adulthood comes maturity and either decline or a reinvigoration of the business and the start of a new curve. It's a choice, however, a choice which has to be made before the business achieves adulthood; it may be too late to start the new growth before the decline sets in.

Business Life Cycle

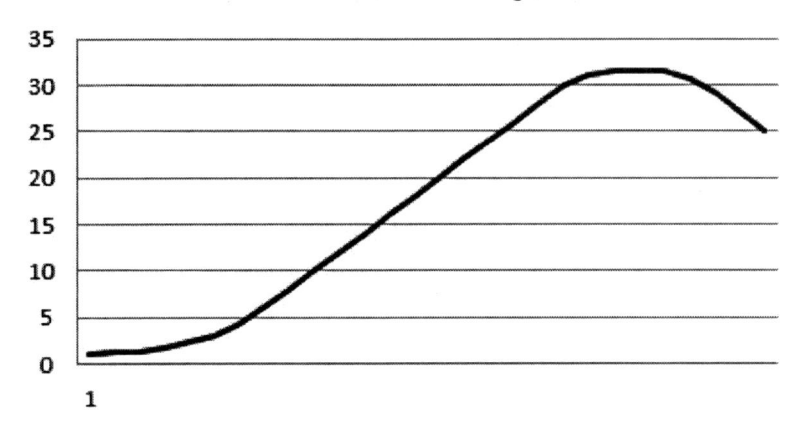

Innovation and reinvention has to be on your mind almost constantly. There should be a background unease about the status quo or concern over apparent calm stability. Your business should be in a state of controlled agitation, with new ideas, strategies, and tactics forming a part of the daily routine – not to destabilise what you have but to maintain the tension and passion that keeps your business alive and continually attractive to customers.

Your new product or process needs to be under development while your existing ones are doing well. Research and development should be funded by the profits from your existing products and must be put in to your budgets and cash flow forecasts. If you don't have research and development, training and allowances for the generation of ideas that may never even make it to market, you are underselling yourself.

Business Immortality Cycle

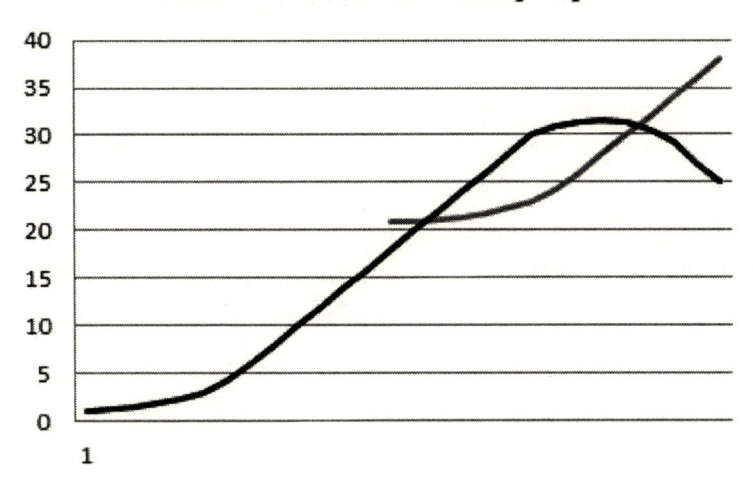

For your business to achieve immortality, it needs a new lease of life every so often. The second line on the curve represents the introduction of new products and services, or processes and procedures. The second line starts well before the decline of the first such that as one product declines, the new one takes its place.

Product Innovation – Your product or service may have to change or adapt due to the demands of your customer, legislation, or technological advances. If I was in the business of producing VHS video recorders, I would be out of business now. Your customers may demand that your product changes and adapts. As much as Morgan have kept their product reasonably consistent, the engines and drive train are modern under the traditional shell, few people would rush out and buy an Austin Allegro if it were brought back in to production; few people bought it the first time round.

Your product innovation strategy is customer dependent and should be designed to maximise the quality and experience customers derive from using the product or service you provide. Dentists who hand out bottles of whisky as an anaesthetic will appeal to a marginal niche market. However, those that guarantee no pain and use the latest techniques will be the growth players in the market in the future.

Process Innovation – Improvements in technology, efficiency, techniques, and materials may not fundamentally change the overall perception of the product. However, efficiency and quality improvements will be expected by the customers. Even Morgan uses modern engines and materials.

Your product innovation strategy should be focussed on improvements to your margins and the quality of the service you provide. Your customers do not really take a lot of interest in your processes, providing they are environmentally friendly, safe, and legal, and in some cases, moral. Your processes are for you to stay ahead in terms of productivity and efficiency by benchmarking yourselves against the best in the world and then finding a way to improve.

Risk – Innovation is risky because there is always a danger that a new method, process, or product will fail. If you fire someone for making a mistake, then you will stop all innovation and ideas. Whilst clearly mistakes should be minimised, the acceptability of risk taking within the boundaries you set must be part of the rules of the game.

Hewlett Packard and 3M allow between 10% and 15% of workers' time to be invested in 'pet projects'. These bootleg projects are not officially sanctioned, although the time and resources are allocated by the company. The company lives in hope that these projects will result in the next transformational product or service development; famous results of this bootlegging approach include the 3M Post-it notes and Google's Gmail, Google News, and Orkut services.

The risk these companies take is that they invest 15% of payroll and get no return. In reality, these programmes can return the investment several times over.

An alternative strategy is to use a 'skunk works' approach. The term was the name given to the Advanced Development Program at the Lockheed Martin Company in the USA. Skunk Works was responsible for the development of the U2, SR71 Blackbird, and the F22 Raptor. The skunk works approach is where a team of highly skilled engineers, technicians, or designers are seconded to work as individuals, or as a team, without interference from management, with a brief to develop the extraordinary. Boeing has a similar approach with secret developments using the term *Phantom Works*.

Maybe if my dad had developed a clandestine skunk works operation at the back of the shop where we stored the potatoes, we could have seen off Carrefour, Tesco, and Wal-Mart.

So innovation is important, but don't innovate for the sake of it. Innovate for the sake of your customers and your profitability and growth.

And to prove there is an exception to every rule ...

In the town of Malvern in the UK, there is an unusual and typically British car manufacturer – The Morgan Motor Company. The company was founded in 1909 and is currently run by Charles Morgan, the grandson of the founder, Harry Frederick Stanley Morgan.

The standard cars are still built around an Ash frame, and the basic design of the cars hasn't changed since the Plus 4 model was introduced at the 1950 Earls Court Motor Show in London, and the company endeavours to deliver a new vehicle within twelve months from date of order. Due to the length of the waiting list, the actual price of the vehicle cannot be determined or guaranteed until nearer the delivery date.

The classic car on which the company was founded was the Morgan Three Wheeler, and from 1909 to 1953, around 30,000 of these vehicles were built in the UK, with more being made in France by Darmont Morgan. Amazingly, one of these three-wheeler cars actually won the French Grand Prix in 1913. In 2011, the Morgan Three Wheeler was launched and is, according to the company web site, a fusion of modern technology into a classic design. With an 1800cc V-twin engine connected to a Mazda 5 Gearbox, the car produces around 100h.p. at the wheels and will get to 60 mph in under 4.5 seconds, around the same as a Ferrari 360, or just slightly behind a Lamborghini Gallardo.

Morgan cars have updated their product and process to keep pace with advances. However, their philosophy of producing high quality, traditionally built vehicles has remained intact since the company first started over 100 years ago. Morgan will never be the world's biggest car maker, and thank goodness for that. However, they have found a niche that suits them, and the loyalty of their customers means that extreme innovation could actually kill the brand and the business.

Remember, your philosophy is the basis for your business. Innovation should not take the company away from that. Your products and processes may change, and innovation here is important. However, sometimes the roots of business need to remain intact – fancy schemes and technology have a place. They also sometimes need to be kept in that place.

Morgan Motor Company is a glorious and refreshing exception to the rule that businesses must innovate and change all the time, and whilst we may yearn for this to be the case in our businesses, regularly it is not and innovation and change is indeed critical to our success and growth.

Notes

Rule No. 8 – It's Not About You Anymore

All that is valuable in human society depends upon the opportunity for development accorded the individual.

Albert Einstein

Congratulations. Having got this far, your business is not dependent on you anymore. It has the framework and systems in place that mean it is systems dependent and not person dependent. The monarchy has been replaced by the hierarchy.

Your role now has changed. Yes, you are still the owner, but you are now the chair of the board. You add value now by supporting, coaching, and leading your team, and also looking for ways to expand the business. It may be that you want to sell the business, franchise the model and duplicate it, pass it over to your children – or simply enjoy being involved in your business at a different level. Whichever route you choose, having a business that is structured and systemised with excellence at its core will make the journey easier.

For your business to achieve immortality and realise its full potential, you may have to get out of the way. At some point, we business owners become the single biggest limiting factor in our businesses. You have a life cycle too, and recognising when the best time to pass control over to the next generation or the professional CEO that will continue your legacy is a tough call but a necessary one if the true potential of your creation is to be realised.

Your business will always be about you but not dependent upon you.

Now, as a cautionary tale, and as a final thought from me on your journey through ***Your* Business RULES OK,** I want to leave you with a thought, and it concerns the case of a fisherman and the businessman. There are several versions of this story, and I was unable to identify the originator. So whilst I don't claim to have written it, I am not able to acknowledge the author.

A very important business man is on holiday in a fishing village in Brazil. He notices that a small row boat has come in to the harbour and has started to land the day's catch, so he wanders over to find out more. The fisherman had caught plenty of fish, although he was only using small nets and fished alone in that small boat; the businessman was impressed.

'How long does it take you to catch these fish?' he enquired.

The fisherman replied, 'Only about two to three hours.'

'If you stayed out longer, you could catch more fish then, couldn't you?' asked the businessman.

'But there is enough here to feed my whole family. I don't need any more fish,' replied the fisherman.

'And what do you do with the rest of your day?' asked the businessman.

'Well, I usually get up to catch the early tides, go fishing for a couple of hours, go home and see my children, and help prepare lunch. In the afternoon, my wife and I go walking, and in the evening, we go to the town and sing and dance all night with our friends,' came the reply.

'As a management consultant with a PhD in business and marketing, I could help you grow your business; it has great potential. My advice would be that you spend more time catching fish, and you sell the surplus for a profit. With the profits you can buy a bigger boat, catch even more fish and with those profits invest in a fleet of trawlers. When the fleet is running at capacity, you should consider a strategy of vertical integration and start your own processing, canning, and distribution network, and within ten years you can franchise the operation and have outlets on every continent.'

'And then?' asked the fisherman.

'Well, then we will take your company public and have you listed on the stock exchange. You will be rich beyond your wildest dreams.'

'And then?'

'Once you are truly rich, you can buy a place by the sea, do a little fishing in the mornings, spend time with you family, have relaxed lunches with your wife, and in the evenings you can meet with all your friends in the town, singing and dancing all night.'

'Thanks for your advice – *you are clearly a genius.*'

The reason I have included this is because as your guide, it is not my role to advise you to quadruple your business just because you can. My role as your guide is to help you build the business that will enable you to have a lifestyle that will make you happy and fulfilled. If that means you need to build a global business, that's great; let's get started.

You may of course not need to build a global empire; the currency of your happiness and fulfilment is yours to choose, and remember that some of the most contented people in the world have nothing. Having a business of any size that is not totally dependent upon you is a great objective, regardless of the size of the business you have. If your business needs you every day, then you have a job not a business, and the benefits aren't that great.

So choose your objectives and goals with care. Be ambitious, be determined, but above all, enjoy the ride. I wish you well in your ventures, and I look forward to your thoughts, comments, and feedback about the book we have just shared. It has been my privilege to be on your reading list.

Finally, come along to one of our events so I can thank you personally, and if you believe that I could help you achieve your objectives, drop me a line, and let's have some fun together building business.

Notes

Index

3M 254

Above the Line 212
absenteeism 185
Abyssinia 22
Accidental CEO 228
acquisition cost ... 196, 197, 198, 199, 200, 201, 212, 217
Advanced Development Program 254
advertising ... 191, 193, 204, 212, 217, 218
Albert Einstein 258
All Blacks 231, 232
Alum Rock 15
annual sales ... 96, 97, 98, 101, 152, 165, 191
Apple 37
artefacts 227, 229, 231
assumptive cross sell ... 162, 163
attendance . 86, 152, 153, 210
Australia 21
Average Debtor Days ... 144, 145, 148
Average Order Value ... 144, 145, 151, 154

Babylonia 19
balance sheet 48, 85, 140
barter system 18, 19
Bartering 18
basics 56
*Be My Guest (*Hilton*)* 42

Bedford TK Truck 17
Below the Line 212
benefits of a systematised . 66
Bill Gates 37
Birmingham ... 15, 17, 29, 52, 107, 112, 123, 167, 184, 187
Blanchard, Ken 226
BNI (Business Networking and Referrals 232
BoB (Business over Breakfast) 232
Bob Geldof 21
Boeing 129, 255
BOGOF (buy one get one free) 158, 159
booked miles' ... *See also* KPI
Bowman's Strategy Clock 109
break-even point ... 87, 134, 135, 200
Break-Even Point 134
British Hospitality Association 214
Buckminster Fuller 8
budget ... 81, 83, 85, 87, 121, 180, 210, 211, 217
bundles 155, 156, 157, 209
bundling ... 139, 155, 156, 162, 187, 201
Burger King 24, 25
Business Coaching 271
business tree model 72
business vision 34

262

Carrefour 255
cash ... 18, 21, 29, 33, 34, 38,
   45, 46, 47, 65, 67, 76, 79,
   81, 85, 87, 90, 98, 99,
   100, 103, 139, 141, 142,
   148, 149, 150, 158, 177,
   180, 184, 217, 252 *see
   also profit*
Cash Flow Forecasting 85
Castro, Fidel 114
Chao 20
Charles Handy 8
Charles Morgan 255
cheques 148
Cliff Bowman 109
Coca-Cola 113, 114
Code of Hammurabi 19
Coldstream Guards 16
Colgate 113
Columbo 206
commitment 7, 41, 238
Commitment 41
commodity money ... 19 *see
   also* barter system
community 171
Community 174
Companies House 38
Competitive Strategy
   (Porter) 109
compound growth 94
conversion rate ... 192, 194,
   195, 196, 202, 207, 208
Conversion rate percentage
   196
Cost Leadership 109
cost of goods sold 83, 200
credit cards 41, 148, 173, 175

Creditors 141
crisis 245
Cross Sell 162
culture statements 56
customer service ... 56, 57, 58,
   88, 97, 114, 121, 123,
   124, 229, 245, 248
Cycle of Business . 28, 34, 35

David Faulkner 109
David McClelland 225
Dean Martin 24
debits 148
debtors 120, 141
Default Diary ... 103, 105, 106,
   107
Deming Prize 88
Deuteronomy 22
Differentiation 109
Dilbert Mission Statement
   Generator 56
direct costs 83, 140, 183, 185
direct mail ... 193, 212, 213,
   215, 219
DISC profiling system 235
discounts ... 101, 137, 158, 183,
   184
Diversification 92
Donald Keough 114
Dorian Gray 59

Earls Court Motor Show . 255
Edwards Deming .. 8, 88, 240
efficiency ... 32, 47, 83, 88,
   128, 130, 131, 133, 181,
   182, 184, 193, 196, 197,
   254

263

Electronics 56
email...10, 45, 149, 151, 212, 219
Emotional intelligence......42
energy 41
enquiries...191, 192, 203, 204, 211, 217, 220
entrepreneur...15, 45, 46, 47, 236
EPOS
   (Electronic Point of Sale) system 18
Ethiopia.......................21, 22
exclusivity.......................219
Exclusivity 176
Exhibitions and Events ...219
Exodus 22

F22 Raptor 255
Fashion Show Mall,..........31
Ferrari 256
Fiat money 20
filters...193, 194, 195, 201, 203, 209, 211
focus...7, 45, 46, 48, 60, 61, 62, 63, 64, 86, 88, 98, 103, 105, 113, 163, 184, 212, 215, 224
Focus...............41, 61, 63, 89
Ford...........................37, 89
franchise...23, 25, 26, 27, 48, 65, 67, 92, 113, 173, 258, 259
Franchises 23, 228
Frank Holland...................16
freedom...32, 66, 119, 121, 124, 233, 234, 237, 249

GAP analysis...143, 186, 188, 212
Gay Mullins 114
Germany 21, 216
Gmail 254
goals...34, 42, 50, 70, 81, 83, 103, 105, 107, 260
Goldilocks Sales Technique
  111
Google 105, 230, 254
Google News 254
Gordon E. Moore............176
gross contribution 83
gross margin...99, 134, 137, 144, 146, 158, 178, 179, 180, 181, 200
Gross Profit.83, 99, 100, 200
growing business...96, 97, 98, 99, 185
growth...20, 34, 44, 46, 47, 48, 51, 54, 56, 62, 64, 65, 67, 72, 74, 79, 88, 90, 93, 94, 95, 97, 98, 99, 103, 126, 191, 192, 251, 254, 255, 256
growth potential................64
Growth Potential...144, 145, 189

Harrah's 173
Harry Beckwith 8
Harry Frederick Stanley
   Morgan. 255
Hersey.............................226
Hewlett Packard..............254
hierarchy...63, 64, 65, 66, 222, 240, 258

264

Hillman, Neil 187
Hilton, Conrad 42
hyperinflation 20

IATA 127
ideal customer. 144, 145, 150
Igor Ansoff 90
immortality 253, 258
Industrial and Commercial Temporary Employment Agency 86
Influence (Cialdini) ... 21, 235
In-N-Out Burger ... 24, 25, 27
innovate 59, 251, 255, 256
innovation... 35, 47, 48, 127, 176, 228, 253, 254, 255, 256
Innovation... 62, 251, 252, 253, 254, 256
inspiration 51, 107
Intelligence 42
International Air Transport Authority 127
International Franchise Association 23
interpretation... 139, 222, 224, 238
Investors in People 52, 53
invoice... 39, 45, 85, 148, 149, 150, 151
Iraq 19

J. F. Kennedy Stadium 21
Japanese Union of Scientists and Engineers 88
Jay Abraham 8
Jeffrey Gitomer 8

jet ski... 201, 202, 203, 204, 205, 206
Jim Collins 8
Jim Rohn 60
Joe Girard 166
Jonathan Holland 139

Ka Mate Haka 231
Ken Blanchard 226
KFC 24
knowledge... 7, 8, 10, 12, 23, 29, 37, 42, 49, 54, 59, 76, 91, 107, 111, 119, 162, 211, 217, 228, 229, 230, 236, 237, 272, 275
Knowledge 37, 42, 237
Kojak 30, 107
KPI... 85, 86, 87, 88, 128, 165, 187, 196
Kublai Khan 20

Lamborghini 256
Las Vegas... 24, 31, 57, 115, 167, 237
leadership... 51, 121, 222, 223, 224, 225, 226, 227, 228, 229, 232, 234, 238
Leviticus 22
Lewin 225, 251
Lewin's Rule 251
life cycle 251, 258
Life Cycle Theory of Leadership' 226
Lisbon 53
Live Aid 21
local businessman 15

location...31, 54, 76, 111, 145, 189, 220
Lockheed Martin Company 254
Los Angeles. 25
Loyalty Schemes 170
Lynn Holland...7, 21, 25, 31, 39, 107, 116, 121, 123, 152, 170, 210, 236, 247

Mailbox................29, 30, 107
maintenance programme...175, 203, 206
Malcolm Gladwell, ...8
management accounts.....140
Manchester United..........230
Mandalay Bay Hotel.......115
Maori 231
Margins...135, 144, 177, 181, 185
Market Development 91
Market Penetration 91
Market Segmentation......109
marketing...11, 23, 32, 33, 44, 46, 52, 57, 61, 74, 76, 89, 92, 97, 99, 107, 110, 111, 112, 113, 143, 168, 185, 189, 192, 193, 195, 196, 198, 200, 201, 203, 208, 211, 212, 213, 214, 215, 217, 219, 220, 222, 259
mark-up...135, 136, 137, 138, 158, 179
Marshall Thurber 8
Marston, William Moulton 235
Martinez, Lynsi................25

MBA 275
McDonald's...24, 25, 108, 228, 231
Mexico.......................21, 22
Michael Gerber.............8, 15
Microsoft 37, 50
Midge Ure........................21
Milton Friedman philosophy 29
Ming dynasty, ...20
Ministry of Defence........177
mission...28, 34, 52, 53, 54, 55, 56, 58, 70, 72, 88, 108, 111, 118, 123, 151, 153, 165, 216, 219, 222, 228, 229, 232, 233, 238, 245
Mission statement.............52
MoD(Ministry of Defence) 177
MOIRA...................164, 220
monarchy...64, 66, 222, 240, 258
Moore's Law 176
Morgan ...253, 254, 255, 256
Morgan Motor Company 255, 256
Mussolini, Benitto 22

net margins 33, 181, 185
net profit 134, 181
Net Promoter Score 88
networking........39, 218, 232
New Coke 113, 114
Nordstrom...31, 32, 163, 246
Novak, David..................228
NPS...................................88

number of orders...151, 152, 153, 165, 174, 176, 191, 199, 209

Offer Biggest First..........160
Old Coke...........................114
Old Cola Drinkers of America 114
On Heroes, Hero Worship, and the Heroic in History 225
one-year plan 79
online payments...............148
operating expenses.............83
operations chart 118, 240
opportunities...15, 22, 23, 35, 37, 56, 69, 72, 73, 74, 76, 77, 108, 121, 131, 175, 218
Order of the Sacred Treasure 88
organisation chart...118, 126, 150, 234, 237
Out of the Crisis (Deming) 89
overheads...83, 85, 100, 134, 140, 177, 185, 186

P&O.........................247, 248
Papa o Pango Haka..........231
paper money 19, 20
Penha Longa Hotel 53
Pepsi 113
Permission 39
person profile...........237, 244
Personalised Rewards......174
pet projects.......................254

Peter Drucker.............29, 222
Peter Falk.........................206
Phantom Works 255
Philadelphia 21
philosophy...25, 26, 27, 28, 29, 30, 32, 33, 34, 35, 43, 44, 45, 46, 47, 49, 55, 56, 58, 65, 67, 88, 119, 121, 122, 126, 165, 167, 194, 205, 219, 222, 223, 224, 232, 238, 249, 256, 271
planning model 70
Porter, Michael 109
Positioning.......................210
price...99, 109, 110, 111, 112, 135, 136, 138, 139, 154, 156, 158, 159, 160, 175, 177, 178, 179, 180, 184, 255
principles of Statistical Process Control,.............88
Process Focus 62
processes and procedures 119, 246, 253
Product Development 91
Product Leadership 176
Productivity...127, 132, 181, 182
profit and loss account...85, 135, 140, 141
profit path 198, 199
Promotion Focus..............61
Pulp Fiction 112
purchasing decision 157
Purchasing Decision 174

Quarterly Plans 103

Ralph White 225
raw materials...101, 141, 179, 183
real-life examples 86
Recipe for Success 23
reciprocation 20, 22, 232
Recruitment and Training 101
Referrals...144, 145, 186, 217, 232
Reichheld, Fred 87
Renault Megane 161, 162
reputation...32, 44, 54, 62, 76, 86, 91, 108, 109, 175, 188, 196, 212
Research and development 252
Results Rules OK mission statement 54
Richard .11, 37, 92, 139, 150
Richard Branson ...11, 37, 92
risk...24, 43, 91, 92, 98, 108, 111, 113, 127, 160, 209, 210, 254
Risk Taking 43
Ritz Carlton Credo' 53
Robert Burns 69
Robert Kiyosaki 8
Rogers, Caden 56
Ronald Lipitt 225
Royal Navy 242, 245
Royal Ordnance 9
Royal Small Arms Factory 183
rules of the game...34, 56, 58, 70, 72, 88, 108, 111, 118, 119, 122, 123, 151, 219, 222, 228, 229, 233, 238, 245, 254
Running Rate 95

sales delivered not invoiced 141
sales graph 96, 97
sales income...83, 131, 134, 153, 157, 158, 192, 199
sales manager 99, 100
sales revenue...88, 93, 95, 96, 97, 98, 99, 100, 101, 157, 185
sales value 145, 177, 200
scenario 35, 128, 152, 248
script 117
SDNI (sales delivered not invoiced) 141
shareholders 39
single-page business plan .70
Situational Leadership Theory 226
Skinner 228
Skunk Works 254
SME (small and medium enterprise)...91, 108, 109, 212
Smithfield Wholesale Market 17
Snyder, Esther 25, 26
Snyder, Harry 25, 26

Song dynasty 19
South West Airlines 56, 57
SR71 Blackbird 255
Stacy Perman 25
standards...26, 28, 43, 44, 53, 59, 112, 114, 127, 151,

170, 176, 177, 222, 224, 225, 230, 234
Standards 43
Starbucks 172
Statement of Purpose 34
statements of account 149
Stella Artois Lager advert 112
Steve Jobs 37, 251
stock ... 123, 124, 126, 133, 139, 141, 157, 158, 176, 178, 184, 201, 245, 260
Stock 141
Straight-line growth 93
strategic choices 90, 109
Subway 24
Sumerians 19
SWOT process and analysis 76
systematised consistency .. 27
systems ... 18, 19, 24, 26, 27, 31, 32, 34, 45, 48, 114, 116, 118, 119, 121, 124, 125, 126, 140, 151, 160, 169, 177, 184, 193, 195, 220, 227, 228, 238, 240, 242, 244, 245, 246, 249, 251, 258

task and relationship behaviour 226
telemarketing .. 217, 218, 219
Telly Savalas 30
Temp Agency 86
Tesco 184, 255
THE hotel 115, 116

The Ultimate Question (Reicheld) 87
Thomas Carlyle 225
threats 74, 76, 77
Three-Year Plan 79
Thurman, Uma 112
To Win 41
Tom Hopkins 8
Tony Robbins 8
Topological Psychology' 225
Total Revenue 95
Total Rewards 173
Trade-In's 160
trading ... 18, 19, 23, 100, 110, 139, 140, 145, 148, 161, 183, 191, 197, 198, 223
training ... 9, 13, 37, 51, 54, 60, 121, 123, 124, 125, 128, 157, 164, 192, 218, 228, 232, 237, 244, 245, 249, 252
Training 271
Training and Review 163
Transport Security Administration 57
Travolta, John 112
Tropicana 24

Ullman, Harlan K. 153
underlying principles 22
Unique Sales Proposition 110
University Degree 37
Upsell 161
USP ... 110, 112, 118, 153, 170, 191, 194, 205, 209, 271

value statements 56

VAT 18, 41
Video 126
Virgin 'empire' 92
vision 271
Vision 42, 50, 93
vision statement 52

Wade, James P. 153
Waldorf Astoria hotel 42
Wallace, Mia 112
Wal-Mart 255, 274
weaknesses 76
Web Design 87

web site ... 10, 13, 25, 44, 58, 70, 106, 115, 160, 172, 216, 219, 255
Wembley Stadium 21
Wilde, Oscar 59
WIP 141

Yuan dynasty 20
Yum Brands 228

Zappos 237
Zig Ziglar 8

Notes

About Results Rules OK

Results Rules OK was created with a simple and clear 2020 vision;

To enable everyone to enjoy learning, achieving, doing and being more...

This is achieved through the delivery of World Class Business Coaching, Training, and Development Programs designed for business owners and entrepreneurs just like you...

We recognise that all businesses are different, as are the people that build, own and run them so we have a range of products and programs that will help, inspire and support you – whatever stage of development your business is at...

You can register for our newsletter, check out David's latest blog and even download documents and templates from our website at www.resultsrulesok.com

If you'd like to come along to an event – either to join one of our Webinars or participate in a Workshop or Seminar – visit our website www.resultsrulesok.com to find our full schedule of events.

David is offers a limited number of **FREE Business Strategy Sessions** for qualifying businesses, to arrange a meeting or discussion with David, simply got to www.resultsrulesok.com, scroll down and press the "**Book Free Session with David**" button...

Our USP is our people, our delivery, the results our Clients achieve and our philosophy of Fun in Life and in Business. We are a growing profitable business, and we believe in making contributions to charity and causes that are aligned with our values.

David's unique experience, background and passion for adding value to the business and personal lives of others have enabled him to become not only a top Business Coach, but an accomplished Speaker and Author. Having worked in 23 countries so far, his presentations and key note presentations are compelling, informative and fun and his books reflect his knowledge and personality...

David's first book is available now...

If you have got this far then maybe we should talk...!

Contact Us;

Web – www.resultsrulesok.com

Email – info@resultsrulesok.com

Other Books by David Holland now available

Business Results Rules OK Volume I

Business Results Rules OK Volume II

Life Results Rules OK Volume I

Presenting Excellence

Would you like Fries with That?

Success Rules OK

Learning How to Fly

Unlucky for Some

The Case of the Ego in the Corner

The You Tree

Lights, Camera, Action

Goals, Objectives and Precession

Every Day in Every Way, I'm Getting Better & Better

Success Matters

The Professional Tarot

Scared of the Dark?

Leads United

Selling & Closing

The Franchise Connection

Only Read at 4am

Is Business Coaching Hornswoggle…?

How to Surf the Tsunami…

Strength in Numbers….

Dutch Courage...

Surfing the Wal-Mart Tidal Wave

Negotiating Success

The 9 Rules

Drumming and the Art of Business Maintenance

The 5 P's for Every Professional who Own's a Business

Growing Pains

The Sales Meeting

Customers for Life

Contrary to Popular Belief

The 4 Keys

Captains Blog

The Time that People Forgot

Results RULES OK

The YOU Tree

Business Coaching
FOR Professionals
BY Professionals

Looking for someone inspirational, competent but also kind & honest? He's THE guy. A true leader that's always there to make you better.'

"David Holland MBA is FUN, he is extremely engaging and shares his wisdom generously with an intent to always be of service to others."

'David is always able to add just the right bit of humour to his professional endeavours'

'David is a superb coach with extensive business experience and knowledge - oh, and one of the funniest people I have ever met! '

www.resultsrulesok.com